When Riot Cops
Are Not Enough

CRITICAL ISSUES IN CRIME AND SOCIETY

RAYMOND J. MICHALOWSKI, SERIES EDITOR

Critical Issues in Crime and Society is oriented toward critical analysis of contemporary problems in crime and justice. The series is open to a broad range of topics including specific types of crime, wrongful behavior by economically or politically powerful actors, controversies over justice system practices, and issues related to the intersection of identity, crime, and justice. It is committed to offering thoughtful works that will be accessible to scholars and professional criminologists, general readers, and students.

For a list of titles in the series, see the last page of the book.

When Riot Cops Are Not Enough

THE POLICING AND REPRESSION OF OCCUPY OAKLAND

MIKE KING

RUTGERS UNIVERSITY PRESS
New Brunswick, Camden, and Newark,
New Jersey, and London

Library of Congress Cataloging-in-Publication Data

Names: King, Mike.
Title: When riot cops are not enough : the policing and repression of
occupy Oakland / Mike King.
Description: New Brunswick, NJ : Rutgers University Press, 2017. |
Series: Critical issues in crime and society | Includes bibliographical
references and index.
Identifiers: LCCN 2016024608| ISBN 9780813583747 (hardback) |
ISBN 9780813583730 (pbk.) | ISBN 9780813583754 (e-book (epub))
Subjects: LCSH: Occupy movement—California—Oakland. | Police—
California—Oakland. | Social control—California—Oakland. |
Port of Oakland. | Social movements—United States—History—
21st century. | BISAC: SOCIAL SCIENCE / Violence in Society. |
HISTORY / United States / 21st Century. | POLITICAL SCIENCE /
Political Freedom & Security / Civil Rights. | SOCIAL SCIENCE /
Criminology. | POLITICAL SCIENCE / Political Freedom
& Security / Law Enforcement.
Classification: LCC HC103 .K455 2017 | DDC 322.4/40979466—dc23
LC record available at https://lccn.loc.gov/2016024608

A British Cataloging-in-Publication record for this book
is available from the British Library.

∞ The paper used in this publication meets the requirements of the
American National Standard for Information Sciences—Permanence
of Paper for Printed Library Materials, ANSI Z39.48-1992.

www.rutgersuniversitypress.org
Manufactured in the United States of America

Contents

ACKNOWLEDGMENTS

VERY MUCH LIKE the movement it documents, this book is a product of accumulated knowledge and experiences, of influences seen and unseen, and of trials and efforts that stretch far beyond the discrete episodes and events that we come to examine. As I tried to do in my *Counterpunch* essays during Occupy Oakland's existence, it has been my objective in this book to humbly and honestly document what I see, understanding that I don't see everything and that whatever analytic insights emerge are derived from ideas and lenses that have been gifts to me from others, which I hope to pass on with minimal damage done to them on my part.

I am very grateful to my mentors at University of California–Santa Cruz who contributed to my intellectual and personal growth in my years of graduate research there. My appreciation is due especially to Ben Crow, Herman Gray, Dana Takagi, and Barbara Epstein. I would also like to thank Kitty Calavita for her insights and wisdom. My deepest thanks to Craig Reinarman and Wally Goldfrank, who helped me through this process, whose patience and dedication as advisors were essential to this project coming to fruition. They also serve, in different ways, as my models for how to mentor my own students—most of whom, thankfully, are not as difficult as I am. The lessons, mentorship, and encouragement provided to me as an undergraduate at University of Massachusetts–Amherst by Agustin Lao-Montes and the late Stephen Resnick will be forever foundational in my scholarship and my understanding of the world.

Great appreciation is due to Luis Fernandez, who provided the encouragement and direction this project needed to get it to this point. Lesley Wood and Peter Kraska contributed valuable feedback on earlier drafts of this book, providing both general and specific comments that were of great value to the finished manuscript. Thanks to Jeffrey St. Clair at *Counterpunch*, where many of these ideas were first put forward on a platform and in a context that was very much a part of a movement trying to make sense of, and progress in spite of, repression.

I would like to thank everyone at Rutgers University Press who had persistent faith in this project, and patience with me, as I drafted and redrafted this text. Special thanks to Ray Michalowski and Peter Mickulas for their effort, time, and support in making this book a reality.

A debt is also owed to my colleagues at UC–Santa Cruz for the various forms of support, encouragement, and collaboration; particularly Nik Janos, Rachel Bryant-Anderson, Jennifer Burke, Travis Williams, Shannon Williams, Stuyvie Bearns Esteva, Liana Gamber Thompson, and Chris Dixon. Special thanks are due to Derrick Jones, who spotted me in different ways when I had loaded on more weight than I could lift.

Particularly in relation to understanding social movements and state repression I have learned the most from experience, from lessons learned through and alongside innumerable people over the last twenty years. The people I have marched with in the streets, sat in long meetings with, or on front stoops with until the wee hours of the morning—from Western Massachusetts to the Bay Area—have left a lasting imprint on me, and by extension this work. Special thanks to Geert Dhont, Thais Brodeur, Dave Taber, George Ciccariello-Maher, Sam Stoker, Barucha Peller, Laleh Behbehanian, Gerald Sanders, George Russell, and Mickey Fitzpatrick.

I am forever indebted to my family, particularly my mother, Pat, and stepfather, Steve, for their love and support over the years.

Above all, this book never would have come into being without the unflinching support and dedication of my partner, Emily Brissette. For not letting me give up on this project for various reasons, and in various ways, over the past four years, this book is as much hers as it is mine. And for helping me edit and reorganize a text that was painful to read—not simply because it retells a heavy and painful history we share—she deserves more praise than I can give. Unending love and thanks to our children, Sophia and Ian, who sat through more meetings, and missed more trips to the park, than they remember.

Love and respect is due to everyone involved in Occupy Oakland who made it what it was, which was far more than I could even attempt to cover in this book.

*When Riot Cops
Are Not Enough*

CHAPTER 1

The Commune by the Bay

THE ORIGINS
OF OCCUPY OAKLAND

SCORES OF PEOPLE filled the park in front of Oakland's city hall on a rainy Monday afternoon in early October 2011, for the formation of Occupy Oakland. I joined that gathering of about five hundred with my two kids, donned in dripping wet ladybug and duck raincoats, climbing halfway up light fixtures to get a better look at the landscape dotted with multicolored umbrellas and various speakers engaging those present through a small P.A. system. It was a familiar place to me, at the corner of Fourteenth and Broadway—a familiar place to many people there. The intersection at which the park was located had served as a convergence point on many nights during the movement that had militantly demanded justice for Oscar Grant. Grant was the young man shot in the back and killed while being detained, face-down, on the Fruitvale Station train platform on January 1, 2009, in Oakland by Bay Area Rapid Transit (BART) Police (Chimurenga 2014; Raider Nation Collective 2010). This park, renamed by Occupy Oakland that day in honor of Grant's memory, had also been the site of a series of large grassroots protests in opposition to the city's gang injunctions in the preceding months. The plaza that we were claiming was one where we had previously run from the cops, and also where we had stood up

Image 1   Occupy Oakland General Assembly in Oscar Grant Plaza
(January 2012). (Photo by Daniel Arauz)

to the cops—enough so that those small uprisings led to the first
criminal conviction of a California police officer for an unlawful
on-duty killing. Now we stood here in the rain, the newest node
in a global movement that had emerged in the United States
three weeks earlier, with an encampment that occupied a New
York City park. No cops in sight, quite yet.

Just weeks earlier, my kids had also joined me as we tailed
a few winding marches through these same downtown streets,
marches that opposed ongoing budget cuts to social services in
the city of Oakland. The one that sparked the most outrage in
our small, familial affinity group was the closing of several Oakland public schools and libraries.[1] On this wet day, my kids, aged
six and four, tired of listening to grown-ups talk, just wanted to
know if we were going to march already (and if we could get
pizza). While we ate pizza across the street I told them we'd be
marching soon enough. Like anything truly beautiful and excit-
ing, it was hard to conceptualize exactly what this new thing was,
or to rationally explain the specific reasons I had for feeling the

way that I did. We left the park that day and descended to the BART platform. I couldn't shake that anxious-in-a-good-way feeling and a shared sense of connection with those who waited on that platform with us, their cardboard signs soggy now, but still legible. Nominally waiting for a train, really waiting for a "what next?" that we couldn't define, but we knew we were a part of.

What Was Occupy Wall Street?

Occupy Oakland was one of dozens of Occupy sites in the United States—following from the public occupations of city parks and squares during the Arab Spring of 2011, first in Tunisia and most visibly in Egypt, where the Mubarak regime was ousted in February 2011. The first Occupy site in the United States was Zucotti Park, in New York City. It was there in Lower Manhattan that the movement got its name—"Occupy Wall Street." Zucotti Park, like the dozens of encampments that would follow in the coming weeks (Oakland included), was tactically defined by protesters living in the camps and practicing direct democracy as a mechanism for making movement decisions (Cornell 2012; Garces 2013; Maeckelbergh 2012).

The encampments were not without their problems and they proved to be less than immune to various forms of repression, but within a few weeks Occupy was everywhere. It was a living, breathing political force with a visible day-to-day existence. As a movement, while ultimately failing to meet its objectives (which are part of a longer and deeper process), Occupy was both disruptive and popular. Its demobilization would require innovation on the part of city administrators and local and federal police. In no city was this struggle to repress the Occupy movement more pronounced or protracted than in Oakland.

The politics of the movement (like any movement) were somewhat varied, but the unifying concerns stemmed most immediately from the most recent economic crisis and the social crises that it furthered—including deeper cuts to education and social services, the 2008–09 bank bailout and its cost, the foreclosure crisis, and the years of recession that followed the financial crisis of 2008. A common chant—"Banks got bailed out, we got sold out"—encompassed a general sentiment of frustration and anger with the neoliberal governance of the past decades (led by both major political parties). These neoliberal policies (also known as free market or trickle-down economics) and their associated political logic had expanded the gap between the rich and poor, fueled an enormous expansion of prisons, shrunk the middle class, facilitated the loss of manufacturing jobs through free trade agreements, shifted the tax burden from the rich onto workers, privatized essential social services from telecommunications to education, and deregulated industries like banking and healthcare (Harvey 2005; McNally 2011; Parenti 1999). The results were persistent economic crisis, the inflation and bursting of a series of speculative investment bubbles, and the steady expansion of social inequality to degrees not seen in this country since the Great Depression. While it did not have a shared, detailed platform (most mass movements do not), the movement was intent on turning these economic and social crises into a political crisis—to disturb the neoliberal politics as usual that fostered these crises and then respond to them by rewarding the corporate criminals responsible for the crisis with taxpayer money, as average Americans lost their homes and jobs.

The conceptualization of "the people" in Occupy Wall Street was "We are the 99%"—a referent to the bottom 99 percent of the income bracket. This populist framing, despite glossing over significant inequalities and tensions that existed within that 99 percent, was effective at both projecting a broad movement base and identifying an enemy—the 1 percent. While starting in New York City, after a call by the magazine *Adbusters*, the movement in the United States, as elsewhere, was largely decentralized and not led by any organization or coalition. Decisions were made by direct democracy and consensus, in face-to-face meetings called General Assemblies that were transparent and accountable if not always terribly efficient. These populist politics of opposition to a rich elite appealed to a broad base—students who were taking on enormous debt for futures that were increasingly uncertain, homeowners who owed more on their houses than they were worth due to the housing crisis, those who had lost their homes when the housing bubble burst or to predatory lenders, those who had lost their job in the recession, those who had less secure and lower paying jobs than they once had, those getting displaced out of cities by gentrification, those who were opposed to recent environmental disasters aided by government deregulation, and those who saw a lack of social justice (however they happened to define it) and wanted to do something about it.

The act of occupying parks was publicly visible and disruptive without being overly risky. The encampment tactic was also easily transferable to any location—the necessities being a few people with tents and signs. The localization and decentralization of the movement was a clear advancement in relation to other movements. People didn't need to wait for a march, and the protest wasn't over a few hours after it started. The camps built and fostered community, discussion, and debate that was more open than traditional forms of mobilization.

The movement, centered around this tactic of park encampments, took off after the initial camp in New York City was erected on September 17, 2011 (Gould-Wartofsky 2015). Dozens of camps were erected in the first two months of the movement, with hundreds of rallies and protests taking place throughout the United States, Canada, and Europe.[2] The decentralized, self-led nature of the movement, combined with the visibility of the camp/tent tactic and the broad appeal of the populist frame with which the movement promoted itself, helped to produce camps, rallies, and bank protests in places where mass movements rarely reach. In small towns from Alaska to Mississippi the movement was both something people wanted to be involved in and something they could easily be an active part of.

THE EMERGENCE OF
OCCUPY OAKLAND

Oakland's encampment began on October 10, 2011, after three planning meetings that took place twenty blocks north, at Mosswood Park. Those meetings established the basic logistics of the first day. Furthermore, resolutions were passed at the first General Assembly (on October 10, 2011) that there would be no negotiation with police over permits in relation to any of Occupy Oakland's activities.[3] From previous experience, and for reasons I will discuss in the next chapter, the overwhelming majority of Occupiers in Oakland viewed appealing to city officials or the police for permission to protest as inherent dead ends, at best.[4] Things like official permits to assemble (in this case quasi-permanently) in the plaza, permits for amplified sound, the expectation that the movement maintain "order" as determined by the police or by city officials, the expectation that the movement would police itself, were almost universally rejected by Occupy Oakland.

This orientation of rejecting communication, cooperation, and collaboration with the police or mayor's office would come to play a significant role in the nature of the Occupy Oakland encampment. The encampment conceived of itself as a commune, with hundreds of residents and hundreds more as active participants in planning protests, creating committees, resolving conflicts, making posters, cooking food, providing basic healthcare, and helping to care for children on a daily basis. The camp and the broader community that was Occupy Oakland was a prefigurative movement—a collectivity premised on self-sufficient mutual aid that attempted to model a different and egalitarian set of social relations. It was also very much a militant movement that was far more hostile to existing political structures than disillusioned by them. From the very first day, the stage was set for an inevitable conflict between the movement and the administration of the city. The unfolding of that conflict, the creativity of various forces of repression, and the resilience of the movement form a story no one could have foretold.

The Failure of Social Control and Repression in Oakland

The two main mechanisms of protest movement social control[5]—physical force and negotiation, techniques of hard and soft repression—failed dramatically in Oakland in the fall of 2011. This book provides an explanation of why they failed but also of how they were eventually successfully restored. Beyond the simple ebb and flow of movement activity, there was a clear and conscious, if not always centralized, set of efforts to reestablish social control and destabilize the movement. These efforts came from a range of actors—the police, the mayor, the city administrator, the mainstream press, pro-police groups, the Chamber of Commerce—sometimes in a coordinated fashion, other times not. Occupy Oakland overcame negotiated management, and the thousands who came out to support and expand the movement saw repression as illegitimate and ultimately unsuccessful at demobilizing Occupy Oakland protests, *for a period of time*. These tools of social control were reconstituted relatively quickly.

The fall of 2011 presented a political opportunity initially seized by Occupy Oakland and then lost. The course of events illustrates how that opportunity was an effect and not a cause, as a reality forged by the movement itself. On October 25, hundreds of people withstood ongoing barrages of less-lethal weapons for several hours. It was the critical wounding of marine veteran Scott Olsen that put a face on the police violence of that night.[6] That violence opened up a significant political opportunity that simultaneously mobilized and expanded the movement while demobilizing aggressive street policing in the coming weeks.

That chain of events would not have taken place if people had simply dispersed or been deterred by the waves of less-lethal weapons. As in any society, stability and social control are the norm; therefore, studying how the social control of movements works illuminates not just the repression of social movements, but the terrain upon which they operate and the most immediate struggles they must transform in order to succeed. The term "social control" is used in relation to social movements throughout the book to refer to the symbiotic relationship between both "hard" and "soft" techniques of repression. Hard repression refers to the range of mostly police techniques of preemptive arrests, restriction of free assembly, surveillance, riot police, less-lethal weapons, arrests, prosecution, and incarceration (Noakes and Gillham 2006). Soft repression refers to efforts by various state and nonstate actors that have the intent or effect of politically delegitimating, dividing, coopting, or intimidating movement actors or movements.

For various reasons all of these contexts that shape the viability and efficacy of social control—whether negotiated management or police repression—were unfavorable to the police and city officials in Oakland in October 2011. Negotiation proved impossible in an encampment that fashioned itself as an autonomous commune, self-styled after the Paris Commune, where anticapitalist and antipolice sentiment were not only present, but widespread. Not only could police find no one to negotiate with, they were physically confronted and verbally abused when they would attempt to even go near the perimeter of the camp.[7] Letters from City Hall were burned at General Assemblies.[8] In terms of public opinion, the police themselves had been the target of many recent major protest movements. Tactics used against anti–Iraq War protesters as well as general police abuse and misconduct, including the Oakland Riders scandal,[9] had further tarnished a police department already well known for political repression and abuse of subaltern communities (Bloom and Martin 2013;

Murch 2010). Physical repression of a progressive/radical populist movement, which was riding the momentum of democratization movements in the Arab world earlier that year, in what is arguably the most Left-leaning urban area in the United States, held with it the serious risk of blowback for the city. When police in Oakland were incapable of getting the movement to abide by its wishes through persuasion, force was the only option left. The fears expressed by Mayor Quan and others, that repression would create a martyr of the camp and the movement, engendering public support and ultimately proving counterproductive, turned out to be particularly astute.[10]

"When the Smoke Cleared . . .":
Two Brief Vignettes from
Occupy Oakland

At 4 A.M. on the morning of October 25, 2011, several hundred riot police arrived to evict the Occupy Oakland encampment.[11] Angry, weary, and anxious Occupiers erected barricades around the perimeter of the park that were made primarily out of wooden pallets and folding tables. But with only a couple of hundred Occupiers present at that hour, there were only enough Occupiers to defend a small part of the park, and the idea of defending it was abandoned as the police closed in on the plaza.[12] With the exception of those who stayed to commit passive civil disobedience, there were few arrests, as the police cleared the park and tore up the camp—shredding tents, dismantling makeshift social centers, and trampling belongings. A hundred Occupiers marched throughout downtown for hours, followed but not confronted by police, but went home amid the bustle of the morning commute and what the police hoped was a return to normalcy in downtown Oakland.

Later that day a few thousand came out to protest and march in opposition to the eviction, finding the park where the camp had stood cordoned off by several hundred riot police. Hundreds of mutual aid police from seventeen other surrounding cities pursued a coordinated strategy of controlling urban space in downtown Oakland.[13] That night they successfully prevented Occupy Oakland from retaking the plaza in front of City Hall where their encampment had stood until being evicted early that morning.[14] As night fell and the number of demonstrators dwindled to about a thousand, the police attacked the demonstrators with less-lethal weapons for several hours. As Occupiers would approach Fourteenth and Broadway (at the perimeter of Oscar Grant Plaza where the camp had stood) to meet the rows of riot police assembled from more than a dozen Bay Area police forces, volleys of concussion grenades, tear gas, CS gas, rubber bullets, and bean-bag munitions were fired at the retreating crowd.[15] The police held their line, but demonstrators kept coming back, and were met with more aggression in the form of wave after wave of police projectiles and chemical weapons. This process went on for several hours. During this series of police attacks, marine veteran Scott Olsen was hit with a tear gas canister from very close range, critically wounding him and putting a bloodied human face on the now martyred movement.[16] The police violence was immediate global news. Other centers of the movement in Cairo, New York City, and elsewhere were quick to express solidarity.[17]

The following evening, October 26, more than three thousand people descended upon downtown Oakland and reclaimed Oscar Grant Plaza, as police were now ordered to desist.[18] The encampment was re-erected that night as the movement's largest ever General Assembly voted in favor of a General Strike, which would bring downtown Oakland to a halt and shut down the Port of Oakland on November 2. Police repression evicted the camp, but for a mere thirty-six hours. On the evening of October 26, as the police were ordered to stand down, the encampment returned. The movement quickly seized this opportunity, as the police orders extended to two subsequent Port shutdowns. The bravery of the movement in the face of repression was turned into emboldened and legitimate mass action after the application of that repression on the evening of October 25. I was one of several hundred who found themselves coughing up chemical weapons for days after that night, but those days also included taking back the plaza, voting for a General Strike, and beginning to plan actions that would take advantage of the political moment that had been created by the failed police repression.

There was a visible anger among the broader Left in the Bay—over the eviction of a protest camp, over the excessive force of the Oakland Police. Local sympathy and support for the movement were heightened by the police repression. The movement was able to use this support to expand and take on bigger and bolder actions. As Scott Olsen lay in his hospital bed and many others nursed contusions from various police projectiles, the only political victims of the police violence on the night of October 25 were the forces of social control themselves—a reality made visible worldwide when more than fifty thousand people descended on, and shut down, the Port of Oakland a week later. The window of political opportunity that was created on October 25 showed that repression does not always work, that there are more forces at play in relation to demonstrations than simply tactics and their material effects. That window of political opportunity was slowly and steadily closed by a range of actors, but *not* primarily through the use of riot police force or through convincing the movement to negotiate with police. Three months later those same police tactics that had helped mobilize and embolden the movement produced a very different effect.

On January 28, 2012, more than two months after the last camp eviction in Oakland, members of Occupy Oakland attempted to occupy the long-vacant Kaiser Convention Center and restore the social services and social center the movement had had with their two previous encampments. The same riot squad used the same tactics and weapons—tear gas, concussion grenades, and rubber bullets—against a crowd that included several children. Occupiers carried shields and assembled in formations designed to withstand police attack. The objective was to carry out a mass seizure of vacant public space, in broad daylight, for the purpose of reconstituting the camp. After an afternoon of being outmaneuvered and attacked by the police, more than three hundred people were mass-arrested.[19] These events sparked no mass support and created a clear turning point toward the movement's decline.

Why did repression mobilize and expand the movement in one moment and demobilize it in another? Theories of the policing of social movements focus predominantly on police tactics. The tactics in both of these instances were quite similar, yet their impacts on protest mobilization were polar opposites. The literature on police repression currently focuses primarily on police tactics—the use of riot squads, their formations, weapons, strategies of geographic containment. I hope to broaden the discussion

Image 2   Jon-Paul Bail producing iconic Occupy Oakland screen prints on December 12, 2011—Oscar Grant Plaza. (Photo by Daniel Arauz)

here by centering my work around policing strategies (as well as tactics). In fact, the impetus to write this book emerged from the ways in which the story of Occupy Oakland deviated from a linear narrative of protest–repression–demobilization. My analysis highlights the need to go beyond an analysis of repressive tactics to a broader examination of techniques of social control with an emphasis on the contentious social and political context in which they are deployed.

TOOLS OF REPRESSION IN CONTEXT

The days, weeks, and months that followed January 28 involved numerous and diverse attempts at regaining a momentum that the movement simply could not find. The same aggressive police tactics did not elicit that same protest mobilizing effect; the movement was instead successfully marginalized, demonized, criminalized.[20] What do these two instances, tactically similar in terms of repression but diametrically opposed in terms of strategic impact on mobilization, tell us about the nature of protest policing and the possibilities for the persistence of popular protest in the face of aggressive policing? What other facets of policing and social control, as well as their contexts in relation to movement tactics and popular support, need to be analyzed in an effort to make sense of the potential for social movement persistence and growth, or the persistence of social control? How should we conceptualize the overall logic and practice of social control in relation to protest and social movements today? These are the questions that animate this book. It is my aim to not simply detail police tactics, but to also contextually analyze how police tactics are but one variable in a much broader patchwork of social control.

Simply looking at police tactics and techniques of repression (i.e., surveillance, riot squads, less-lethal weapons, permits, etc.) glosses over the social contexts that produce and are produced by repression. As someone who has been active in major protest movements since the 1990s, and as a scholar, I feel that theories of social control need to cover more ground than describing what the protest repression tools are and where they came from. Why is police force seen as legitimate in some instances and not others? Beyond equipment and training, what relation does the war on drugs/crime have on the policing of protest? What is the contemporary role and scope of federal agencies in the policing of protest? What is the role of the press, or other knowledge producers like city officials, in delegitimating movements, dividing movements, and criminalizing them? I feel that exploring these questions helps us see not just what the new techniques of repression are, but how and why they work, as well as providing a map of fault lines and contradictions that exist within these methods of social control.

As researchers trying to make sense of the policing of protest, we need to build upon emerging theories like strategic incapacitation by situating them within the political contexts in which they are deployed, taking into consideration the orientation, tactics, social resonance, and goals of the movement (understanding these facets are often changing as movements progress), as well as broader forces of criminalization and delegitimation, that make those police tactics politically operable. Participants in social movements also must look beyond tactics (i.e., "nonviolence" versus "diversity of tactics" debates) and street-level policing, toward defining what political success means for modern movements today in the short- to mid-run. If social control is not just about controlling physical space, but negating political space for social change, what are its weaknesses and contradictions and how can they be exploited?

THE POSITIONALITY OF THE RESEARCHER AND METHODS

The breakdown of social control in October and November made me realize that there were lessons to be learned about how and why repression tactics break down, and also that the academic and movement literature could benefit from a broader view of

repression, beyond simple police tactics. My role as a participant observer and ethnographer grew out of my already existing
extensive involvement in Occupy Oakland as well as my writing
a series of popular analytic reports on Oakland and the broader
Occupy movement. The impetus behind this book is partly an
effort to document a popular movement and the barriers it tried
to overcome, and partly an effort to advance the analytic understanding of repression within the academy and social movements
themselves. Each chapter is centered around data from numerous
empirical sources, from ethnographic fieldwork and discussions
with hundreds of participants, but also from internal police documents, declassified materials, and newspaper data.

My experiences attending the vast majority of General
Assemblies from October through January and beyond, as well
as conversations and relationships built during this period, have
given me a broad knowledge of what the pulse of the movement
was in these months. I spent hours attending meetings, shivering
outside in the park, in apartments, union halls, bars, and base-
ments. I facilitated meetings, made flyers, talked and organized
with workers. I was a press liaison for the December 12 Port
Shutdown and afterward, which brought me into contact with
several journalists. This allowed me to get a sense of some of the
assumptions and frames driving their writings. My focus here
is on the social control tactics used against the movement, and
not a proper ethnography of the movement. However, because
of my involvement in the movement, I have knowledge of the
significant moments of repression, including some, like the raids
on the Occupy Oakland Vigil discussed in chapter 4, that got
little public attention but are fundamental to understanding both
the movement and efforts to repress it. My fieldwork provides a
contextual backdrop for the wealth of declassified city and police
documents, internal city communications, as well as purposive
uses of the mainstream press, legal documents, movement documents, and city press releases.

My interest, questions, and theses were originally geared to help create change, and later, in popular writing, to make sense of the evolving tensions between police and protest tactics, and ultimately as a social scientist to map the broader trajectories of protest and strategies of control—how they sit in relation to history and the literature. My extensive involvement as an organizer in Occupy Oakland has, in my view, made my analysis stronger. My initial hypotheses about police repression were predictive rather than descriptive, coming from my experiences in the movement planning actions, talking with other Occupiers about when the raid would most likely take place and what it would look like, what the police would do at the next march, seeing friends go through the legal system, debating tactics, repression, and history with newspaper reporters, calling a friend on the East Coast in the middle of the night after the plaza was retaken on October 26, asking for help starting an article to get published later that day, explaining to the world how repression had failed in Oakland and the complex terrain the police would now have to navigate to regain control (King and Ciccariello-Maher 2011). This text benefits from those extra layers of analysis that were made from a different angle than that of a "detached observer." Coupled with the wide range of empirical data that is the foundation of this text, I feel confident that the reader will find this work well grounded and insightful.

Structure of the Text

The primary story this book tells is quite divergent from the emphasis of this chapter. Occupy Oakland started as a militant movement that successfully refused negotiation and cooperation with the police, and weathered the resulting repression in the short term to orchestrate successful mass actions. However, effective social control reemerged, not simply through policing tactics, but through broader sets of coordinated and uncoordinated efforts to divide, discredit, and demobilize the movement. The bulk of the text is devoted to these broader forces and the contexts that helped shift the perception of repression from illegitimate to warranted. What these contexts and supportive structures are, how they coalesce with each other and with police tactics, and how these forces navigate the various social and political contradictions entailed in suppressing movements are questions I will answer in the remainder of the book.

Chapter 2 traces the dominant protest policing methods in the United States over the last half-century—why and how they have evolved and how they relate to each other. In recent decades there has been a shift away from policing practices that sought to negotiate the terms and nature of demonstrations with protesters, toward more aggressive forms of policing. Despite the fact that formal negotiation has declined, the chapter shows how the era in which negotiation was dominant (1970s–1990s) continues to help legitimate repression against protests who do not negotiate with, or more importantly defer to, police. The chapter also provides discussions regarding how various forms of repression are socially contextualized and also interrelated with each other.

Chapter 3 provides a narrative and analytic account of how the Oakland Police and city officials lost control in the initial weeks of the movement. Occupy Oakland was conceived as an autonomous commune in downtown Oakland—formally barring negotiation with police or other officials. Internal City Hall email discussions (made available through a FOIA request) portray the level of confusion and political paralysis created by this lack of desire on the part of the movement to negotiate and the lack of a clear plan by the newly elected mayor to repress the movement. The first police raid on the encampment brought with it dramatic police brutality that expanded the movement significantly, while momentarily dampening police repression. The movement took advantage of the political opportunity, shutting down the Port of Oakland twice in a six-week period. I provide firsthand accounts of both encampment raids, including the evening where marine veteran Scott Olsen was critically wounded by the OPD, as well as interactions between Occupiers and the police within the camps. This chapter shows how the militancy of the movement was a founding characteristic of Occupy Oakland, a characteristic that was furthered by the events that would quickly unfold.

Chapter 4 examines the role of federal coordination in the second encampment raid in Oakland, part of a nationwide eighteen-city sweep of Occupy camps in mid-November. The mayors of these eighteen cities were on conference calls with the Police Executive Research Forum (PERF), a think tank specializing in policing protests, as well as joint calls with the Federal Bureau of Investigation (FBI) and the Department of Homeland Security (DHS). DHS denies that it was in command of local policing in all of the cities with encampments, and the exact nature of PERF/FBI/DHS advice is still a point of some contention and mystery. What is clear is that all eighteen of these cities pursued an almost identical strategy for evicting their camps in mid-November. The whole world saw the Oakland Police's disastrous handling of the October 25th eviction; clearly there was a universal concern among political leaders to not replicate that failure on a mass scale in their effort to destroy the movement's camps nationally. The November raids were successful at destroying the visibility and physical centers of the movement on a national scale, without significant blowback. Oakland's camp was torn down and never reemerged; the police controlled the space without having to revert to the mass deployment of less-lethal weapons. Aside from that difference, the goals of destroying the camp and the tactical policing means used to achieve that end were largely identical to those of the first raid. It was not the tactics of strategic incapacitation that explain the difference in the public's response, but the supporting political and ideological processes that justified, normalized, or rationalized those tactics. I argue that it was the incorporation of elements of negotiated management as a normative structure that helped to situate the police and their objectives as legitimate.

Chapter 5 provides a micro-level examination of the application of negotiated management and strategic incapacitation methods, which drew from existing anti-gang techniques in the City of Oakland, to surveil, target, and criminalize specific actors and control public space. Beginning in November 2011, a combination of smaller-scale physical repression and surveillance efforts were deployed, enhanced by the issuing of a permit for the plaza after the second raid, as well as restraining orders issued against many Occupiers to restrict their access to the plaza. Activists with criminal records and those who continued to distribute food and maintain a presence in the plaza were targeted by police in an effort to control urban space and targeted populations. The police drew upon civil and criminal law, and its interpellatory power,[21] refashioned from anti-gang initiatives, to target specific individuals and geographic areas while furthering a public image of the movement as being inherently apolitical, dangerous, and criminal. These were themes that would persist in the following months, shaping Occupy Oakland and the repression of it.

Chapter 6 details the last major direct action that Occupy Oakland attempted, the occupation of the vacant, publicly owned Kaiser Convention Center (briefly discussed earlier in this chapter). Using press releases, declassified police documents, primary documents from the *San Francisco Chronicle*, and participant observation from my interviews with various news reporters, the chapter illustrates the relationship between the criminalization of social movements and aggressive policing.

Chapter 7 illustrates the period from January to May 2012, which saw numerous efforts by Occupy Oakland to expand its base into working-class communities around issues of police brutality, housing, grassroots labor organizing, and the reclamation of unused space, and to build toward a major mass action on May 1. On the national scene, MoveOn.org and the major labor federations launched a cooptive campaign, the 99% Spring, to appeal to liberal activists to break from Occupy, which was portrayed as apolitical, disorganized, and directionless. Within Oakland, the movement saw a series of events (some externally imposed, others organic to the movement) that fostered divisions and conflicts. Three of the more important conflicts involved three Occupy Oakland (OO) participants being arrested and charged with an anti-gay hate crime (charges that were later dropped), the disbanding of the OO Media Committee after several members falsely accused a prominent member of the movement of being on a terrorist watch list, and the protracted harassment of the OO Anti-Repression Committee and false accusations that some of its members were embezzling money. As the movement weathered these controversies while trying to build a broader base and planning for a mass action (which would fall far short of expectations), the Oakland police were training in new crowd-control tactics (utilizing what activists refer to as "Snatch Squads"). In spite of a court order barring the OPD from altering its crowd-control tactics, and legal challenges made by the ACLU, the OPD's aggressive control of urban space on May 1 against a crowd that was a fraction of the size of early marches was tactically successful and marked Occupy Oakland's last attempt to initiate a mass action. The book concludes by briefly summarizing the arc of social control tactics from October 2011 through May 2012, highlighting the roles of legitimacy and criminalization in the policing of protest and the various factors beyond police street tactics that inform modern strategies of social control.

This book illustrates the wide variety of repression techniques deployed against Occupy Oakland, mutually reinforcing tactics of hard and soft repression. Repression seeks to not only aggressively contain street demonstrations and movement tactics of strategic disruption, but to undermine the constituent power of movements through a combination of physical force and discursive power that defines the movement as a criminal problem and as a threat to the common good. It was Occupy Oakland's radical politics and militancy, coupled with widespread popular support locally, that made it the flashpoint that it was within the US Occupy movement. The success of the two shutdowns of the Port of Oakland as well as effective organizing against foreclosures and the continued neoliberal restructuring of the city, and in support of striking workers and victims of police brutality, all hinged upon this foundational nexus of autonomous radical politics combined with mobilizable popular support. The various forces seeking to contain, disrupt, and demobilize the movement did so through various efforts to undermine this foundational nexus of radical militancy and popular support.

The spectacle of police repression in late October 2011 helped transform the movement from a small but intractable movement into a mass movement when the police descended on a small crowd of less than two thousand on October 25, hoping to extinguish the small but well-crafted fire that was a young Occupy Oakland. They failed to extinguish the movement that evening, and 50,000 people showed up less than a week later like a strong wind fueling a fire that was now hotter and larger. Through repression efforts that divided and contained the movement, police, city officials, the corporate media, and others formulated a strategy of a controlled burn. By May 2012, the Oakland Police were stamping on the remaining embers of that great conflagration in the exact intersection that had ignited the blaze six months earlier.

I contend that public *legitimacy* is central to successful policing and the repression of dissent, and that gaining and maintaining legitimacy is a sociopolitical process, not a tactical issue. Both repressive power and the constituent power of social movements are ultimately rooted in their ability to transform the social world, a process that is ultimately determined not just by the ability to act in the face of opposition, but to also successfully define the context of the social conflict in which they are engaged and the actors involved in that conflict. The ability of hard repression and aggressive street policing to demobilize and disrupt movements ultimately hinges upon the successful *criminalization* of its target— in this case Occupy Oakland. The movement had mass support from one of the more progressive urban centers in the country. After the first raid thousands came out in support, not know-ing if they would be subject to the same brutality they had seen via mainstream and new media after October 25. Rather than driving people fearfully back into their homes, the initial repres-sion drew out tens of thousands to take direct action. Where did those people go? The answer is hard to quantify, but a facet of social control in the context of social movements that gets under-analyzed is the role of ideological supports, the state and media as educators, and the construction of a common sense around the social control of movements that nonetheless resonates with the public. Despite standing against police brutality, foreclosures, and budget cuts, in a Left-leaning city with a radical past plagued by these problems, how did the movement go from being a martyr in the eyes of the public to being defined as a social problem, all within three months—with a progressive (formerly Maoist) mayor declaring the movement a criminal enterprise rather than a social movement? How were both negotiated management and strategic incapacitation intertwined through political discourses and press coverage? What does this tell us about social control generally and the efficacy of police tactics specifically? The arc of this text illus-trates how the successful repression of Occupy Oakland ultimately had more to do with effectively painting the movement as violent, apolitical, socially marginal, dangerous, irresponsible, and internally fractured than it did with street policing tactics.

CHAPTER 2

From Permits
to Storm Troopers

REPRESSION, SOCIAL CONTROL, AND THE GOVERNMENTALITY OF PROTEST

THE SOCIOLOGY AND criminology of protest policing is usually developed from observing protest movements failing to overcome various techniques of social control (Fernandez 2008; Gillham and Noakes 2007; Starr, Fernandez, and Scholl 2011; Vitale 2007). Studies of repression tend to emphasize an overwhelming, and seemingly insurmountable, array of policing techniques. Overall, scholarship on protest policing presents different models of policing that have been predominant in different eras. The era of the 1960s was defined by a police approach referred to in the literature as "escalated force." Escalated force was a policing approach "in which the militancy of protesters was met by increased militancy by the police. Any show of force or violence by the protesters was met with overwhelming force in return" (Vitale 2005, 286). In the 1970s, a significant shift took place, toward a legalistic method of controlling protest that used negotiation between protesters and police, usually resulting in protest permits that defined the nature and details of the protest in order to decrease both protester disruptiveness and the use of police force. The police use of militarized equipment and tactics against protesters at the 1999 World Trade Organization in Seattle

Image 3   Police line at Fourteenth and Broadway. (Photo by Daniel Arauz)

is seen as marking a second shift, this time away from the model defined by negotiation between protesters and police and toward a new model of protest policing termed "strategic incapacitation" by John Noakes and Patrick Gillham (2006). This new form is defined by more preemptive, militarized, and surveillance-driven policing. There is a general agreement that these most recent models—negotiated management and strategic incapacitation—are mutually exclusive and temporally separated. Following Antonio Gramsci, my argument is that these strategies of force and consent are mutually constituted and, separately, that the effectiveness of modern police aggression is predicated on criminalizing protesters through the use of the norms and expectations of negotiation and nondisruption.

THE POLICING OF PROTEST IN HISTORICAL CONTEXT

The literatures on negotiated management and strategic incapacitation, taken collectively, create a historiography of evolving normative models of protest social control. The history of protest policing in the United States can be read, in a very generalized way, as shifting from "escalated forced" in the 1960s, to "negotiated management" from the mid-1970s through 1990s, followed by a second shift to "strategic incapacitation" as negotiation became less likely (Gillham and Noakes 2007; McCarthy and McPhail 1998). Clark McPhail, David Schweingruber, and John McCarthy describe escalated force as "characterized by the use of force as a standard way of dealing with demonstrations. Police confronted demonstrators with a dramatic show of force and followed with a progressively escalated use of force if demonstrators failed to abide by police instructions to limit or stop their activities. . . . Arrests were forceful and were used strategically by police to target and remove 'agitators.' The main exception to the rule of immediate arrest was when police used physical punishment in lieu of arrests" (1998, 53).

McCarthy and McPhail note that the shift to negotiated management was driven by the legitimacy crisis brought on by everything from indiscriminate police force at events like the 1968 Democratic National Convention (1998, 86) to the FBI's COINTELPRO (counter-intelligence program) of disrupting, discrediting, and destroying radical movements using a range of illegal and sometimes murderous tactics (Churchill and Vander Wall 1988, 1990; O'Reilly 1989). While this analysis is correct, it is also incomplete. It was not just the brutality of 1960s policing that produced the negotiated management model; it was the political threat posed by various social movements—the extent to which the social order was challenged by both entrenched grassroots efforts and widespread rioting and social upheaval, and the degree of legitimacy and support these movements had both domestically and internationally. It was disorder and the threat of substantial social change that prompted the illegal state violence of the 1960s as well as the legalistic incorporation of protest in the 1970s (Piven and Cloward 1977). The successes (if mostly partial) of the movements of the 1960s, in spite of repression, forced the state to innovate its strategy of controlling protests.

Negotiated management arose via various legal decisions, mostly in the 1970s, amid the backdrop of numerous riot commissions, the Church Committee hearings, Watergate, and widespread disillusionment with the government (National Advisory Committee on Civil Disorders 1968; Platt 1971; Skolnick 1969). Jerome Skolnick led a team of researchers that reported to a national commission on protest and violence in the late 1960s, highlighting the interaction between police tactics and protest escalation in the pre-negotiated management moment. The report states:

> [U]nnecessary police violence can only exacerbate the problems police action is used to solve. Protesters are inflamed, and a cycle of greater and greater violence is set into motion— both in the particular incident and in future incidents. More fundamentally, the misuse of police force violates basic notions of our society concerning the role of police. Police are not supposed to adjudicate and punish; they are supposed to apprehend and take into custody. To the extent to which a nation's police step out of such bounds, that nation has given up the rule of law in a self-defeating quest for order. (1969, 249)

Politically at this time, the contradiction inherent in the need to contain popular protest while maintaining police/government legitimacy was acute. Police forces, particularly in major cities, were pressured to uphold First Amendment rights to free speech and assembly while maintaining social order and limiting police aggressiveness (McPhail, Schweingruber, and McCarthy 1998, 55–62). Negotiated management emerged as a strategy and set of practices to resolve this tension (heightened in the 1960s) between upholding the First Amendment and controlling protest—without eliciting a generalized questioning of police/state legitimacy. Negotiated management came to be characterized by situations in which "protest organizers give notice of their intent to demonstrate or obtain a permit to protest. In each case, an opportunity is created, if not required, for contact, interaction, and negotiation between police and protest organizers regarding the purpose, the time, place and manner of protest" (McPhail and McCarthy 2005, 5).

McPhail and McCarthy argue that this constitutes a clear improvement over the escalated force era, putting limitations on both police and protesters, marking negotiated management as an improvement and an evolution of democratic assembly, assuring freedom of speech and limiting (the need for) police violence. The police are seen as markedly more tolerant and utilizing minimum force, the First Amendment is better protected, communication is more open and extensive, and arrests less frequent and more civil (2005, 5). They note the predictability and institutionalization that has come to define most major protests, but conclude that the decrease in violence facilitated by police–protester cooperation outweighs the drawbacks, "as protest has been incorporated as a normal part of the political process" (McCarthy and McPhail 1998, 109).

By incorporating protest as "a normal part of the political process," negotiated management has contained protesters' ability to disrupt or fundamentally change that process. Permits grant more power to police, incorporating police into the nature of permitted protest, while also drawing permit holders into aspects of policing. Negotiated management is designed to make protest less disruptive, to decrease the threat posed, which invariably diminishes the need for brute force. Given that Frances Fox Piven and Richard Cloward define social movements themselves as fundamentally disruptive and defiant (1977, 4–5), it is probably more accurate to say that negotiated management has created a lower form of protest, highly controlled externally and internally, stripped of its disruptive capacity, rather than arguing that it has created a higher standard of policing (Seferiades and Johnston 2012, 5). The police do not need to contain and manage protest because the protesters are doing it themselves.

Negotiated Management as Repression

Negotiated management has often been understood in the academic literature and within movements as a means to protect First Amendment rights and mitigate police violence through the normalization of protest permits and other formal and informal means of communication, coordination, and mutual agreement between protest organizers and police (McPhail et al. 1998, 51). Negotiated management emerged from the crisis of the 1960s, where violence at protests was common and police were increasingly seen by the public as illegitimate because of the repression used against protesters. While noting the banalization of protest in some respects, McPhail, Schweingruber, and McCarthy (1998) see negotiated management as a form of progress, away from the "escalated force" norms of police repression in the 1960s. Statistical evidence supports the thesis of a trend away from police violence from the 1960s through the 1990s. Sarah Soule and Christian Davenport (2009) found that police aggression in the 1970s and 1980s occurred at half the rate of the 1960s, but note that we should view police repression as correlated to the threat posed by protesters—the nature and tone of the protests in the two eras.[1] Soule and Davenport (2009) and P.A.J. Waddington (1998) problematize the argument that negotiated management constrains police violence, arguing that it is not so much whether or not there is a permit agreed to but the level of protest disruption that prefigures the police use of force. It is the level of disruption, the threat to social order, which determines the aggressiveness of police tactics or innovations in police strategies. These analyses do not examine the lack of effectiveness among social movements whose tactics involve cooperation with police. What is missing in much of the existing scholarship is how negotiated management, itself, is a form of repression.

Jennifer Earl (2011) defines repression as "state or private action that prevents, controls, or constrains protest, including its initiation" (262). This definition broadens the source of repression to include nonstate actors and further defines the general ways in which repression takes shape—which include important factors like discrediting protesters, channeling protests toward certain tactics, and/or intimidating participants. Gary Marx (1998) and McPhail, Schweingruber, and McCarthy (1998) themselves note how negotiated management gives police influence over the nature, time, place, and particulars of protest. These serve as a large set of obstacles to protest disruptiveness, made all the more powerful by the extent to which they are incorporated through the segment of the movement that takes on the negotiating. The permit-holding (police-sanctioned) leadership of the movement—those who have their name on the flyers, those who control the stage and microphone, those who lead the march, those who receive tax-deductible donations (so long as they have a permit), those who get to take out the next permit so long as there is no disruption at the previous protest (McCarthy and McPhail 1998, 94, 100–104)—agree to these terms on behalf of the whole movement (while defining the parameters of "legitimate protest"), internalizing repression by acting as adjunct "staff" for the police, while also legitimating, normalizing, and making less visible the restrictions on free speech imposed by negotiated management.

Several authors have referred to negotiated management as a form of repression designed to neutralize threats before they emerge, preserving order, while reserving violence and maintaining legitimacy for the police (Fernandez 2008; King and Waddington 2006; Starr et al. 2011). Theories of protest must take into account disruption and repression, as well as the question of legitimacy, since they are foundational aspects of both protest and social control. It was the perceived illegitimacy of the police in the eyes of the public, combined with subsequent legal rulings calling for the reform of protest policing, that ushered in the era of negotiated management in the first place (McPhail et al. 1998, 63). The tumult of the 1960s necessitated development of new methods to manage and contain future protest that did not rely on physical force as a first option. While negotiated management is more complex than this, its use as a tool to neutralize disruption and to serve as an invisible form of discipline and repression that maintains police legitimacy is key to making sense of the modern social control of protest movements generally. This invariably influences the tactical repertoire and strategy of social movements themselves, and over time has played a significant role in shaping how many participants and the general public view the nature and process of popular protest.

While negotiated management altered how, when, and if force was used, it was never designed to displace force. Negotiated management was a complementary tool of repression, as police capacities to violently repress protest continued to advance from the 1970s through the 1990s, regardless of how often the deployment of those capacities was deemed necessary in the context of protests. Drawing on the Kerner Report (in Platt 1971, 343–377), a major impetus for the police reform in the 1970s that produced negotiated management, Kristian Williams (2007) highlights how police militarization and negotiated management were never separate but were developed alongside and through each other: "In short, it is military discipline that makes Negotiated Management a possibility, restraining the individual officers while maintaining the potential for a coordinated attack. This requires careful planning for the operation itself, and a higher level of discipline among the officers so that each one acts according to the established plan. Hence, militarization may *increase* the organization's overall capacity for violence, but may decrease individual acts of brutality, owing to a higher level of discipline" (195).

Christian Parenti (1999), Peter Kraska (2001), and Williams (2011) note how the insurrections of the 1960s prompted massive changes in policing generally, from crowd-control strategies to advances in police technology, from police education and training to a plethora of new laws, from new social control techniques on the ground to federal-level coordination. In terms of the policing of protest, negotiated management and militarization of the police have their root in the same social crisis (of the 1960s), and seek the same social control ends. Negotiated management is not simply peaceful coordination, but a multilayered form of social control. Modern riot policing, despite the way it often plays out in practice, is not designed to be simply the wanton unleashing of police force. "The use of force is not an end in itself, nor is it indiscriminate. Instead, rearranging and incapacitating protesters allows the police to control and defuse protests without risking the legitimation crisis faced at the end of the escalated force era" (Noakes and Gillham 2006, 114). What separates modern protest policing from the (in some respects) similar, force-oriented strategies of the 1960s is the development of police praxis (street policing derived from empirically tested and theoretically informed training) as well as the use of surveillance and communications technologies and less-lethal weapons. Furthermore, modern protest policing "does not represent a return to escalated force because it attempts to avoid the use of force through planning and careful management of the protest" (Vitale 2005, 287). Force is reserved for disruptiveness, a social control problem that negotiated management was and is designed to preempt—either directly through permits, or indirectly through expected nondisruptive modes and methods of protest. Negotiated management is not an evolution away from police aggression: Police aggression and negotiated management are two sides of the same coin (Williams 2011).

MILITARIZED POLICING:
THE EVOLUTION OF ESCALATED
AND STRATEGIC FORCE

Luis Fernandez (2008), Amory Starr, Luis Fernandez, and Christian Scholl (2011), and Williams (2007) also draw attention to the apparent contradictory forces of modern protest policing—that of negotiated management coexisting with the militarization of protest policing in the last decades—including many years when negotiated management was still dominant. This seeming contradiction of less common police aggression along-side the evolution of militarized policing in the era of negotiated management is clarified by seeing negotiated management as a form of repression, but also seeing that the use of police violence was never rescinded but restrained, reserved for instances when the subtler repression of negotiation failed. If that discipline of negotiated management were to fail, riot police would be waiting to hand out forceful reminders about the appropriate comport-ment of dissent.

While the militarization of protest policing in the United States is substantially different in practice from other forms of police militarization, they share a common lineage as well as overlapping uses of equipment, training, and organization. In defining the overall militarization of the police, Kraska (2001) offers a broad conceptualization that points to police equip-ment and practices, but also importantly to the social context and meaning of this form of policing that, as the course of this book will illustrate, is fundamental to successful hard repression. Kraska defines militarization as "the social process in which society orga-nizes itself for the production of violence or the threat thereof" (16). My partial conceptualization of general police militarization involves a variety of connected facets: military *equipment* (vehi-cles, weapons, body armor, surveillance equipment), new forms of *specialized organization* and the proliferation of Special Weapons and Tactics (SWAT) teams and riot squads (ACLU 2014; Balko 2013), *training* with domestic and foreign military (Williams 2007, 2011); the socially diffused ideology/discourse of war, as in the Wars on Drugs, Gangs, Terror, etc. (Kraska 2001); milita-rized *police culture and psychology* (Herbert 1997); and the *milita-rization of geographic spaces and zones* (Beckett and Herbert 2010; Herbert 1997). We see all of these facets of police militarization translated and incorporated into the modern policing of protest. From MRAPs (Mine-Resistant Ambush Protected Vehicles) and body armor, to crowd-control lessons from the Israeli Defense Forces (IDF),[2] to the definition of protesters as internal enemies or criminal syndicates, and the militarized securing and cordoning of specific urban spaces, protest policing is a microcosm of broader police militarization, tailored to the circumstances and contexts of protest. Contemporary US protest policing is defined by processes, practices, and discourses that draw on military equipment, training, and organization to control space, intimidate or contain targets, and strategically deploy force to neutralize the disruptive capacity of protest.

THE LOGIC OF NEW PENOLOGY AND THE TECHNIQUES OF STRATEGIC INCAPACITATION

Although distinct in many respects, changes in protest policing cannot be fully understood outside of the context of more generalized policing trends (Oliver 2008). Whether in terms of changes in technology, equipment, and weapons, or surveillance capacity in the process of police militarization (Kraska 2001, 15–17; Williams 2007, 195–196) or the increasing political power of the state and police to expand their sphere of influence in the name of security (Garland 2012, 40–43; Rigakos 2011, 57–84), the policing of protest, and protest itself, are shaped by broader political, economic, and cultural changes in the nature of policing in society. New penology is an extension of the logic of zero-tolerance policing, the use of new technology and intelligence to target and preempt marginal populations that pose an implicit or explicit threat to the social order. Many of the tools and strategies used against street protesters over the last decade and a half are derived from law enforcement techniques developed in the wars on drugs, gangs, terror, and immigration. These techniques of generalized new penology in the broader field of policing, which find derived parallels in the strategic incapacitation model of protest policing, include new forms of surveillance and profiling (Marx 1988; Neocleous and Rigakos 2011; Tirman 2004), the normalization of preventative policing measures (as opposed to reactive criminal investigation) (Harcourt 2001; Williams 2006), the control of physical space by police (Davis 1990; Herbert 1997), as well as aggressive, militarized policing (Davis 1990; Kraska 2001).

Noakes and Gillham (2006) have provided a useful framework to understand the "new repression" that emerged after the Seattle WTO protests of 1999, and the different facets of social control used to confront the "new breed of protester" that has emerged, one that increasingly refuses to cooperate with police, organizes in a decentralized and often leaderless fashion, and pursues disruptive direct action. Noakes and Gillham (2006), King and Waddington (2006), and Vitale (2007) all argue that protest policing over the past fifteen years has taken on the logic and many of the methods of urban policing more generally: of zero-tolerance and preemptive methods of policing (Beckett and Herbert 2010; Harcourt 2001; Vitale 2005); tighter police control over geographic space (Herbert 1997; Wacquant 2009); and an increased use of surveillance and intelligence gathering (Graham 2010; Haggerty and Ericson 2001; Parenti 2003; Marx 1988). This shift in the dominant model of policing, derived from broader policing changes under the rubric of "new penology" (Feeley and Simon 1992), has been termed "strategic incapacitation" (Noakes and Gillham 2006)—the application of militarized policing in the context of protest control, to neutralize (potential) threats to public order (Oliver 2008). Strategic incapacitation encompasses a variety of aggressive police tactics designed to neutralize disruptive protesters through police control of geographical space, the deployment of new weaponry and tactics (Noakes and Gillham 2006, 108–111), and, more specifically: "a range of tactical innovations aimed at temporarily incapacitating transgressive protesters, including the establishment of extensive no-protest zones, the increased use of less-lethal weapons, the strategic use of arrests, and a reinvigoration of surveillance and infiltration of movement organizations. This shift in police tactics during protests is consistent with broader changes in the ideological underpinnings of crime control, including an emphasis on risk management and the prevention of (rather than reaction to) crime and disorder" (Gillham and Noakes 2007, 343).

While this police strategy usually works, it is not without weaknesses or contradictions. Tactically, the police in Oakland deployed all of these measures before and after the critical juncture of police violence on October 25, 2011, yet these methods were counterproductive at first. The four facets of strategic incapacitation serve as an accurate assessment of the tactical core of modern protest policing.[3] Attention to how these tactics are situated in a broader strategy of legitimated social control allows us to see how and why they work, as well as explain moments in which they do not—illuminating the broader social contexts that are the hinge that determines whether repression closes the door on social movements or allows them to travel through it and make social change.

The common objective of brute force and negotiation is simply to maintain order and prevent or contain disruption, which, in the context of street demonstrations, is achieved through relatively indiscriminate force in the 1960s, through incorporation of police objectives within agreed terms of protest and the use of bureaucratic, legalistic, and institutionalized methods of control under negotiated management in the 1970s, 1980s, and 1990s, and increasingly through militarized and targeted policing at present. In a very general sense, this can be seen as a cyclical return back toward a reliance on brute force, but one in which surveillance, advanced methods of controlling space, and preemptive policing against socially marginal actors (as well as the discursive criminalization of disruptive protesters) allows for a much more targeted and effective use of force.

Reconstructing the Theory
of Negotiated Management

The story of Occupy Oakland illuminates two major omis-
sions in the literature on the policing of dissent. First, in contrast
to almost all of the theoretical work analyzing it, negotiated management is squarely, and always has been, a form of repression.
Permits, protester liability mandates, movement self-policing,
sharing information with the police, are all forms of social control even when there are no arrests or police aggression. Second, negotiated management is a form of repression even if and
when it is rejected. Not only is negotiated management a form
of repression, it is intimately entwined with strategic incapacitation. Police violence can elicit future cooperation, while failure
to cooperate enables and legitimizes police violence. Negotiated
management has become a normative expectation of protesters,
and if it is refused, becomes the sociopolitical grounds upon which
the delegitimation and criminalization of movements (or movement sectors) is established, and through which effective strategic
incapacitation is enacted. Delegitimation and criminalization are
separate but often connected processes. Delegitimation refers to
repressive actors (the state, media, or police themselves) defining
and portraying movements or groupings within movements as
confused, marginal, or threatening. Although rarely directed by
the state, media reporting often helps to delegitimize protesters: "Mass-media accounts of social movement activity frequently
follow the lead of the state, which not only fails to focus on the
issues and ideas of social movement participants but also frames
matters in ways that actually deprecate the participants as ridicu-
lous, bizarre, dangerous, or otherwise out of step with the general
public, thereby undermining social movement efforts" (Boykoff
2007b, 293).

This process of politically marginalizing protesters is often
taken a step further, toward labeling them as violent, criminal
threats that must be placed under control through police force.

Criminalization is "a political, economic, and ideological process through which individuals and identifiable groups are selectively policed and disciplined" (Chadwick and Scranton 2001, 68–69, quoted in Aksyutina 2012, 169). Beyond legitimizing potential police violence, criminalization seeks to depoliticize repression— to fundamentally redefine the terms of the conflict between police and protesters as simply a matter of crime control: "The state constantly asserts its respect for the rights of 'peaceful,' 'law-abiding' political expression. Those who refuse to follow the rules of protest permits, routes, and styles do not deserve the state's respect. Thus, by definition, all those who disturb in the slightest the channel provided by police are threats, are violent, unpredictable, preternaturally out of control, beyond the bounds of social mores. Political policing cleverly merges social decorum with the architecture of state control" (Starr et al. 2011, 95).

"Hard" and "soft" repression, while often functionally separate and emanating from different and sometimes unconnected actors, not only share the same ends, but are mutually constituted and reinforced. The ability to successfully define someone as a "violent anarchist" or "domestic terrorist" enables far less publicly scrutinized efforts to materialize and use whatever means are seen fit to contain that threat (Potter 2011). Recognition of these relationships should help us establish a broader view of the policing and social control of protest, and help show how strategic incapacitation is legitimated in the existing political culture.

The case of Occupy Oakland demonstrates how negotiated management is much more than simple permits. Only one permit was taken out during the course of the movement's existence, and it was effectively used as a tool of repression, as discussed in chapter 5. A facet of negotiated management not theorized in the literature arguably had more bearing in terms of the social control utilized against the movement. The literature sees negotiated management as both a model of policing and an era of protest policing that has been significantly waning since the Seattle

World Trade Organization demonstrations in 1999 (Gillham and Noakes 2007; McPhail and McCarthy 2005; Noakes and Gillham 2006). In terms of permits, this is largely the case (Vitale 2007, 406), but that does not mean that the logic or normative expectation of protester cooperation has disappeared. This normative expectation of cooperation with police and city officials, whether it takes the form of permits or not, is an element of negotiated management not yet examined in the academic literature, but is a central aspect of my analysis in this text.

This book seeks to provide and emphasize the importance of sociopolitical context for the dominant methods of controlling social movements and to analyze repression through a discussion of social movement tactics, the state's need to project legitimacy, and the role of popular support and solidarity. Scholarship tends to describe tactics of repression and their effects, with much less focus on how and why they work. Protest and repression do not exist in a vacuum; ultimately they are both driven by the need for popular support. With movements trying to pursue systemic changes, the police are tasked to preserve the existing order. This obviously elicits conflicts between protesters trying to disrupt, and police trying to preserve, the social order. Starting from this very basic relationship, the question of popular legitimacy invariably comes into question—when there is conflict, who has support? As Max Weber outlined in 1918, the power of the police, and government more broadly, is rooted in the legitimate use of force, the creation and application of law, and jurisdictional control over social space (Weber 1946, 77–80). But as Weber also noted, and Gramsci would explore in greater detail, the legitimacy of the state's force is not immutable or permanent, though it is the norm. The repression of protest (as with any type of policing) is political. It is rooted in bureaucracies, legacies of governmentality, and discourses of legality, normalized in relationships and routines,[4] and hegemonic ideas and roles. But repression is ultimately contingent upon public cooperation and support. In Oakland, this cooperation and support broke down after the police vio-lence on October 25, 2011—creating a political opportunity that the movement quickly capitalized on. Repression mobilized solidarity with the movement while simultaneously demobilizing hard repression during the two Port Shutdowns on November 2 and December 12. The political costs of maintaining order had overcome those of preserving any semblance of traditional order in downtown Oakland or on the Port in the weeks to come.

AN ONGOING TENSION BETWEEN POLICE VIOLENCE AND LEGITIMACY

Seeing the overlap in the strategic goals of negotiated man-agement and strategic incapacitation is necessary to gain a full pic-ture of the logic, strategy, and practice of police repression. When examined at the level of normative definitions of protest, protest behavior, and justified police force, the two decades in which negotiated management was dominant laid the groundwork for the efficacy and perceived legitimacy of strategic incapacitation when directed at those who shun negotiation. Strategic incapaci-tation is, itself, a more sophisticated and technological application of the escalated force approach, the dominant model of the 1960s, which forged the crisis of legitimacy that ushered in negotiated management in the first place.

A factor in this evolution that requires more examination is the role of legitimacy in the process of police repression. Police force is more than a question of tactical capacity. As Jonathan Jackson and colleagues (2012) succinctly put it, "Police legiti-macy and public consent are necessary conditions for the justifi-able use of state power" (1051). Dating back at least five hundred years to Niccolo Machiavelli's writings (1961), this dynamic of social legitimacy in relation to the state's use of force has received its share of attention. The social control of protest repeatedly puts pressure on this tension: "In a democratic society, where open coercion cannot be used too often without losing legitimacy, the state must come up with subtler ways to maintain social control" (Boykoff 2007b, 303). The legitimacy of police repression, or the lack thereof, in the eyes of the public was the driving force behind the shift to negotiated management as a means of social control. The weakness of formalized negotiated management was its reliance on the cooperation of protesters, an acceptance that became increasingly less likely after the Seattle protests in 1999. However, negotiated management was, and is, more than an immediate tactic of social control. It became, and still is (even when not pursued or accepted), a normative structure that seeks to define the very nature of dissent, legitimate certain methods and tactics of protest, as well as clearly demarcate identities for protesters, through which, from a policing standpoint, disruption of any kind is coded as criminal rather than dissent (King 2013b).

As police have increasingly used force to suppress dissent over the last several years (Federici and Caffentzis 2004; Redden 2002; Vitale 2007), questions around the legitimacy of that force have largely been suppressed by a range of factors. The most immediate of these are the targeted and preemptive nature of this new mode of repression, as well as the normative understandings of what legitimate protest is, that were established in the previous three decades, of which negotiated management is but one part. Under certain circumstances the tension between police repression and police (and broader political) legitimacy can reemerge, expanding possibilities for social disruption. While I examine how the four facets of strategic incapacitation were deployed against Occupy Oakland, my starting point is their initial failure. In examining how they were eventually made effective, I draw attention to the various processes and institutions that serve as connective tissue between police repression and legitimacy.

As discussed further in the next chapter, the preconditions for negotiated management were lacking in Oakland. While police and city officials originally pursued a strategy of passive containment, in keeping with the policing goals of negotiated management, it quickly became clear that the camp was not interested in negotiating with them, prompting a contentious shift in thinking toward overt repression. The assumption about police repression within the literatures on both negotiated management and strategic incapacitation suggests that repression against protesters who do not cooperate with police and can be labeled "troublemakers" will be met with minimal sympathy from the broader public. In the raid of the camp on October 25, 2011, and the police force used later that night, the techniques deployed were textbook strategic incapacitation. However, these techniques were not only ineffective, they were ultimately counterproductive, leading to the emergence of a second encampment and the almost complete negation of hard repression during two subsequent mass actions. The obvious question of why is one I will answer over the course of the book, through illustrating how those techniques were later made functional for the police. It is first important to see how strategic incapacitation was deployed in mid-October 2011.

What the theory of strategic incapacitation introduces, an aspect that needs to be more fully examined, is the role of criminalization in legitimating modern protest repression tactics. Strategic incapacitation was applied in late October 2011 and failed miserably, not in a tactical sense but in a strategic one. Because the movement was not seen as criminal or illegitimate at that point, the repression was seen as illegitimate, and the movement grew stronger and expanded. This exposes a major fault line in the policing of protest—that quasi-military tactics alone cannot contain popular movements. The broader contexts of protest—specifically the history of police-protest interactions, the normative roles that have been established through the past, and the inherent relationship between police violence and coerced or consented non-disruptiveness on the part of demonstrators—all highlight important factors that explain how and why repression typically succeeds.

POLICE VIOLENCE OR POLICE PROTECTION: THE PATERNALISM OF SOCIAL CONTROL

Whether a protest is permitted or not, the threat of police force is ever present, whether through the visible presence of militarization (extensive riot suits and equipment, less-lethal weapons, tanks, helicopters, surveillance cameras, assault rifles, etc.), periodic displays of police violence, or significant impositions upon the freedom of assembly (Noakes, Klocke, and Gillham 2005, 241; Starr et al. 2011, 43–46; Wood 2014, 40–41). Beyond being two sides of the same coin, there is a dialectical relationship between physical repression and negotiated management, in that the lack of negotiated management usually elicits police violence, while the threat of that police violence elicits acceptance of negotiated management. The dynamic that emerges is a paternalistic strategy of controlling social movements, akin to a protection racket, whereby demonstrators are offered protection from violence by the state, which is simultaneously threatening the use of violence if the terms of protection are not accepted (Peterson 1977; Tilly 1985; Young 2003).

Feminist theorists have shown how paternalistic political relationships are internalized by and shape the political subject itself. Choices that individuals make are shaped, constrained, and understood within the context of various social hierarchies of power. Susan Rae Peterson's discussion of state power (though in a much different context) encapsulates the capacity of the state to define political choices so that the subject is left with two negative options—in this case, force or negotiated management—which both serve to replicate the state's power at the expense of the subject. Peterson (1977) points out that: "The state needs to justify interference which is both deliberate and forceful, and does so usually in two basic ways: according to desert or paternalism" (363). Iris Marion Young (2003) posits this same relationship through the metaphor of the patriarchal household, where paternalistic protection demands submission and the acceptance of inferior positions (under a constant, implicit threat of violence): "Central to the logic of masculinist protection is the subordinate relation of those in the protected position. In return for male protection, the woman concedes critical distance from decision-making autonomy.... The head of the household should decide what measures are necessary for the security of the people and property, and he gives the orders that they must follow if they and their relations are to remain safe" (4–5).

These analyses of state paternalism provided by Peterson and Young make the implicit power dynamics between police and protest explicit, noting how the terms of their engagement are defined, in every instance by the state, and how these roles are inherently disempowering to social movement actors. The social control function of negotiated management stretches far beyond the permit as a discrete mechanism to proscribe tactics and the terms of protest. Whether a permit is signed or not, the modern relationships between police and protesters revolve around negotiated management. It has established itself as the commonsense rubric through which protesters understand protest as a process and understand themselves as protesters.

Upon close examination, the threat of repression, the internalization of that threat by social movement actors (Fernandez 2008; Starr et al. 2011), and its bearing upon their decision to accept or forgo permits, cannot be separated from each other when making sense of movement decisions or repression. In the context of hard repression, negotiation is never simply a rational or moral choice, a conflict between two evenly matched sites of power, or a value-neutral peace. The work of Antonio Gramsci (1971) provides an essential schematic framework for how political power is maintained, and also how it can be challenged, that emphasizes state force, but also the institutionally diffuse mechanisms through which power is typically maintained, largely without having to resort to the use of force. The concept of hegemony is central to Gramsci's work, examining the processes through which order is maintained, mapping Karl Marx and Frederick Engels's maxim from *The German Ideology* ([1947] 2001, 64), that: "The ideas of the ruling class are in every epoch the ruling ideas, i.e. the class which is the ruling *material* force of society, is at the same time its ruling *intellectual* force." Understanding that the modern state not only has an overwhelming material advantage in terms of the deployment of force against opponents, Gramsci's theory of hegemony is premised on how hegemony—this combination of cultural, political, and economic dominance—functions, and where and how to effectively challenge it.

Derived from his conceptualization of hegemony, Gramsci's discussion of coercion and consent conceptualizes the inherent mutual constitution of both (Thomas 2009, 166). Instead of protesters having a real choice between coercion or consent—and rather than seeing coercion as a product of consent, or consent a product of coercion—both coercion and consent are part of the same whole, theoretically distinguishable but practically interwoven. From the standpoint of negotiated management as social control, consent and coercion constitute a hegemonic praxis that establishes norms, in which disruptive challenges to the social order become alien to the process of protest itself. Looking at disruption and social control broadly, effective protest (protest that is disruptive and protracted) must not only overcome coercion and reject consent, but also actively challenge and displace the hegemonic power that supports and is reproduced by this nexus of coercion and consent—even if only partially, among certain groups, and only in certain places and times.

TOWARD AN ANALYSIS OF THE GOVERNMENTALITY OF PROTEST

In trying to get from "what social control is" to "how and why it works," Michel Foucault's concept of governmentality is helpful in tracing techniques of repression and placing them within broader logics of social control (Foucault 1994, 201–222). Governmentality refers broadly to the "art of government" (Foucault 1991, 87, 92), the production and maintenance of social behavior, relationships, and orders. This art of government involves the activities of the state, but is not limited to them—it is an assortment of disciplines that regulate morality, politics, and the economy. Governmentality refers to the various normative regulatory regimes of power in society that present themselves as essential mechanisms for promoting the public good through the maintenance of social orders. As Ronjon Paul Datta (2011) notes, "The concern with security in governmentality is not then the protection of the population, but it is about ensuring the integrity of regulatory mechanisms" (229). Although he did not employ the concept, Foucault's work is largely concerned with the question of what Gramsci has called "hegemony"—drawing upon not just institutionalized power to explain the social orders of the day, but also the various "dominant ideas" and socially accepted roles and behaviors that govern everyday life and serve as barriers to social change.

This lens provides a broad and holistic way to think about power and social order that highlights and emphasizes the production of social roles and practices as well as the dominant ideologies that surround them. As almost every chapter in this book touches on, using very different examples, repression was also situated within, or contextualized by, normative social practices and jurisdictions beyond formal police practices. From the city's need to protect public health, to the invocation of protester etiquette, to the city's ability to define people as a "public nuisance" so as to control where they are allowed to be—repression has to do with much more than formal policing, and rarely involves policing alone. Police force and permitted acquiescence are two primary, but not exclusive, repressive means to the social control end. They are obviously situated within and constituted by various social, political, economic processes, which all contain their own set of normative moral orders and invoked roles and expectations. For instance, the logic and practice of negotiated management is thoroughly imbued with concerns about protest liability; the lens and logic of liability make permits seem natural and necessary. The ability to identify a movement or movement sector as a violent, criminal threat creates a political rationale in which police violence will be far less scrutinized than if the demonstrators were not portrayed in this fashion. This stretches beyond framing to the coupling of two separate but combinable logics of social control. The goal of government is to maintain the social order and not simply to repress. Despite important and measurable changes in the use of police force, impediments placed upon the rights of free speech, assembly, and association, and the general predominance of neoliberal values and policies in the Global North (the United States in particular), the object of protest policing and governmentality is not to annihilate opposition, but to marginalize it, contain it, and ultimately make productive use of it, in the project of maintaining a certain social order. Ultimately the means of repression (strategic incapacitation and negotiated management) are not autonomous or disconnected, nor do they exhaust the techniques of social control used against protest movements.

CHAPTER 3

The Oakland Commune, Police Violence, and Political Opportunity

OSCAR GRANT PLAZA (Frank Ogawa Plaza) sits on a triangular block in the center of downtown Oakland. Within the space of about three acres, a small, functioning commune was built overnight on October 10, 2011. There was a medical tent with basic medical supplies and trained medics around the clock. There was a children's village that provided a kid-friendly (and fun) space for kids to utilize, with toys, books, and frequent activities. There was a full kitchen that served hot meals three times a day to hundreds of people. There was a library stocked with donated books, and a media/information tent powered by a stationary bicycle. The rest of the camp was comprised of densely settled tents, with wooden pallets serving as a walkway throughout the interior of the camp. The physical and infrastructural functioning of the camp and all of its facets developed much like the future projects of Occupy Oakland. Ideas were put forward and people gravitated toward projects that interested them, applying skills they had and developing new ones. Based on a mixture of political desire and immediate need, the Oakland Commune established itself quickly. In terms of social roles and relations, as well as models of politics and community, the camp sought to embody a new world on a small scale in the midst of the normative late-capitalist structures the movement sought to destroy, including the sedimentation of those structures in the identities, minds, and actions of those involved.

THE OAKLAND COMMUNE

While the tactic of camping was characteristic of the Occupy movement, not all camps were the same. Around the country, some were erected with the permission of city administrators or the police, others were not.[1] The demographics of the camps differed by location, as did their longevity. Many had first aid tents, others had kitchens. Across the variation, Oakland itself was unique—both politically and tactically. This difference was essential in the events that would follow. Although Occupy Oakland was comprised of a range of actors with differing politics, anticapitalism was a dominant philosophy. Occupy Oakland was not so much protesting on the lawn of City Hall as occupying it. What that meant in Oakland was that the park now belonged to the movement, and they were not going to give it back. Occupy Oakland conceived of itself as a commune, as an autonomous, self-governing space. This orientation goes beyond "framing"; it fundamentally shaped how participants saw the movement (themselves and each other), and shaped how they acted.

The name of the occupied park in Oakland was immediately changed from Frank Ogawa Plaza to Oscar Grant Plaza, in honor of a young man killed by the police in Oakland. An agreement to physically bar police from the camps was passed, and implemented on more than one occasion. A resolution was also passed not to negotiate with city politicians or to grant them a voice within the movement. A diversity of tactics within actions were adopted as well, that established agreed-upon tolerance for a range of different protest tactics.[2]

Although the camp was rarely overtly framed as such, it was prefigurative (Brissette 2013). Prefigurative movements try to model new, liberatory social structures in the present (such as the General Assembly as a political institution), as well as inhabit new forms of social roles and relations in a deliberative way (Breines 1989; Poletta 2002). Prefigurative politics are not inherently antagonistic to strategic action or organization (Maeckelbergh 2011, 4). However imperfect and contradictory the camps were, they represented a coherent effort at political autonomy, the fulfillment of social needs through mutual aid and social struggle, and the usage of direct democratic processes to shape daily life in the camps as well as the political efforts and actions that the movement took on. More in terms of form over content at times, the Oakland Commune was prefigurative in the sense of physical, public refusal of the established order. Despite the many incredible things that emerged from the camp, one would be hardpressed to offer it as a model of a new society. Sexual harassment, violence, drug use, and mental health crises were not uncommon. While groups like Occupy Patriarchy emerged as an organic and necessary response to sexual violence in the camps, an urban commune with a porous perimeter that lacked enforced guidelines for personal behavior will likely be riddled with conflict, whether from within or without.

Occupy as a Tactic: General Obstacles to Repression

The Occupy movement in the United States, and Occupy Oakland in particular, presented a series of new obstacles for police and city administrators in three distinct ways—*tactically*, *organizationally*, and in terms of *public support*. The tactic of occupying public space is, itself, not new.[3] But open, public encampments presented a series of problems for the police, and potential liabilities for cities. On the first day of the encampment in Oakland, police ceded that the camp could be used as a cover for petty criminal activities, but also that they would have to weigh the enforcement of the law with the need to maintain general order.[4] This approach falls within what John Noakes and Patrick Gillham (2006, 101) define as the policing logic of negotiated management—tolerance for minor violations and disruption so as not to provoke more serious disorder from protesters or instigate escalated disorder in the process of police repression. This policing approach was quickly deemed untenable in Oakland, given the widespread militancy and anti-police sentiment of the movement. In a private email conversation with other city officials, Assistant to the City Administrator Arturo Sanchez, discussing a failed attempt to negotiate the terms of Occupy Oakland's first major march on October 19, 2011, said: "They [Occupy Oakland] consider any OPD attempt to escort marchers an escalation. They indicated they have burned all notices and intend not to ever comply because the city has not asked for compliance but attempted to direct the occupation. 'Any attempt to favilitate [sic] the march will be considered an escalation and lead to riots.'"[5]

Compounding this clear refusal of negotiation, in this private email conversation, police and city officials expressed concerns with legal liabilities and health and safety issues from the first days of the camp.[6] The potential legal liabilities the camps posed would eventually be used as rationales for a coordinated national raid on almost twenty encampments in late November 2011, including Oakland (discussed further in chapter 4). City officials in eighteen cities cited real, but largely exaggerated, public health and safety risks that the camps presented—including sickness, sanitation concerns, fire hazards, and various interpersonal crimes. The *tactic of occupying urban space* in city centers, drawing attention to inequalities and injustices through communal civil disobedience, garnered widespread support from students, workers, immigrants, victims of foreclosure, and retirees from inside and outside of the traditional Left, drawn to general political messsages that opposed the political and economic trends that had produced the ongoing economic and social crisis at that time. The tactic of camping, which spread all over the country in a matter of weeks, was disruptive but low risk, easily spread, and a tactic for which the police and city officials had no immediate plan. The eventual solution drew upon the same paternalistic logic and bureaucratic legalisms that define negotiated management, which have always been premised around reducing risk and disruption—channeling protest into forms and methods that are predictable, manageable, and (ultimately) ineffectual.

Unlike the Anti–Iraq War movement, where the primary tactic was mass marches, or the Alterglobalization movement,[7] which featured more disruptive mass marches, blockades, and actions, often aiming to obstruct major trade summit meetings, Occupy was entirely different. Where negotiated management largely defined the Anti–Iraq War movement, in which marches were almost always permitted and orderly and orchestrated to mitigate the need for aggressive policing, the Alterglobalization movement was more decentralized and less likely to cooperate with police, leading to a wide array of militarized police repression (Fernandez 2008; Gillham and Noakes 2007; King and Waddington 2006; Noakes and Gillham 2006, 2007; Noakes, Klocke, and Gillham 2005; Starr, Fernandez, and Scholl 2011; Vitale 2007; Wood 2007). As discussed in chapter 2, negotiated management and strategic incapacitation are the two main policing methods to control protest movements, despite the increase in the prevalence of militarized policing since 1999. Simple, hard repression of the encampments ran the risk of being seen as unjustified, as it was in Oakland in late October, particularly in light of the public support discussed below. In general, negotiated management was highly limited in many Occupy sites and basically nonexistent in Oakland. This presented a conundrum for police and city officials for which there was no easy answer. When negotiated management proved impossible to establish in Oakland, the remaining option of police repression became a counterproductive strategy of social control in the existing political context. The mistakes that were made in attempts to repress the movement quickly turned into political opportunities that were successfully seized, compounding the problem of social control for police and city officials facing a popular and expanding movement.

A second key way in which the overall nature of the Occupy movement frustrated traditional methods of social control was its *organizational and leadership structures* and its decision-making process. The decentralized nature of the movement was a barrier to the establishment of negotiated management in many cities, Oakland in particular (Noakes and Gillham 2006). The model of protest where police and protesters negotiated and cooperated had been fostered over the previous four decades to preempt public outcry against police aggression by making police aggression less necessary (King 2013b). It is erroneous to see police violence or aggressive police tactics (riot police, less-lethal weapons, mass arrests, etc.) as simply misconduct, or as a result of poor training. As several theorists have noted, these tactics have become widespread in the policing of protest since the Seattle World Trade Organization protests in 1999 (Fernandez 2008; King and Waddington 2006; Noakes and Gillham 2006, 2007; Noakes et al. 2005; Starr et al. 2011; Vitale 2007; Wood 2007). Police generally use force when they believe it is necessary to maintain order or to address targeted threats. The threats posed by the social movements of the 1960s, the repression used (often quite violently and illegally) to squelch dissent in that historical moment, and the resulting loss of legitimacy for the police and broader structures of political power necessitated a different approach. The alternative to brute force that maintained order *and* police legitimacy was negotiated management.

Negotiated management is contingent upon political organizations within the movement, or leaders (often self-appointed), negotiating the terms of protest with the police. Occupy, to an even greater extent than the Alterglobalization movement, which was itself largely decentralized, had no official leadership and was basically a horizontal movement.[8] In Oakland, this was coupled with the movement being largely comprised of veterans of previous militant movements that were reciprocally hostile to the police. The lack of official leadership was not the only barrier to negotiated management.

A wholly decentralized movement is not impervious to negotiated management since city officials would simply need to find one grouping in an occupation willing to negotiate with police. The existence of General Assemblies as decision-making bodies and political centers provided protection from small groups seeking to coopt the movement from within or pursue negotiation with the police. The General Assemblies served as autonomous political structures through which major decisions about the movement took place and a process through which legitimate decisions about movement activities (including potential decisions to cooperate with police, negotiate with city officials, take out permits, etc.) were made. The General Assembly as a counter-institution was an organizational component of the movement that allowed for decisions to have legitimacy and for movement decisions to be participatory and directly democratic. It was also strategic in the sense that it mitigated the myriad limitations and shortcomings of top-down models of organizing, while guarding against a complete tyranny of structurelessness, where there is no political center or accountability (Freeman 1972; Garces 2013; Maeckelbergh 2012).

Politically, what gave the movement a center and also served to legitimate movement decisions within the movement was the General Assembly. The Occupy Oakland General Assembly (or G.A.) met four nights per week, usually for two to three hours, sometimes longer. An agenda was approved before every meeting and there was a facilitation team. Comprised mainly of discussion and debate of various decisions, as well as announcements and a period of open discussion on topics important to the movement, the G.A. was a space for people to get to know one another and for camaraderie. The decisions made by the Oakland G.A. on its first meeting would set the tone for the weeks to follow.

Consensus decision-making at General Assemblies, where decisions initially need 90 percent or universal agreement in order to be approved, is typically a brake on any contentious decisions getting approved (Cornell 2012). While this often serves to stifle decision-making on contentious issues and silence minority opinions, in the context of negotiated management the likelihood of achieving consensus in favor of cooperating and coordinating with the police is often extremely slim. In general, this structured horizontalism, the existence of a legitimate political center and collective decision-making institution, created a structural constraint against cooptation and negotiated management while a consensus decision-making process thwarted any contentious proposal, including negotiating with police and city officials. To varying degrees, the lack of any official leadership gave local police departments and city officials no one to negotiate with or hold responsible, and the barriers presented by consensus decision-making processes served to self-institutionalize the movement, protecting it from cooptation—making negotiated management an impossibility in many cities such as Oakland.

A third major factor that frustrated the repression of Occupy was its immediate national visibility and *widespread public support*.[9] After years of bipartisan neoliberalism produced the most significant economic crisis in generations, followed by multi-trillion-dollar corporate bailouts and years of recession, the emergence of a largely populist movement resonating with the public around issues rarely addressed by government leaders—the foreclosure crisis, budget cuts, bank bailouts, and unaccountability, to name a few—created a barrier to repression. Public opinion can be a structural constraint upon repression, bringing into question the legitimacy of police and the political order, if and when applied (Waddington 1998, 66–68). Social movements and the repression of social movements, like any political processes in society, are not simply based on resources and official positions of power (whether financial, legal, or political); they are, to varying degrees, questions of public legitimacy. In Oakland, as city officials were becoming aware of the substantial threat the encampment posed for social order, there was confusion and tension as to how to disrupt it without creating significant blowback, as repression might be publicly perceived as an illegitimate attack on a social justice movement, against a movement that was simply camping in front of City Hall.[10] Oakland's Mayor Quan privately expressed to other city leaders that she was "concerned about [the] perception of clampdown, creating martyrs."[11] Those fears were soon realized, as police violence after the first encampment raid garnered massive public sympathy and forged a political opportunity for the movement, which the movement translated into mass action the following week—bringing out more than fifty thousand people to successfully shut down the Port of Oakland on November 2, 2011.

THE FIRST ENCAMPMENT: FROM KID GLOVES TO AN IRON FIST

Occupy Oakland emerged in a local political context marked by ongoing tensions between the Oakland Police Department and the newly elected mayor, Jean Quan. The political tensions between the mayor and OPD had begun as soon as she took office in January 2011, most comically highlighted by the OPD's putting a parking boot on Quan's car after she won the November 2010 election, but before taking office.[12] Mayor Quan, a one-time radical who was elected with a minority of the popular vote in a ranked-choice election, was not well received by the OPD:

> In one instance, pictures of Quan and [Thelton] Henderson [federal judge overseeing the Oakland Police Department] were found at OPD headquarters covered in racially charged graffiti, including one depicting Quan as a dragon. In another, photos were found of Quan and her predecessor, Mayor Ron Dellums, believed to have been used as dartboards. In 2012 an OPD Sergeant told a Citizens Police Academy—an

educational series open to the public—that Henderson "has an agenda" and was "in the SLA [Symbionese Liberation Army]"—a left-wing guerilla organization in the 1970s. In case their intentions were not clear, another flier was left at the OPD shooting range depicting a World War II pilot with the text, "You shut the fuck up. We'll protect America. Keep out of our fucking way, liberal pussies." With these attitudes flaunted around the department, it should be no surprise that OPD has refused to cooperate with the court's reform efforts or follow orders from City Hall. (Jay 2014)

In addition to the hostility Mayor Quan faced from the OPD, a fierce battle between her office and then City Attorney John Russo ended with Russo resigning from his position in a conflict over the city's much-contested gang injunctions, of which Russo was a key architect. Dan Siegel, Quan's legal advisor, was Russo's adversary in court, with Siegel representing those named in the injunctions pro bono. In a city where the police are even more of a political force than in most cities (Jay 2014), this conflict over the direction of policing in Oakland created an atmosphere of tangible hostility and distrust between the mayor's office and the OPD. The morning after tents went up in Oscar Grant Plaza, OPD Chief Batts handed in his letter of resignation, citing a lack of resources and control over the direction of the police force. While the camp cannot be identified as the primary reason for Batts' departure, the emergence of an encampment full of radicals on the front lawn of City Hall surely compounded the lack of resources and lack of autonomy that Chief Batts referenced when stepping down.

That same morning, as Chief Batts announced his departure, an email with official talking points for the heads of communications within City Hall from the OPD Chief of Staff Christopher Bolton made it very plain that the police had no intention of raiding the camp, despite the fact that he notes that camping on public property is a violation of city codes and that the camp could be used as a cover for petty criminal behavior.[13] The official messaging from the police was that they "would continue to weigh the need to cite citizens for minor infractions against their overall need and right to assemble peacefully in public."[14] This was the overall tone of internal dialogue within City Hall and the OPD during the first week of the encampment. There were concerns that the public address system was too loud and a three-day discussion about how to go about getting a canopy taken down.[15] By the end of the first week the OPD brass would be pushing for an immediate raid of the camp, but on its second day were cognizant of the need for a deliberative approach to dealing with it, a strategy that was not yet clear. Even early supporters of evicting the camp, like Assistant to the City Administrator Arturo Sanchez, were mindful of the potential resistance the city and police would face during and after police repression, saying on October 13: "A confrontation now [before a planned October 19 Occupy Oakland march] may provide more reason for them to act out on Saturday when there may be more anarchists and or people here."[16] Deputy Police Chief Jeffrey Israel (later demoted to captain) expressed the tenuous situation the Occupy Oakland camp posed for police: "If directives are not followed and there are no consequences it is likely seen as an opportunity to do whatever. On the flip side, we have to pick our battles."[17]

The mayor, the assistant city administrator, and the deputy police chief all had concerns about the lack of (externally accountable) leadership to communicate with at the camp and the fact that Occupiers were not following the rules laid out by the city and police; however, their overriding concern was that a confrontation could prove counterproductive for the city. Several city leaders voiced hope that the camp would just disband or dwindle, which it never did. Sharon Cornu, the co-deputy mayor, sent a prescient email to the city administrator and her assistant on October 13, saying that the mayor "is concerned about perception of clampdown, creating martyrs."[18] Quan would be in Washington, DC, when the raid took place, leaving ultimate command over the police in the hands of City Administrator Deanna Santana. However, Quan admitted knowledge that a raid had been imminent, saying, "I didn't think it was going to be last night. . . . I only asked the chief to do one thing: to do it when it was the safest for both the police and the demonstrators."[19] Quan's foreknowledge of the eviction logistics is still somewhat unclear. However, it is clear from the internal discussions that the city did not know what to expect during and after the raid.

A shift in thinking took place in the second week, when it became clear that there were several differences between Occupy Oakland and the earlier encampments on the East Coast. The encampment had called itself the Oakland Commune since the first day, in reference to the Paris Commune—and the name was more than a rhetorical device. Unlike the situation in Zucotti Park in New York City, police were confronted by Occupiers and not allowed to enter the camp under any circumstance. This was agreed to at the first Occupy Oakland General Assembly on October 10, 2011. Police efforts to enter the camp were repelled several times in the camp's first two weeks. Oakland police officers would show up at the edge of camp in marked squad cars, after midnight, usually numbering a half dozen. As they would attempt to enter the park, several dozen people would form a supported line, preventing them from entering, often yelling "Pigs, go home."

> The police would strike up conversation (or sarcastic back-and-forth exchanges) with people on the perimeter, and on a handful of occasions they used these exchanges as a pretext to move from the curb into the park. What followed was the application of the Occupy Oakland mandate against police in the park. On one such occasion, sometime after midnight on an ordinary night in the camp in mid-October, four police tried to make entry into the camp—maybe out of

boredom or aggravation, or perhaps it was a pre-planned test to see how Occupiers would respond. As the police left their squad cars parked along 14th Street and approached a group of about a dozen Occupiers in the park, the latter yelled at the cops to "go home." Other Occupiers announced that the police were trying to enter the park and might be trying to snatch somebody. Within a minute over fifty Occupiers were assembled along the edge of the park, forming a thick barrier of flesh—not impenetrable, but not interested in moving either—and shouting "pigs, go home" continuously. The police hesitated, seemingly embarrassed, angry, and perplexed. One officer went back to his car, returning moments later with instructions. As the police retreated to their respective cars, the crowd continued to chant: "pigs, go home." The Oakland Commune was not the Paris Commune—not even a single musket among us. Nevertheless, a rag-tag group of campers was able to repel uniformed Oakland police officers intent on walking through the park when every official law in the State of California gave them full mandate and jurisdiction to do so. (King and Brissette, forthcoming)

At every attempt, the police would leave, which only bolstered the confidence and militance of the encampment. In addition, the camp had its own security, which was lackluster at first, but eventually would deal with interpersonal conflicts, assaults, and theft.[20] Oscar Grant Plaza was no longer governed by the City of Oakland in any meaningful way; the administrative and physical control of the plaza had been lost. This was both a conscious goal of the movement and a legal and political nightmare for the city. In that second week, key leaders of the OPD, the Chamber of Commerce, and conservative local newspaper columnists all voiced outrage over the passive stance of the city administration. Deputy Police Chief Jeffrey Israel, in relation to the loss of effective police control over the Plaza, stated in an email to city administrators, "This is a very dangerous situation and one that exposes the City to liability if another person needs our assistance and we cannot provide it."[21] *San Francisco Chronicle* columnist Chip Johnson, whose visit to the camps drew attention and concern as expressed in the emails between city leaders, would write, "In Oakland, protesters have pretty much had their way on most issues, and when they've pushed, the city has so far failed to push back."[22]

Beyond the loss of immediate control over public space in the city, the establishment of a dynamic where the protesters successfully ran off the police every time they showed up emboldened the camp as a whole, and fundamentally altered normative power relations between protesters and police. The loss of police control over the Plaza—right down to the fact that the movement had changed the name of the space to Oscar Grant Plaza, in homage to a young man unjustifiably killed by police in Oakland—provoked an aggressive assault on the movement during the first eviction, which would backfire on the police and the city, and incur significant costs to the Port of Oakland.

While the tactic of occupation of public space through constant encampment took law enforcement somewhat by surprise, and though their initial efforts at negotiated management failed, the police had developed a plan to implement strategic incapacitation before and during the raid of the camp on October 25. The objective of the raid was clearly stated in OPD's operation plan.[23] The goal was to surround the camp, declare an unlawful assembly, announce imminent arrest, clear the camp, arresting anyone who had failed to leave, and then secure and control the space, preventing "outside agitators" from reentering the park. The police used military tactics, including less-lethal weapons and a riot squad consisting of mutual aid forces from more than a dozen Bay Area cities, pursuing clear goals to transform the occupation of Oscar Grant Plaza into a coordinated police occupation. A City of Oakland Emergency Operations Center press release sought to criminalize the occupiers, emphasizing threats to law enforcement and public order,[24] though they came out quickly right before the raid. Police also conducted extensive surveillance of the camp, making note of: its security force; numbers of people and sleeping patterns in the camp; potential weapons in the camp; tactics (suspected or) likely to be used by protesters in conflict with police; movement communication via social networking, the Internet, text, and telephone networks; movement contingency plans in the event of a police raid; as well as other information gathered through physical surveillance.[25] The police operations plan squarely encompassed all four facets of strategic incapacitation—controlling space; using militarized formations, techniques, and weapons; targeting socially and politically marginal protesters for arrest; and utilizing surveillance and intelligence. The camp was cleared on the morning of October 25, but that night's defense of the area by police, using a wide array of less-lethal weapons in keeping with the same logic of strategic incapacitation, created public outcry and police withdrawal, fearful of protest escalation and loss of control. The application of strategic incapacitation directed as a means of social control led to the strategic incapacitation of social control itself.

On October 25, 2011, when the movement was just two weeks old locally, Oakland police conducted a predawn raid of the camp. A City of Oakland notice of violations on October 21 made clear that a raid was imminent.[26] Rumors circulated daily within the camp about when and how the raid would take place. Around 3 A.M. on the morning of October 25, a text message went out to everyone who had signed up for alerts from Occupy Oakland, announcing that a raid was immediately imminent. The scene in the camp was frenzied as hundreds of riot police slowly made their way toward the park. Occupiers built barricades out of tables and wooden pallets, which had previously served as a walkway through the tents, tied to lampposts and other fixed structures in the park. With little more than one hundred Occupiers present, it soon became clear that it would be impossible to defend the plaza as the police got closer. Police outnumbered protesters by a factor of four, with about 600 police evicting approximately 150 occupiers. The police announced a dispersal notice and gave adequate time for people who wanted to leave to do so. Tear gas was used in the raid as police swept the camp around 5 A.M. amid little physical resistance; almost all arrests were passive resisters who refused to evacuate. Immediately after the eviction a group of slightly more than a hundred snake-marched throughout downtown into the morning, followed, but not directly attacked, by police. As this group was blocking an intersection two blocks from Oscar Grant Plaza, a middle-aged worker in an old pick-up truck instructed protesters in the street to keep fighting. As the morning commute continued, those in the streets agreed to reconvene that afternoon at the downtown public library. The police seemed content to have met their objective of eviction and had done little to physically attack, or attempt a mass arrest of, the small group in the streets that morning.

As discussed in chapter 1, the police tactics later that day, in the evening of October 25, 2011, were very aggressive. After Oscar Grant Plaza had been fully secured by the police all day, rubber bullets, concussion grenades, tear gas, and other chemical weapons were used repeatedly that evening for more than four hours against an initial crowd of about one thousand people. Volleys of tear gas and concussion grenades would clear the intersection of Fourteenth and Broadway, where the main police skirmish line was and would remain throughout the night. Demonstrators would retreat for a few blocks, wait for the chemical gasses to clear, loosely regroup, and return to the intersection of Fourteenth and Broadway. This cycle repeated itself several times, as the police lines were never seriously challenged, with the exception of empty plastic water bottles periodically lobbed from across the intersection. Late that evening, as this cycle of police aggression, protester retreat, and return continued, marine veteran Scott Olsen was shot in the head with a tear gas canister at close range, leaving him critically wounded with a cracked skull. The violence of the policing, coupled with both the popularity of the movement and the city's failure to justify the raid effectively in the press beforehand did, in fact, lead to a blowback.

THE RECLAMATION OF
OSCAR GRANT PLAZA

A few thousand people came out the evening of October 26 and retook the Plaza, constructing a new encampment and calling for a general strike the following week. The police had completely stood down as the Plaza was reoccupied, with no visible police presence downtown. A simple chain-link fence had been erected around the grass area of the Plaza where the camp had been; the fence was eventually torn down by Occupiers during the General Assembly as the number assembled exceeded two thousand. Where the police had been tactically successful, clearing the camp and using aggressive techniques to drive people out of the area, they had failed miserably on the level of political strategy.

The planning for the November 2 actions was harried, chaotic, and energetic. Ad hoc groupings organized outreach and logistics and the General Assembly endorsed working groups, actions, and a framework of actions for the day. Materials were gathered or donated. People who had been strangers two weeks earlier met into the night at parks, bars, and apartments; inevitably, efforts overlapped in some respects and left some issues unattended until the last minute on November 2. Within a week, more than fifty thousand people would converge to shut down much of downtown and the Port of Oakland, as the police were relegated to a role much closer to that of a convenience store security guard than a militarized force empowered with keeping downtown and the Port of Oakland open. The violence that took place the night after the first eviction had helped translate public sympathy for the movement and outrage at the police, from all over the Bay Area, into tangible mass social action that would shut down the Port of Oakland a week later. It also helped facilitate the immediate reestablishment of the camp and prompted the city to severely limit police presence during the November 2 General Strike and the December 12 Port Shutdown. The interrelation between police tactics and protest tactics had its clearest manifestation in the week from the end of October 2011 into the beginning of November. Banks were shut down in the morning, and there were marches throughout the day, culminating in the occupation and closure of the entire Port of Oakland that afternoon and evening. The only significant confrontation between demonstrators and the police came late that evening with the attempted occupation of a shuttered homeless relief office. The illegitimacy of police tactics on October 25, in the eyes of the public, helped to empower the movement to such an extent that they were able to escalate their tactics, while the police additionally had their hands tied politically as no effort was made to prevent protesters from occupying the Port of Oakland.[27]

The counterproductive nature of the first raid's aggressiveness was by no means the only tension or limitation that the policing of the movement would face. Ongoing federal oversight of the Oakland Police Department,[28] political tensions between the mayor and the OPD, as well as divisions within city government (Jay 2014) all played key roles in frustrating any type of simple repression of the movement. The OPD had been under federal judicial review since 2003, stemming from numerous abuses and violations—most notably the use of less-lethal weapons against a small group of anti–Iraq War protesters in April 2003 and the Oakland Riders scandal, where police officers beat citizens and fabricated evidence. With numerous killings of unarmed civilians and $57 million paid in abuse settlements over the previous ten years, by a small city of less than 400,000 residents, the OPD has been on the verge of federal receivership for several years.[29] While impossible to quantify, this looming threat

Image 4   December 12 West Coast Port Shutdown, Oakland. (Photo by Daniel Arauz)

of federal takeover did serve as a deterrent to future abuse. Even though police misconduct and abuse in Oakland never ceases, their emergence as public scandals prompts efforts to create the perception of reform and restraint, if nothing more. In relation to Occupy Oakland, this meant the OPD would be forced to rely on less visible forms of physical repression, legal harassment of movement participants, and innovations in crowd control at large demonstrations.

November 2: OPD Get "Sent to Their Room" and Occupy Takes Over the House

On November 2, tens of thousands took to the streets of downtown Oakland, engaging in various direct actions and marches. The size of the protest on November 2 drew from the visibility of the national movement at that point, surely aided by anger over the eviction of the first camp and the subsequent police violence.

Several banks were closed down, including by foreclosed families who moved their furniture into the branches of banks that had foreclosed on them. Many businesses chose to shut their doors for the day amid the imminent tumult, as many workers struck for the day by calling in sick. The anti-capitalist march broke the windows of banks and a Whole Foods that had threatened retaliation against employees who did not go to work that day, with no police response to the property destruction. By 4 P.M., there were more than thirty thousand people in the streets. Even as the march approached the Port of Oakland, it was still uncertain how the police would respond, whether the march would be rerouted or blocked by hundreds of police defending the Port from the inside out. There were no police to be seen as the march entered the Port of Oakland. Because of the police overreaction on the night of October 25, the OPD had been quietly instructed to allow demonstrators to occupy the Port, which they did, halting all Port activity that afternoon and evening, causing an estimated loss of $4–8 million in revenue.[30] The OPD briefing for the day preceded the November 2 Port Shutdown, describing officers' roles as controlling traffic for the march to the Port and assisting in the patrolling of the Port *after the protesters had occupied it.*[31]

The events of November 2 further emboldened the movement, making the idea of shutting down the Port of Oakland for an entire day, along with the whole West Coast five weeks later, a conceivable possibility. The looks of surprise, elation, and empowerment in the eyes of almost everyone as they entered the Port and shut down terminal after terminal was a clear, effective collective advance for the movement (King and Brissette forthcoming). While on the one hand this can be seen as a miscalculation on the part of OPD and the city, on the other hand it marks pragmatism on their part. In some respects the policing of the movement was stuck in a Catch-22. If they had assembled their mutual-aid riot squad of approximately one thousand officers they certainly could have blockaded the entrances to the Port and used various aggressive tactics to attempt to disperse the crowd of tens of thousands. The Port likely still would have been block-aded by the turmoil for most of the evening, with thousands of people being directly politicized by police violence, compound-ing and expanding the militancy and vitality of the movement.

Although the day had been a success for the movement, with a diverse set of tactics being deployed during the day and a suc-cessful Port shutdown in the afternoon, and the movement had now seen the police's strategy of (very) passive containment on a mass scale, the day was not quite done. Most people had gone home after closing the Port, but a few hundred people occu-pied Travelers' Aid, a vacant former homeless services building adjacent to Oscar Grant Plaza. Drawing from mutual aid forces from all over the Bay Area, the OPD's Mobile Field Force Pla-toon descended upon the building in a SWAT/military forma-tion. An OPD tactical team advanced east up Fifteenth Street and clashed with protesters outside of the Travelers' Aid building and then cleared the building. Protesters and police exchanged projectiles, with police using concussion grenades and chemi-cal weapons and protesters throwing rocks, bottles, and M-80s. The police eventually cleared the area. The next morning ush-ered in broad condemnation for Occupy Oakland in the press; the Travelers' Aid events overshadowed the success of the Port shutdown, beginning a lasting trope demonizing the movement for not adopting a strict code of nonviolence. What had been a day of strategic advance for the movement was overshadowed by tactical adventures before the sun came up on November 3.

Conclusion: Repression and Escalation

October 25 was a triple failure for the police and city—negotiated management and brute force both failed, the goals of repression were not met and the movement grew stronger, and there was now increased structural constraint on the police, with legal and political pressure coming from City Hall, the public, and the courts. Even though negotiated management was rejected by the movement, the physical repression used to disrupt it was seen by many in the broader Bay Area as unjustified, excessive, and illegitimate. The militancy and refusal to cooperate with authorities that the police were aware of before the raid was now given a free hand after the raid, with city leaders not wanting to re-create October 25 on a much larger scale during the general strike on November 2. Beyond Occupy Oakland seizing the political opportunity presented in this moment, the legitimacy of the police was further tarnished, and the "martyr" status of the movement that the mayor had expressed concerns about very early on materialized, exacerbating the public relations damage and political balance of power. These miscalculations would end up having a tremendous effect on the subsequent strength of the movement due to public support, while concomitantly tying the police's hands during the next two mass demonstrations (November 2 and December 12)—both resulting in the successful occupation of the Port of Oakland. To compound this boost to the movement, the OPD was now under further legal and judicial scrutiny, in terms of lawsuits, an independent review of OPD malfeasance on October 25, and the (now looming) potential of federal receivership. Reporting on the receivership process, a *Mother Jones* article quotes the federal judge overseeing the Oakland Police, Thelton Henderson, saying that "the police response to Occupy Oakland protests raised 'serious concerns' and that the department remained 'woefully behind its peers around the state and nation.'"[32]

The refusal of Occupy Oakland to negotiate with, or even communicate with, city leaders and police, was at first puzzling and troubling to officials, but eventually became a way to delegitimate and criminalize the movement under the normative power of negotiated management. John McCarthy and Clark McPhail (1998) and McPhail and McCarthy (2005) have brought attention to the role of negotiated management, a process usually involving the legal permitting of protests, in which "an opportunity is created, if not required, for contact, interaction, and negotiation between police and protest organizations regarding the purpose, the time, place, and manner of protest" (McPhail and McCarthy 2005, 5). While the authors suggest that negotiated management is an advancement and a check on police violence, chapter 2 illustrated that it is, itself, a form of soft repression, adding layers of constraint and liability on protest organizers, stifling disruption and spontaneity, and imposing normative rules where only state-sanctioned protest and tactics are deemed legitimate or, as the discussion of January 28 in chapter 6 will show, whether some forms of protest cease to be protests and become simply criminal (King 2013b).

Occupation as a tactic posed many problems for the police and city officials; their internal discussions in the first week of Occupy Oakland illustrate this clearly. The movement had a great deal of support locally and nationally, which lent initial hesitation to the use of force. The popular understanding was that people were peacefully camping in a public park as a mild form of civil disobedience against austerity, inequality, and a lack of responsive government. The tactic of encampment itself was something the police had no clear plan for initially, pursuing tactics of passive containment when negotiated management failed to materialize, which only bolstered and further radicalized the movement, leading the police and city to eventually conclude that the encampment presented an untenable situation of ungovernable space at the heart of downtown. The short-term strategy of passive containment, of police ignoring city code violations and petty criminal activity in fear of sparking a militant response from the movement or sympathy from the public, proved to be counterproductive. If people got hurt, the police and firefighters were not allowed into the camp and inquiries from the city about camp conduct were universally ignored. Initially, passive containment was a logical choice for the city and police since immediate brute force would have been seen as illegitimate. However, the hands-off approach, instead of creating a generalized set of mutually agreed-upon norms for the camp, in keeping with the logic of negotiated management, gave the movement extra space to make the original idea of an autonomous commune a reality, if an imperfect one. Occupy Oakland's refusal of negotiated management was also a tactical advantage in the context of the camp, in that it not only eliminated potential mechanisms of control for the city and police, but also precipitated police aggression against what was a basically peaceful, if ungovernable, camp.

The police and city administrators would need to (re)establish their upper hand on all three of these contextual fronts that shape the policing of protest—tactical advantage against the movement, the establishment of a political common sense that legitimated repressive police tactics against protesters, and freedom from further constraints on policing. The OPD would need to regain tactical advantage over the movement, to put it on the defensive, to resituate police tactics as neutralizing threats to the public, rather than police tactics being seen as threats *to* the public. The police and mayor would need to bolster and broaden the legitimacy of social control against the movement while turning the movement from a martyr into a villain. Lastly, the primary structural constraint on the OPD, legal and judicial oversight, would need to be held at bay through adopting policing methods that were both more effective, in line with professional policing standards, and less likely to jeopardize police autonomy and legitimacy. The remainder of this book is the story of how the Oakland Police Department, city administrators, and other powerful actors navigated this complicated terrain and were largely successful at imposing social control from a variety of angles.

Chapter 4

Legitimating Repression through Depoliticizing It

Federal Coordination, "Health and Safety," and the November 2011 Occupy Evictions

The second Occupy Oakland encampment was erected the night the plaza was retaken, October 26, 2011. It would last until November 14, when police again evicted people from the camp in a predawn raid. In this second iteration of the camp, police and city officials were once again unwelcome. Police and city administrators demanded cooperation within a framework of negotiated management: "We need to have direct communications between City staff and Occupy Oakland representatives"[1]—and once again Occupy Oakland refused. Faced with this intransigence, city officials groped for a strategy: They would come to frame the camp as a threat to health and safety and justify eviction and hard repression as both necessary and in protection of the public. Locally this was used to justify the evictions from the camp, alongside a long list of complaints from the city ranging from damage done to the grass, contested claims about the financial effects on small businesses, and accusations by the mayor (later admitted to have been false) about a spike in crime in the surrounding area, to the fear of fire hazards and

Image 5   Fourteenth and Broadway. (Photo by Daniel Arauz)

communicable illnesses.[2] Where health and safety concerns were raised in internal discussion among city leaders right before the first raid in Oakland,[3] they became extremely widespread in the press in the lead-up to the second raid, not just in Oakland, but nationally. The widespread frame of public health and safety concerns, and the terms used to discuss them, turned out to be more than coincidental.

THE NATURAL DEFENSES OF OCCUPY WALL STREET'S CAMPS

Writing in *Homeland Security Today*, Ian Oxnevad noted, "So far, Occupy protests in the United States exhibit a mostly peaceful nature. However, certain elements within Occupy that have been seen both here and abroad have the potential to inflict major damage to governments, people, and the private sector." If not monitored and mitigated carefully, he continued, "these elements pose a significant threat to modern democracies."[4] The tactic of occupying public space in urban centers all over the country was unexpected, including many cities and towns not used to protests, let alone ongoing occupations of city squares. Quite often on the lawns of city halls, these camps presented a number of obstacles and problems in terms of effective repression. In the previous chapter, I identified three primary obstacles to repression that the movement as a whole presented: (1) the uncommon tactic of occupying public space; (2) the structured decentralization of the movement; and (3) the popularity of the movement. These obstacles were highlighted by the disastrous attempt to repress Occupy Oakland in October 2011. In response, city officials and national and federal agencies devised a scheme to evict the camps with bureaucratic justifications that were effective, largely through depoliticizing the subsequent repression of the camps. Depoliticization refers to a process by which political decisions or choices are publicly presented in such a way as to preclude all but one option, in an effort to minimize opposition while portraying any dissension as irrational.

In Occupy Oakland and across the country, city officials did not know what to make of the encampments at first.[5] The morning after the first encampment went up, Alber Lujan, Oakland's community services coordinator, sent an email message asking several City Hall administrators: "Do we have a position or statement regarding the encampment in the plaza? Are we in solidarity? Do they have a right to be there as long as they want? Are there any city ordinances that prohibit their actions?"[6] Other questions in this email discussion included: Would the Occupiers go home after the first night? The first week? Would they defer to the requests of city administrators? As the days went by, the question shifted to "aren't they going to get tired and leave?" In the aftermath of October 25, 2011, in Oakland, as the city's second encampment became more militant, and as the weeks wore on and encampments around the country became more entrenched, the question for city politicians and police became: *"How do we get rid of these encampments without creating counterproductive outcomes or greater disruption?"*

In late October 2011 in Oakland, those in power found hard repression ineffective and counterproductive. The camps themselves were a form of nonviolent civil disobedience and democratic decision-making in a country riddled with economic crisis and political unresponsiveness to social crises (foreclosures, healthcare costs and access, unemployment, education cuts, police violence, etc.). The camps were disruptive but hard to portray as violent, threatening, or criminal. They brought together a wide swath of the Left—from anarchists and communists to progressives to centrist Democrats—under a populist banner of the 99% versus the 1%. The camps were also prefigurative and served social needs; this was both a strength of the movement and a physical highlighting of the social and political failures the movement was opposing:

> The state's concern is not just about people occupying space, but the social and political significance of that occupation embedded in activities such as feeding hungry people and keeping visible the memory of the camp. The public threat of self-determination, represented by mutual aid in public places outside of the sanctions of the state, produces reactions from the city and police that on one level seem absurd, but on another level speak to the state's need to control and manage poor populations such that if their needs are met, they are met in conventional ways, and if they are not met, the poor suffer in isolation, invisible to the general population. (King 2012, 23)

The encampments were a constant political challenge to the cities in which they were built, a contestation over public space, not just in the sense of occupying public parks without a permit, but in Oakland and elsewhere (in a deeper, more prefigurative sense) an overt assertion of power over social space, not just in terms of physical control, but political legitimacy. Writing about a precursor to the US Occupy movement, the Indignados movement in Spain, which arose in spring 2011, Puneet Dhaliwal speaks to this process of contesting power in and through controlling social space: "The Indignados movement's occupations of public space, then, are not simply a seizure and re-organization of physical space, conceived as an instrumental resource for the purposes of mobilization and publicity. They are also interventions in the very process of the production of social space. That is, they are attempts to produce an alternative form of public space to that which currently pervades society" (Dhaliwal 2012, 256).

Occupy Oakland was located in the heart of downtown, amid intensive ongoing processes of gentrification in downtown Oakland (Drummond-Cole and Bond-Graham 2012). This has brought with it more than a rebranding of downtown, but a refashioning of the nature of public space toward consumption and leisure (Smith 1996, 52). Mike Davis describes the refashioning of urban centers in the context of capital flight and gentrification: "The universal and ineluctable consequence of this crusade to secure the city is the destruction of accessible public space" (1990, 226). The fact that homeless people were a significant part of the second encampment in Oakland was both a rupture in the segregation of classed bodies in terms of social norms and a political delegitimation of the city of Oakland, which has been steadily cutting homeless services while maintaining a public safety budget that monopolizes two-thirds of the city's resources.[7]

Oakland's camp had a kitchen that fed hundreds of people three times a day, a library, a children's village, a health clinic, and open, democratic meetings. These daily actions of the movement garnered broad support. An October 2011 *National Journal* poll showed that 59 percent of Americans completely agreed or mostly agreed with the Occupy protesters,[8] despite the fact that the movement's goals/demands were both fairly broad and generally vague. For supporters of the movement—even those who only saw it on the news or the Internet, or those who had reservations about certain aspects but still embraced it—the movement was a positive development and a reason for hope. The degree of public support was evident in Oakland after the first eviction and police violence on the night of October 25: More than fifty thousand people (most of whom had never been to the camp while it was standing) came out to voice their opposition to repression and stand in solidarity with Occupy Oakland. In the face of this public support, and in the absence of negotiation,[9] police and city officials had to find a way to regain social control. A broad-based effort was initiated to shift the public perception of the camp. Here, Oakland was not alone.

REPRESSION AS SAFETY, SAFETY AS (DEPOLITICIZED) REPRESSION

In an interview the day after the November raid in Oakland, Mayor Quan noted that media messaging was important for how policing was perceived, and whether police tactics (and how they were understood) mobilized or demobilized people: "And then, unfortunately, at the demonstrations (on October 26th and November 2nd), it was clear that people were not clear on why the camp was closed. We've taken this time over the last two weeks to really talk to the community about the impact of the camp."[10] This concern with political messaging and legitimacy is central to this chapter, as not only Mayor Quan but other mayors and federal agencies became acutely aware of the potential costs of taking the public's acceptance of repressing Occupy for granted. These mayors took part in a coordinated effort to manufacture consent for the eviction of Occupy camps in several cities across the United States. The objective went beyond simply evicting the camps to doing so without popular blowback. With assistance from the Department of Homeland Security (DHS) and the Police Executive Research Forum (PERF),[11] Quan and seventeen other mayors collaborated on a strategy to evict the Occupy encampments in a strategic and depoliticized fashion.

A main way in which hegemonic power operates is through the reinforcement and political deployment of normative ideas and assumptions about political, economic, and social orders and the necessary functions, roles, behaviors, and relations connected to them, roughly what Antonio Gramsci calls "common sense" (Gramsci 1971, 419–425). "Hegemony, for Gramsci, is a process by which a hegemonic class articulates (or co-ordinates) the interests of social groups such that those groups actively 'consent' to their subordinated status" (Slack 1996, 117). Often, arrticulation links widely held ideas, beliefs, and values, connecting them to new policies or government actions. The national trope that emerged in city after city and the common sense it forged was that the cities respected and were committed to upholding the First Amendment right of free speech, but were left with no choice but to evict the camps because of health and safety concerns (Gramsci 1971, 330).

In the two weeks from mid- to late November there were raids on Occupy encampments in eighteen cities; the mayors, chiefs of police, and other prominent city officials in these cities all reiterated this basic, two-point message. The raids were conducted in the middle of the night, with little media presence, with media actually instructed to stay away for *their* safety.[12] In New York, the "NYPD actively rounded up members of the press, escorted them to a predetermined location removed from the park, and detained them there until the eviction was completed" (Gillham, Edwards, and Noakes 2013, 96). As in a modern war zone, certain media outlets were allowed to be embedded with police during the raid, but had to agree to not use their cell phones during the events.[13] Within a four-day period, from November 11 through 15, major raids took place across the country—in St. Louis, Salt Lake City, Denver, Portland, Oakland, Seattle, and New York City.

Although the Department of Homeland Security denies it, there seems to have been explicit coordination and federal assistance, even if federal agencies did not assume direct command and control throughout the process. There were also calls facilitated by the Police Executive Research Forum, a think tank that specializes in crowd control:

> The AP reports that another set of conference calls on October 11 and November 14 were organized by the Police Executive Research Forum and included representatives from 40 different cities. A spokesman for the group said that the timing of the calls was "completely spontaneous" and had nothing to do with the recent raids. "This was an attempt to get insight on what other departments were doing." Including the maxim: "Don't set a midnight deadline to evict Occupy Wall Street protesters; it will only give a crowd of demonstrators time to form."[14]

Chuck Wexler, the executive director of PERF, admitted the coordination on *Democracy Now!* on November 17, 2011.[15] Wexler clarified that the PERF conference calls were separate from the DHS calls: "We did not coordinate the call with the mayors. It was simply with police chiefs. And it originated from Boston and Portland. The police chiefs in those cities asked to just compare notes."[16] The *New York Times* reported that an anonymous source from the Justice Department acknowledged that the FBI and Homeland Security had lent assistance to these eighteen mayors on a separate set of conference calls in the weeks prior.[17] That set of calls where Homeland Security and the FBI lent assistance was arranged by the US Conference of Mayors, as declassified documents would later show. This organization of mayors conducted a survey of mayors with Occupy camps and was clearly oriented in this moment toward repression with an eye on public perceptions of the movement and that potential repression:

> The mayor's conference asked via [an] emailed survey: What are the estimated Occupy-related costs? What are the major

issues relating to Occupy events? Has the Occupy membership changed and if so "describe those involved in the
movement how they've changed in terms of who they are
and what their intentions for the demonstrations are." In the
survey, the organization also called on city administrations to
share tactics. "Please describe any strategies or tactics your
city is employing in responding to Occupy-related events,
including an assessment of their effectiveness if possible."[18]

After requesting and evaluating additional declassified
documents pertaining to these calls, Mara Verheyden-Hilliard,
the head of the Partnership for Civil Justice Fund, concluded:
"These are sessions that were intended in assisting cities in creating the public pretext for the eviction of the encampments. . . .
I think they tried to play a fairly covert role in what was an
extremely significant nationally coordinated effort to shut down
the occupations."[19]

Homeland Security's refutation of these claims is itself peculiar, where officials qualified that they did not give advice to US
mayors, *as a whole*. A DHS spokesperson told reporters at the
Huffington Post that DHS "is not actively coordinating with local
law enforcement agencies and/or city governments concern-
ing the evictions of Occupy encampments *writ large*" (emphasis mine).[20] Freedom of Information Act documents from DHS
included an email exchange between this same spokesperson and
his superior, where he is instructed that DHS has had "standard
coordination calls and face-to-face meetings with our partners to
ensure that the proper resources are available for operations such
as street closures, etc."[21]

Some of the mayors themselves indicated that coordination
took place on these calls. Mayor Quan spoke of the conference
calls many times: "I was on a conference call with big city mayors and of the eighteen of us, we were having the same problem where the people who started the camps were no longer in

control, and that they've become a big drain and have become very dangerous places."[22] The *New York Times* quoted Portland's mayor Sam Adams, who said, "There had been two calls hosted by the organization 'to share information about the occupying encampments around the country.' He described the calls as check-ins to share information and advice on how various cities were handling the demonstrations."[23]

While we know little more of the content of these calls beyond a handful of comments like these, what is clear is that these cities all presented a common message to the public: that the cities had no choice and were forced to raid the camps due to their obligation to maintain public health and safety. This messaging was effective for the wave of raids, creating very little public outcry or swell of support for the movement of the sort that we had seen in Oakland less than a month before. The trope was useful moving forward as a way to portray the future encampments as untenable and dangerous and to smear the movement as dirty and irresponsible. A *USA Today* article quoting Oakland City Council President Larry Reid reported that "the encampment has been a major setback for the area while attracting sex offenders, mentally ill and homeless people, and anarchists. 'This is no longer about Occupy Wall Street. . . . This is about occupying Oakland and extracting whatever you can get out of Oakland by holding our city hostage.'"[24]

Mayor Quan and seventeen other mayors all listed a range of potential liabilities that the camps posed to varying degrees—sanitation, food safety, the potential for the spread of illnesses, fire, and so on. The logic of the public relations effort was to make the raids seem inevitable. The talking points also adopted a depoliticized tone, that the raids would be conducted with great reluctance from the political actors responsible (mostly liberal Democrats) who mostly expressed a deep respect for protesters' rights, but that the raids were essential to maintain public health and safety. As with most things in the social world presented as inevitabilities, the raids were not actually necessary or inevitable, as the persistence of camps after November in more than sixty cities and towns demonstrates.[25] In crafting the discursive strategy that was key to the success of the coordinated raids, there is a deliberate avoidance of frames of repression; the "respect for First Amendment rights" was reiterated constantly. The "but" that followed in this rhetoric served to depoliticize the raids and to center the "public safety and health" mantra. I establish, in the next section, that these were the talking points, that they were part of a coordinated strategy, and that they were designed to mitigate blowback from the ensuing repression of the camps. The final section of this chapter analyzes this strategy and why it was chosen.

FEDERAL COORDINATION AND NATIONAL TALKING POINTS

The November raids played a significant role in stripping the national movement of visibility shortly thereafter. In the parlance of the news media, the camps were "the story," and without them Occupy was seen as a dead movement (Gitlin 2003, 263; Ryan 1991, 31; Sobieraj 2011, 88).[26] As Mayor Quan noted in an interview, the November raids were more successful at framing the media analysis than Oakland's first raid. Instead of a discussion as to whether the camps should be raided, it became more of a question of when and how. Amid all the claims used to attack Occupy Oakland and the other camps that were raided, the trope of health and safety was key; I have seen scant few articles that interrogate its validity or make room for counter-arguments.

The policing was far less aggressive in the second raid, and in Oakland even the most militant folks in the movement were resigned to the raid before it happened. The discourse of public safety and health was key to mitigating public sympathy *before and after* the second round of raids. This was by design.

Health and safety concerns were not entirely groundless, and it would be false to say that there were not significant problems in the camps. These concerns were, however, overblown and taken out of context. In Oakland, sexual harassment was an issue, and a committee was developed and was greatly successful at weeding it out and mitigating it. Internal camp security had nonetheless improved in the second camp, addressing interpersonal conflict and sexual harassment better than the first camp. Despite this fact, a twenty-five-year-old man named Kayode Foster working security for the camp was shot and killed after an altercation with men from outside the camp on November 10. City officials quickly capitalized on the tragedy, with Mayor Quan stating, "It is now clear to most Oaklanders that because of the increased violence associated with the camp and the strain on our city's economy and resources, now is the time for the encampment to end."[27] The use of this tragedy to further a preexisting agenda also decontextualizes the prevalence of gun violence in the city, and on that corner particularly. Four people were murdered on that same street corner the year prior. This does not diminish that young man's life in any way. Occupy did not make that corner violent, because it already was (as Quan herself would later note).[28] Kayode Foster's senseless death became an additional talking point in Oakland as the "health and safety" trope drew the encampment raid closer.

In examining New York, Oakland, Portland, Philadelphia, Denver, and Los Angeles, this trope of health and safety was evident and widespread. It was frequently coupled with the claim that the cities respected people's First Amendment rights to protest, but that those rights needed to be balanced with the cities' obligation to provide health and safety. In city after city, mayor after mayor, this same exact message was conveyed over and over again. All of these quotations come from the days surrounding raids in these cities:

> Mayor Quan in Oakland stated: "The camp had become an unbearable drain on city resources, an economic threat to nearby businesses and a danger to public safety."[29]

In Philadelphia, Mayor Michael Nutter said: "I understand that they have things on their mind as Americans and wish to express their free speech. The things we're talking about, the activities that are going on, are not about free speech. They're public health and public safety concerns that have nothing to do with Wall Street and corporations."[30]

Denver's city attorney relayed the same message: "Denver has worked diligently and done an excellent job of striking the appropriate balance between protecting individuals' First Amendment rights and ensuring the public's health and safety."[31]

And New York's Mayor Michael Bloomberg echoed that he had defended [Occupy's] right to protest, but that "health and safety conditions became intolerable."[32] He added, in a statement after the raid: "Unfortunately, the park was becoming a place where people came not to protest, but rather to break laws, and in some cases, to harm others. There have been reports of businesses being threatened and complaints about noise and unsanitary conditions that have seriously impacted the quality of life for residents and businesses in this now-thriving neighborhood."[33]

Across these different cities, officials all adopted the same language to legitimate the police raids in the eyes of the public. This became the dominant narrative in the media. The logic and nature of this argument is also instructive in illustrating the intertwining roles of local and national government officials, police agencies, and the media in manufacturing a common sense that rationalizes attacks on social movements (Boykoff 2007a, 27–35). A *USA Today* story the day after the second raid in Oakland echoed the national talking points and similarly posed a debate in which only one answer was logical or possible—that of immediate eviction (couched as a "public-safety closure" in the title): "The debate between public safety and First Amendment rights could be reaching a breaking point in the Occupy Wall Street protests in New York City and elsewhere, as police and government officials clear out camps in response to reports of violence, vandalism, death and illness."[34]

The trope of public health and safety that echoed across the country before and after the eighteen-city sweep of Occupy encampments was clearly coordinated. The same discursive strategies supported and sought to legitimate the same policing objective and tactics. The effects were similar as well. Despite the December 12th West Coast Port Shutdown, with solidarity actions in cities like New York, Houston, and Denver, the loss of the camps helped facilitate a decline in interest and growth in the movement nationally. While many in Oakland saw the loss of the camp as a momentary setback (with some Occupiers relieved that the headaches of the camp were over, or feeling that the time used maintaining the camps could be better spent on organizing projects), many commentators from Left to Right used the fall of the encampments to argue the death of the movement.[35] Unlike the recent Tea Party movement, Occupy had a hard time keeping the media's and public's attention after the evictions—a pattern of progressive/radical movement erasure that is long-standing (Davenport 2010, 10–11; Gitlin 2003, 271; Sobieraj 2011, 18).

By framing the movement as a threat to health and safety, the camp evictions met official objectives: There was no repeat of police violence great enough to spark popular blowback. The movement was passively smeared as dirty and irresponsible, but without an overtly politicized emphasis on demonization or criminalization. This effort deployed bureaucratized governmentality situated in a depoliticized political discourse: to repress without being seen as repressive. The politics of how this process worked is important to understand when analyzing the general contexts in which protest and the policing of protest take place.

Situated within the context of paternalistic protection discussed in chapter 2, the core discursive elements of this public relations strategy were to assert good intentions and concerns with First Amendment rights, while placing the policing of the movement in terms of health, security, and the potential for, and unquestionable need to mitigate, a crisis. There was some variation from city to city—with some mayors (i.e., Mayor Antonio Villaraigosa in Los Angeles) emphasizing respect for protesters slightly more than others, and other officials embellishing the camps as imminent social catastrophies (i.e., Mayor Bloomberg in New York); however, the logic and terms of the discourse were universal. To better understand the relationship between politics and knowledge, and the techniques of policing they are entwined with, it is essential to map the logic of the political discourses and policies as well as their social and political contexts and effects.

The ability of public officials to convey messages in the mainstream press, usually completely unchallenged, is a major tool in defining common sense and legitimacy, which is also a tactical advantage in terms of repression and social control (Boykoff 2007a; Gitlin 2003; Ryan 1991; Sobieraj 2011). Instead of relying solely on physical force and policing, these cities utilized their paternal moralistic power as the voice of elected government, alongside their ability to frame the movement as a social problem more than a social movement. This discursive power operated in such a way that the raids were understood as inevitable, even among those inside the movement, while simultaneously portraying the encampments as dirty, dangerous, and uninviting homeless shelters. By situating the eviction of the camps, a major blow to the movement in each of these cities, in the context of "security," legal liability, and bureaucratic necessity, the repression was depoliticized. To the extent that this was seen as repression, it was intelligible primarily as either an unfortunate necessity or an ultimate inevitability.

The strategy solidified on these conference calls was to construct this depoliticizing inevitability within the ideology of security. This catchall legitimation technique is inherently post-political, a largely unquestionable realm of state power. This is a carefully crafted ideological articulation, embedding the raids in a discourse not easily challenged (Hall 1981, 31; Neocleous and Rigakos 2011). Stuart Hall, in his explanation of ideological fields of struggle, discusses the (re)inscription of subject positions and relations of power, and the naturalization of those relations: "Ideologies therefore work by the transformation of discourses (the disarticulation and rearticulation of ideological elements) and the transformation (the fracturing and recomposition) of subjects-for-action" (Hall 1981, 32). This did not take place in Oakland before the first raid; this was the "failure to explain" that Mayor Quan spoke of. It was a mistake that was not made twice, as the highest levels of government lent their voice and insights to make sure that was the case.

Given the popularity of the movement, support for the tactic of occupying (camping), and the strengths of the movement in terms of institutionalized direct democracy guarding against co-optation (and legal liability), local governments were left in a difficult situation in terms of developing a successful eviction strategy. The conference calls helped to foster a widespread strategy of depoliticized safety and sanitation, a common sense constructed around the rationalized duties of city government. In relation to governmentality and the normalization of flexible tools of social control, specifically negotiated management, the objectives of that strategy are to neutralize disruption and to mitigate risk. Chapters 5 through 7 discuss how the rejection of negotiation management can lead to the marginalization and criminalization of those who refuse to police their own disruptive capacity. In the context of the November encampment raids across the country, we see a different normative application of negotiated management. Here, the mitigation of risk is primary, and the evictions are presented as inevitable and apolitical, as city housekeeping essential to the mitigation of potential epidemics and disasters. Here, we have the projection of necessary grounds maintenance done with a sympathetic and heavy heart, instead of the widespread repression of a movement—cutting down beautiful but poisonous flowers because someone planted them on city property and they are interfering with the natural flora and fauna.

Beyond Framing: The Health and Safety Trope as an Exercise in Governmentality

Michel Foucault's conceptualization of governmentality is helpful in understanding the political roots of the public relations campaign and how and why it was successful in simultaneously legitimating and depoliticizing policing. Governmentality, or the "art of government," is increasingly situated around its ability to legitimately control, manage, and make productive three key aspects of the social world—the economy, the natural world and health, and sociopolitical relationships (Foucault 1994, 208–209). As Ronjon Paul Datta (2011) summarizes, "State governing is an exercise of power involving finding out about, intervening in, and shaping what people are doing by facilitating some actions and placing obstacles to others" (226).

How Capital Became "the 99%" (Economic Governmentality)

It is fitting that the language and logic of the market—financial risk and liability, economic cost and budget deficits and the political imperatives that follow from them—would be a cornerstone in the city's strategy to reclaim Oscar Grant Plaza. The economic governmentality of legal and financial liability (as well as city expenditures) runs through the health and safety trope.

The supposed cost to small businesses was another key theme in Oakland leading up to the November 14 raid. The Chamber of Commerce and city officials were eager to insistently posit that the occupation was an economic drain on the city and local businesses, citing figures from the Chamber of Commerce that were not supported by any independent data. The *Oakland Tribune*

quoted Paul Junge of the Chamber of Commerce: "We are seeing serious losses of business. . . . People have lost 40 percent, 50
percent, 60 percent of their sales."[36] Mayor Quan would go on
to add how this was costing jobs, amid the city's long-standing
(and politically unaddressed) high unemployment: "This situation
is costing us real jobs. . . . We can't afford to lose a single job."[37]
A primary function of government is to maintain a prosperous
economy, and framing Occupy as a threat to the health and safety
of private profitability was a responsibility taken seriously and
often couched in the language of Occupy's hurting the 99% by
costing them jobs and resources.

Nor was this line of argument peculiar to Oakland. In Philadelphia, Mayor Nutter made a central issue of Occupy Philadelphia frustrating an urban redevelopment project with its presence.
Two weeks before the raid in Philadelphia, Nutter, who repeatedly spoke on behalf of the 99%, said, "Occupy Philly is now pur-
posely standing in the way of nearly 1,000 jobs for Philadelphians
in a time of high unemployment. They are blocking Philadelphians from taking care of their families."[38] As cities like Oakland
and Philadelphia continued to slash public sector jobs—2,500
layoffs in Oakland, 4,000 in Philadelphia in the months before
and during Occupy[39]—they still remained responsible for protecting the profitability of private businesses from protest (however substantiated the financial costs were).

Nestled into the discourse about public health and safety
were also various claims about the costs of Occupy Oakland, pertaining specifically to policing. The purported costs were both
financial and social. A press release from Oakland's City Administrator on November 4 estimated that economic costs to the city
totaled $1,002,000 for the first eighteen days of the movement's
existence, more than 70 percent of that spent on police over-
time.[40] The social costs were figured in terms of an alleged (and
false) rise in crime (and later, a lack of police response to crime
in other parts of the city). The mayor argued in early November

2011 that Occupy Oakland had caused a spike in crime in the downtown area.[41] While the claims about the costs to small businesses were based on Chamber of Commerce speculation, the allegations about a spike in crime were known to the mayor and OPD Chief Howard Jordan to be false. Local television station KTVU, upon receiving a thousand city emails in a public records request two months after the November raid took place, reported that Chief Jordan knew that the rising crime claims that Mayor Quan was making were, in fact, bogus: "When Jordan received an update that crime was actually down 19 percent in the last week of October, he wrote an email to one of Mayor Jean Quan's advisers. 'Not sure how you want to share this good news,' he wrote. 'It may be counter to our statement that the Occupy movement is negatively impacting crime in Oakland.'"[42]

The safety/crime trope did not go unchallenged at the time of the raids. UC Berkeley professor of law Jonathan Simon, for one, expressed, "But what is regrettable is the use by city leaders of the lame excuse that 'crime' problems necessitated the end of the encampments. It may be that the Occupy Wall Street movement must generate new meaningful actions to build its momentum, but the claims that the encampments were generating unacceptable levels of crime is both false and reflexive."[43] As Jonathan Simon (2007) notes elsewhere, the political expediency of the fear of crime is a central facet of neoliberal governmentality. As we will see, it was one of many nodes in the health and safety discourse used to turn the camps into a social crisis, through which depoliticized state actions become immutable (Agamben 2005, 16–19).

Immunizing the Rabble (Environmental/Health Governmentality)

The emphasis on the threat of accidents or illness, and the possibility that the city would be held legally and financially liable, was another subtheme of the health and public safety trope. The *Los Angeles Times* ran an article on November 9, 2011, three weeks before the raid on the Occupy LA encampment, that spelled out this argument about liability. The article quoted a letter from the Department of Recreation and Parks General Manager Jon Mukri to the mayor: "'The City's liability has increased not only due to potential of fallen tree branches, but also from trip and fall hazards created by tent ropes, holes, and broken sprinklers.' Additionally, the city's open flame and smoking ordinances aren't being enforced at the site."[44]

Five days before the raid on Zuccotti Park, the *New York Times* included an article about an impending health disaster, quoting a doctor who had recently served as an expert for Homeland Security on terrorism and air safety: "Dr. Philip M. Tierno Jr., the director of clinical microbiology and immunology at NYU Langone Medical Center, said the conditions could leave park-dwellers susceptible to respiratory viruses; norovirus, the so-called winter vomiting virus, which can lead to vomiting and diarrhea and which could quickly overwhelm the limited bathroom facilities in the area; and tuberculosis, which is more common in indigent populations and can be spread by coughing."[45]

This highlighting of risks—from second-hand smoke to TB—was part of a national laundry list of sanitation threats and safety concerns. There was widespread discussion of drugs and rats in Oakland;[46] "evidence of excrement, urine, and vomit were observed throughout the park" in San Francisco;[47] it was said that Zuccotti Park in New York had become "an increasing health and fire safety hazard";[48] and inspectors found a clean kitchen but "dirty and stagnant wastewater in the Occupy Portland kitchen."[49] As part of the national strategy, city officials made the issue of health and safety "the story" in the press and threw everything, including the kitchen sink, at the Occupy movement, as city police forces around the country readied themselves to clear the camps.

The day after the raid on Zuccotti Park in New York City, the New York Civil Liberties Union condemned the eviction as not only unnecessary but a threat to health and safety in itself: "The eviction of protesters from Zuccotti Park was not about public health. Rousting hundreds of peaceful protesters from their tents in the dead of night amid a media blackout doesn't promote public safety—it endangers it."[50] To critique this laundry list rationale is not to trivialize the real and potential health and safety threats the camps did pose—a young man was shot and killed in Oakland, women were sexually assaulted in Oakland and other cities, those involved in camp tidying were not always members of the Martha Stewart fan club. However, the existence of risk is endemic to any concentration of human bodies in one place. The health and safety risk of the camps was more comparable to a sporting event, large concert, or county fair, which do not receive this type of scrutiny. Instead of being seen as having similar threats to public health and safety as good old all-American baseball games, the camps were compared to refugee camps.[51] It would be wrong to suggest that sporting events have not also come under the broadening gaze of anti-terror security,[52] but they are not deemed untenable because they are profitable (Police Executive Research Forum 2011, 28).

The (distorted) threat of illness, epidemics, and disease, coupled with the potential for violence or accidents, speaks to the governmentality of public health. Whether the logic of health and safety is used to repress social movements or surveil public events, the process of using security, health, and safety as depoliticized rationales to extend state power is an ever-intensifying process, and one that needs to be politicized in order to be effectively challenged.

Depoliticizing Social Control (Sociopolitical Governmentality)

The sociopolitical dimensions of governmentality in the nationally coordinated public relations campaign revolved mainly around the relational roles of government and citizens, and of police and protesters. The raids displayed a paternalistic logic, of

keeping Occupiers safe from themselves, of "destroying the village to save it," of portraying repression as a public good. This
paternalistic logic was not primarily grounded in criminalizing
and delegitimating protesters overtly, at least in this instance.
Instead, it was manifest in the positing of circumstantial threats,
however well-rooted in probability, that the government has an
obligation and not a *desire* to address (Tilly 1985). The audience for
this maneuver was a public that has become accustomed to being
patronized and manipulated through fear of vague threats (Curtis
2004; Simon 2007, 260–261).

The City of Oakland would invoke broad and vague civil
nuisance laws (as would San Francisco) to justify the razing of
the camp. The civil law language is also rooted in the use of parks
as sites of leisure consumption, to which the camp was allegedly
serving as an unpermitted barrier. A notice posted in Oscar Grant
Plaza and released to the press three days before the November 14 raid reiterated the national talking points and situated the
encampment as a public nuisance, in violation of criminal and
civil law:

> The City of Oakland and its police department support and
> protect the right of all individuals to engage in free speech
> and their right to assemble. However, this encampment is
> a violation of the law. . . . Your activities are injurious to
> health, obstruct the free use of property, interfering with the
> comfortable enjoyment of the plaza, and unlawfully obstruct
> the free passage or use of a public park or square. (California
> Penal Code sections 370 and 647(e) and Civil Code 3479)[53]

As I discussed in chapter 2, in relation to negotiated management, this paternalism—the restriction of peoples' rights under
the auspices of protecting them while implicitly threatening the
use of force—is a heavily gendered process. Paternalistic protection is imposed (not offered); if attempts are made to refuse that
protection, force is often used under the auspices of responsible

stewardship over dependents. The subordinated object of state protection is granted no autonomous agency, and is rendered irrational, infantile, or irresponsible if protection is refused. This is an inherently undemocratic tendency that has become more pronounced under neoliberalism, one that infantilizes citizen-subjects as part of long-standing processes that erode social rights while concomitantly using fear, manipulation, and simplistic Manichean frames to legitimate uncontested/contestable public policy. As Lauren Berlant points out, "Democracies can produce a special form of tyranny that makes citizens like children, infantilized, passive, and overdependent on the 'immense and tutelatory power' of the state" (1997, 27). Although this tendency toward political paternalism/infantilism is an endemic tension of representative government, these roles and relations have taken on a heightened form in the neoliberal era. The withdrawal of democratic rights and process through the unquestionable expansion of state power has become increasingly normalized. This depoliticization of state and policing activities has a symbiotic relationship with infantilized citizenship; government policy has become more autonomous and citizen participation and engagement more atomized, cynical, and disempowered (Eliasoph 1998; Putnam 2000).

Modern policing is enmeshed in this process to a great extent, as police have become more politically insulated and their practices less subject to effective scrutiny.[54] The November raids cannot be properly understood without appreciating the power of the logic of "broken windows" policing and the roles it ascribes to city officials, police, and politically marginalized groups (Vitale 2005). "Broken windows" is rooted around preempting disorder through a mixture of civil ordinances and police practices designed to control space under the justification of protecting the common good from (criminal) nuisances (Harcourt 2001, 127–128; King 2013a). These prevalent policies, in conjunction with other tactics affiliated with the wars on drugs/gangs/crime, have come to inhabit a status of unquestioned necessity among a wide swath of the public. By applying this logic and language to the eviction of the camps, city officials articulated the evictions within a political discourse that erased the grounds for intelligible contestation.

From the fear of crime and "super-predators" (Rios 2011, 176; Wacquant 2009, 243), to fears of disease (Szasz 2007, 3–4), to fears of terror (Curtis 2004; Parenti 2003, 199–200), to neo-nativist fears that immigrants will bring with them everything from car accidents and pollution, to healthcare fraud and drugs (Gerstyle 2004, 87), the dialectic of paternalism and infantilized fear is a driving force in the politics of policing in the United States. These relationships and roles are easily mobilized to justify a wide range of state policies that erode the civil and human rights of marginalized groups.

We see all three of these facets of governmentality—the economic, the natural/biological, and the sociopolitical—used to situate the November raids. This wide range of post-political justifications—from a cost of policing that is too much to bear and a projected economic hardship to small businesses, to the fear of infectious disease epidemics or propane explosions, to the fear of drugs, violence, and generalized disorder—the trope of health and safety was a smorgasbord of vague threats beckoning effective security, intended to resonate as broadly as possible in terms that were hard to contest.

PROTEST GOVERNMENTALITY: DISRUPTION AS RISK, SOCIAL CONTROL AS SECURITY

Jurisdictional power presents itself as both omnipotent and naturalized, often with policies articulated through discourses of crisis and security. As *Anti-Security* illustrates clearly, security has become an "unassailable" rationale and a "blockage on politics" (Neocleous and Rigakos 2011, 15). George Rigakos points to the ways in which projects of pacification are presented and understood as a preservation of the common good, outside of the realm of politics or debate: "Even from a critical or social democratic perspective: how can anyone be against *social* security, *job* security, *personal* security, or *health* security? How about our *children's* security? How could anyone stand against *environmental* security? . . . The more security seems post-political, post-social, or even postmodern the more it escapes analytic scrutiny. . . . The ability for security to latch itself on to most aspects of human relations must therefore be recognized as an analytic and political blockage" (59–60).

Across the country, the repression of Occupy encampments was placed in this post-political protective bubble of "security"— a discursive ground made slippery by the littering of a long list of (potential) risks, liabilities, crises of incalculable probability. The movement was criminalized to a very limited extent in this moment. Instead, it was made a delinquent dependent, govern-mentalized, an object of security. The political discourse made sure that the wholesale extinguishing of the camps' "fire" was achieved through a well-intentioned smothering of paternalistic love, rather than dramatically extinguishing the fire with a police baton beating.

By using a depoliticized logic of security, this coordinated effort to repress without being seen as repressive (i.e., to police without explicit criminalization) was successful at depriving the movement in Oakland (and elsewhere) of a physical base as well as a corner of visibility in the popular imagination and political discourse. In Oakland, the erasure of the camp physically and politically made the reinstatement of governmental control clear, though not unchallenged. It recalibrated social control tactics, specifically negotiated management and strategic incapacita-tion, to their normal functions within a reemphasized common sense of state perogative over social life. As Datta (2011) explains, "The concern with security in governmentality is not then the protection of the population, but is about ensuring the integrity of regulatory mechanisms" (229). The camps, the Oakland camps in particular, were a regulatory and policing nightmare, an autonomous space in the heart of the city. The first Oakland eviction had created a widespread breakdown in social control—meaning that strategic incapacitation had proven unsuccessful and unstrategic. The Oakland camps had rejected negotiated management but retained social legitimacy. The second raid in Oakland proved much more successful from the point of view of city officials, because the "regulatory mechanisms" not only worked but also retained a veneer of integrity. The legitimacy of the raids was imposed by depoliticizing them, making the raids an "unfortunate inevitability." This message became a common sense reinforced by the fact that the raids were taking place all over the country, under the watch of some of the most liberal Democrats in major elected office, all at the same time. This post-political maneuver would be enough to knock the movement in Oakland off balance while the techniques of negotiated management and strategic incapacitation were readied for future use.

CHAPTER 5

Putting the Occupy Oakland Vigil to Sleep

ANTI-GANG TECHNIQUES AND THE OAKLAND POLICE DEPARTMENT'S STATE OF EXCEPTION

SHORTLY AFTER THE eviction of the second, and last, Occupy Oakland encampment, the police undertook a conscious shift to a more targeted and strategic combination of hard and soft repression of the movement, through fusing the discursive strategy of the second raid (to couch repression in the language of protecting public health and safety) with the legalistic and policing methods applied in the city's existing gang injunctions. When the second encampment eviction came, there seemed to be much more widespread sentiment within the movement that—due to both the clear commitments of local and federal agencies and the difficulties protecting and defending camps from repression—the days of encampments that stood for weeks were a thing of the past. In Oakland, however, a group of several dozen Occupiers was committed to maintaining a presence in Oscar Grant Plaza after the second raid on November 14, 2011, many because they were homeless and had nowhere else to go. Different, sometimes overlapping, groups within Occupy Oakland—including the Tactical Action Committee, the Interfaith Tent, the Oakland Nomads, the Kitchen Committee, Occupy

Image 6   Miniature teepee protest in Oscar Grant Plaza during Occupy Oakland vigil, December 2011. (Photo by Daniel Arauz)

Legal, and the Vigil committee—adopted the tactic of a vigil as part of a strategy to maintain a constant presence in Oscar Grant Plaza without formally "camping"—standing by their constitutional right to protest in public space.

The vigil emerged where the camp had stood, originally intending to maintain the community and social services that the camp provided (food, clinic, library, etc.) while not violating the city's ordinance against sleeping. The General Assembly approved the idea in large part to maintain a public presence in the heart of the city. The tactic was intended to preserve a great deal of the camps while proactively avoiding anything that could be construed as a threat to health and safety and also avoiding the enforcement of city laws prohibiting sleeping in public parks. The vigil was intended to be unpermitted and to serve as a tactical innovation in the face of nationally coordinated efforts to eradicate Occupy camps. It would also put pressure on the overt constitutional tension within the state's carefully chosen rationale of limiting the First Amendment rights of some to protect the health and safety of many. If the vigil could maintain many core aspects of the camps without posing a threat to public health and safety, repression against that vigil could easily be seen as unjustified, similar to the failed repression attempt at the first encampment raid. One of the crafters of the vigil idea, Phil Horne, a member of Occupy Legal (an autonomous collective of legal aid supporters from San Francisco), explained the legal logic of the vigil tactic in this way:

> We wanted something that would set a minimum bar, so it was like as long as we do this, we can be there. So we said, let's look at all the [legal] cases pertaining [to constitutionally protected activities in public parks] . . . it was really the maximum, like what's the maximum we can do safely, like rock solid, it's definitely safe. So that if [the police] act on that [repress the protest assembly], then we get a restraining order, and then we get a precedent started, so we can build on that.[1]

As Occupy Oakland adopted a new approach, the city of Oakland and the OPD would as well—extrapolating the logic of the second raid while honing and downscaling some of their hard repression tactics. As the vigil sought to situate itself within the framework of free speech and legal protections, the city was re-deploying the legalistic regulatory tools that had supported the second encampment raid. As with the effectiveness of hard repression largely hinging upon the response of the movement, the level of public support, and the overall social conditions at that time, efforts at soft repression depend upon those same forces. The right to assemble and demonstrate in public is nominally protected by the First Amendment, but (as was often repeated before and after raids on Occupy camps around the country) those rights can be limited to protect the public from amorphously defined threats and nuisances to the public (Mitchell 2003, 122, 65–66). Beyond the struggles social movements are a part of, the act of protesting itself is always entwined with juridical mechanisms of control and legalistic repression: "If . . . the idea of public space and its role in urban life needs to be preserved, then we also need to be aware that the idea has *never* been guaranteed. It has only been won through concerted struggle, and *then*, after the fact guaranteed (to some extent) in law" (5).

Freedom of assembly and speech are commonly limited or rescinded in the actual process of policing (Noakes and Gillham 2006). Tactically and strategically, the OPD and city officials built from their success with the second encampment eviction on November 14 in relation to their approach to the vigil. The OPD were still having their efforts restrained by the mayor leading up to and during the West Coast Port Shutdown on December 12–13 due to fear of a possible repeat of the very visible police brutality on October 25 and subsequent swell of support for the movement right before an already planned major action. In this period the police drew from techniques long-honed in working-class and poor communities in Oakland. The OPD, the district attorney, the mayor, and other city officials combined the successful rhetorical trope of the federally coordinated raids with the micro-techniques of anti-gang policing. Between late December and early January, the OPD conducted a series of targeted raids on the vigil, arresting dozens on obstruction and other misdemeanor charges. Combining the logics of strategic incapacitation and negotiated management, the raids on those in the plaza were successful at not only controlling urban space, but harassing, intimidating, and detaining Occupiers, and preoccupying the movement with jail support, all the while criminalizing the movement in the eyes of the public.

The three major police raids on Oscar Grant Plaza from December 16, 2011, to January 4, 2012, shared much in common with Oakland's much-contested gang injunctions in both strategy and tactics. They also fit squarely within the logic of strategic incapacitation: incorporating the more generalized police logic of new penology and zero tolerance into the repression of popular protest. Like the city's gang injunctions, the policing of the plaza in December/January sought to exert control over geographically specified urban space through the targeting of people with criminal records, and the surveillance and policing of others engaged in constitutionally protected activities that have been criminalized through the use of civil law. To draw out this process, it is useful to revisit the logic of strategic incapacitation and examine its manifestation in the city's gang injunctions before turning to its application against the vigil.

THE LOGIC AND PRACTICE OF NEW PENOLOGY

The general paradigm shift that took place in the 1970s and 1980s within dominant theories of criminology discarded ideas about rehabilitation and prevention in exchange for aggressive policing and prosecution and fear-driven punishment—featuring longer sentences, mandatory minimums, three-strikes laws, punishing juveniles as adults, more aggressive and intrusive policing techniques (such as gang injunctions), and institutionalized racial profiling. What has emerged in the period of new penology is a reorientation of goals: to identify and preempt threats, with methods geared toward incapacitating or containing "criminal elements" through incarceration or surveillance. The intensified criminalization of urban space and subaltern populations, which is used to legitimate the erosion of civil liberties among targeted groups, has become an inherent part of the process (Blacks and Latinos in the War on Drugs, Latinos in the War on Undocumented Immigration, Muslims/Middle Easterners in the War on Terror). Gang injunctions, and other practices such as stop-and-frisk policies, have been introduced in this period, amid a sociopolitical backdrop of elevated fear of crime, drugs, and violence and a new penology ideological landscape that has concluded that there are no alternatives, that historic levels of inequality are natural and normal, that rehabilitation and prevention have been tried and "nothing works." And, as Jonathan Simon points out: "The new penal policies that emerged during the 1980s, combining pragmatic risk management of presumptuously dangerous populations with populist punitiveness belong to, and in many respects anchor, a new political order" (2007, 23).

Policing, under the new penology paradigm, has become about social control and preemption through surveillance, harassment, and detention. The common denominator of several long-standing policing efforts in the past few decades is to identify a criminal threat, criminalize communities and groups associated with that threat, label individuals or neighborhoods as criminal, and contain and control them (Davis 1990; Herbert 1997; Wacquant 2001; Williams 2011). In all of these cases, exceptions to the law (the rescinding of fundamental constitutional rights of those targeted and the communities in which they are a part) are common, and legitimated partially through a logic and a practice of domestic "war"—wars that cannot be lost (or won), that are being fought against enemies that are undeterrable and incapable of rehabilitation (Agamben 2005; Kraska 2001; Simon 2007). As analyses of gang injunctions and similar policies suggest, these practices are about managing subjects who have been labeled a criminal threat and controlling broader populations and space in the process of maintaining the existing social order and relations (Williams 2011).

STAKING POLICE TURF OUTSIDE: FROM GANG INJUNCTIONS TO OCCUPY OAKLAND

John Noakes and Patrick Gillham (2006) situate the logic of strategic incapacitation within the broader new penology that has arisen with the post-1970s policing and incarceration boom (Feeley and Simon 1992). New penology, the governmentality of policing, is focused on managing inherent threats; "preempting" criminal behavior through increasing surveillance and profiling within certain populations rather than investigating and solving crimes; and discursively justifying these measures (which are often labeled as being unconstitutional) through criminalization and a foreclosure upon alternatives (Feeley and Simon 1992; Foucault 1994; Herbert 1997; Noakes and Gillham 2006; Simon 2007).

Gang injunctions and the police techniques used against Occupy Oakland both fit squarely within the policing logics and practices of new penology—in this instance, entwined with negotiated management (King 2013b; McPhail, Schweingruber, and McCarthy 1998). These methods make use of already criminalized bodies (people with criminal records) to profile and criminalize spaces and broader populations in order to establish social control in a given area. Through criminalizing targets and delegitimating their associates, the police posit themselves as a security force whose legitimacy is difficult to question within the dominant formations of knowledge in which they are hegemonic and their targets socially marginal. This normalizes the rescinding of constitutional rights through generalized surveillance, profiling, and harassment. Once this process of the justified rescinding of democratic rights is forged in one context through criminalization (i.e., with gang injunctions in Oakland), that process can be easily translated into different arenas of policing with its (extra-)legal techniques utilized in any context that can be defined similarly as a threat to the social order or public security (i.e., the presence of members of Occupy Oakland in certain public spaces) (Agamben 2005).

Anomie within the Law as Guarantor of Social Order

Giorgio Agamben's theorization of the "State of Exception" helps explain the shift from new penology policing techniques against one target to the next, in this case how the gang injunctions laid the groundwork for the effective repression of post-encampment Occupy Oakland. Agamben illustrates how the mutual constitution between politics, ideology, and the law is being refashioned by agencies of the state (city and district attorneys and police departments with support from city officials), using a self-appointed judgment of emergency necessity to combat a criminal nuisance, interpellated broadly as an "enemy of the people." Agamben's legal theory is that this is neither outside nor within the law, but a blurring of constitutional rights—an "anomie within the law"—or, as the National District Attorneys' Association (2009) says in relation to gang injunctions, an "innovative" legal technique making use of ambiguities in the law. Clearly (and admittedly), the practices of gang and stay-away injunctions are not rooted in objective criminal law, but in emergency technicalities that allow for the bending and blurring of the law—invoked as necessary exceptions to due process and freedom of speech and assembly. As we see in the direct transmission of the legal and political justifications, as well as the tactics and goals, from the injunctions to the stay-aways (as well as the normative requirement of permits for already constitutionally protected protest), this "anomie within the law" quickly becomes the new norm, with chilling effects on dissent, or anyone labeled an internal enemy (Agamben 2003, 23).

The power of strategic incapacitation is rooted in the police's ability to legitimately use bureaucratized force, ideology, and legal techniques to create a certain social order using legal and illegal policing techniques jointly justified by paternal state power and the criminalization of targets. This "innovation" is a shift from an order rooted in laws and rights toward an order rooted in a perpetual state of exception, with subjective political policies aimed at preserving a new penology social order. The epoch of new penology, whether in the War on Gangs or in the repression of social movements, is rooted in a broader logic of governmentality and managerial control of population and spaces. Power is deployed and reinforced through defining threats and preemptively neutralizing them, rather than upholding the law through criminal investigation. Rather than respecting people's right to protest while upholding the law, the policing of Occupy Oakland used the withholding of the law to preserve the social order of new penology.

A Short History of Gang Injunctions

For almost twenty-five years gang injunctions have been an increasingly used instrument of policing in California. They are a civil (rather than a criminal) injunction against groups of individuals suspected of being gang members. Those named in an injunction are allowed limited association with others, are prohibited from wearing colors associated with gangs, and are subject to a 10 P.M. curfew, among other restrictions. Gang injunctions originated in Los Angeles in 1987, and have spread throughout the country, though remaining mostly concentrated in the West, and California in particular. They are promoted as a somewhat flexible tool for combating gang activity, which is seen as a major, if not predominant, source of criminal activity. This logic of (often, suspected) association with criminal networks as a crime in itself can be found in federal law dating back to at least the 1970s (RICO laws; more recently the Patriot Act) (Churchill and Vander Wall 1990, 309–312; Williams 2006, 172–174). All of the people on the injunction list have criminal records, some of them lengthy, some violent.

Because gang injunctions are civil rather than criminal policies, the state has a lower burden of proof in demonstrating gang membership, and those named in the injunction have no right to a pre-injunction hearing or a public defender (Werdegar 1999, 435). The first injunctions in LA applied to activities that were already deemed criminal, such as burglary or writing graffiti, but they were quickly broadened to include curfews, dress codes, and restrictions on association (416). This criminalization of non-criminal activities now extends to activities such as hanging out with friends and relatives or wearing or possessing any article that has colors associated with gangs. The profiling of specific individuals with criminal records in particular places, the use of civil law to restrict free assembly and expression in demarcated areas, and the use of these tactics to profile associates and broader populations in an effort to establish police control of urban space are characteristics common to both the gang injunctions and the vigil raids and stay-away (restraining) orders used against Occupy Oakland that began in late December 2011.

Oakland introduced its first of two gang injunctions in the summer of 2010 in North Oakland, with a preliminary approval for a second injunction in the Fruitvale neighborhood the following summer. The injunctions sparked great community outrage primarily around issues of racial profiling, the overlapping geographies of injunctions and gentrification, the erosion of civil liberties, and the financial costs to a small, cash-strapped city (Critical Resistance 2011, 3–6). The injunctions were a product of the new penology preemptive approach to policing; the Oakland police's own publications argue that the injunctions were designed to prevent crime, rather than prosecute it.[2] In this way injunctions drift away from strategies of community policing or prevention through social services toward a model of broken windows policing focused on "preempting crime." In March 2015, the city of Oakland announced that it had abandoned the gang injunction strategy and ended its two existing injunctions.[3]

Individuals listed in a gang injunction can be incarcerated for activities that are not part of any criminal statute, but based on associations and legal activities that police argue *lead* to criminal activity—wearing certain colors, talking to certain people, being out at night. The one arrest produced by the North Oakland injunction was of this type. Under a logic of new penology, instead of doing the traditional police work of investigating a crime, gathering and following evidence, and making arrests, the police and city attorney interpellate people as gang members under the pretext that they are indirectly responsible for crimes the police have no evidence to link them with—preemptive guilt by association. From there, the police pursue suspected gang members, not for criminal activity, but for suspected membership in a criminalized group, and for violating restrictions that have nothing to do with California criminal law. The police situate their efforts under the rubric of "smart-on-crime" policing, as an innovative tool to preemptively identify criminals and prevent disorder and crime. Critics argue that the police target people considered to be the usual suspects, and instead of demonstrating that they have committed new crimes, use loose and constitutionally questionable means to put them in prison for offenses that are neither significant nor criminal.

Translating New Penology to Protest Policing

Gillham and Noakes argue that many of the general new penology approaches used by police found their translation in the policing of protest: "This shift in police tactics during protests is consistent with broader changes in the ideological underpinnings of crime control, including an emphasis on risk management and the prevention (rather than reaction to) crime and disorder" (2007, 343). Police tactics and strategies, methods, and logics, at their most basic function, are "tools" to "solve problems." As I discussed in chapter 2, policing approaches are contextual to the task at hand and evolve in tension with the tactics of protesters, not unlike their evolution in various other policing contexts. Nonetheless, as Gillham and Noakes have clearly outlined, the commonalities between different policing efforts not only exist at the macro-level of ideology and the bureaucratic self-definition of the police's role in society, but at the micro-level of tactical application.

Attention to police tactics, even the deployment of similar tactics in different settings does not provide a full picture of how these policing practices came to be or why they persist. The normalization of the erosion of democratic rights through new penology policing which has taken place in recent decades is absolutely essential to the police's ability to continue to legitimately use those tactics (Oliver 2008). As noted by several authors (Fernandez 2008; Gillham and Noakes 2007; King and Waddington 2006; Noakes and Gillham 2006; Noakes, Klocke, and Gillham 2005; Starr, Fernandez, and Scholl 2011;Vitale 2007;Wood 2007), the emergence of more aggressive, intrusive, and preemptive protest policing in the last fifteen years has been accompanied by and resulted in the normalization of restrictions on freedom of assembly and expression. Preemptive or unlawful arrest, entrapment, less-lethal weaponry, militarized equipment, and heightened surveillance are now a routine part of protest policing. At the same time, there is an inherent tension at the heart of these practices: they typically entail the violation of civil rights, but despite often being criminal themselves, are nevertheless frequently applied as *legitimate* tools of protester delegitimation. After analyzing the relationship between negotiated management and strategic incapacitation with particular attention to the role of legitimacy and control, the following section will examine the police methods used during the raids on the Occupy Oakland Vigil and the use of "stay-away" orders against protesters as a condition of bail, and their broad parallels with the city's gang injunctions.

A Vigil Permit Enforced with Vigilance

Occupy Oakland never fully left Oscar Grant Plaza after the second encampment raid. Beyond having General Assemblies multiple times a week in the plaza, a tree-sit was erected on the day of the second eviction, and the Interfaith Committee maintained a daily presence with a canopy and informational table from 12 to 6 p.m. The Occupy Oakland vigil emerged officially on November 29, two weeks after the second and final encampment was raided, and two weeks before the second Port shutdown.

The impetus for the vigil was to maintain a constant presence in Oscar Grant Plaza: to maintain public visibility without erecting another encampment to face another (inevitable) eviction. In this way the vigil was an effort to navigate police repression while maintaining some of the original vitality of the camp, the movement's signature. As we saw in chapter 4, the logic of repression had taken on the legal strategy and paternalistic political discourse of negotiated management, the rescinding of protesters' First Amendment rights under the auspices of the police and city's obligation to uphold public health and safety. Even though Oakland and most of the other cities raided in mid-November had not taken out permits for their camps, the logic of negotiated management was imposed and then physically enforced by riot police, with the movement's inability to ensure public health and safety used to negate their right to assemble and speak. The relationship between the vigil and the police/city would be an extension of this logic of negotiated management combined with physical repression. We see in this moment the dialectical relationship between negotiated management and strategic incapacitation discussed in chapter 2, with hard repression (or the threat thereof) eliciting negotiation, and soft repression (negotiation, specifically permits) legitimating further hard repression. In the context of Oakland, we also see the tactical and discursive articulation of negotiated management as a tool of repression coupled with anti-gang techniques, specifically gang injunctions.

The vigil was an attempt at a tactical innovation on the part of some groups within Occupy Oakland, initially an effort to maintain a presence and serve those in need through providing free food in the plaza where the camp had once stood. The vigil sought to maintain core aspects of the camp while undermining the pretenses used by the police and city to repress the movement in the two encampment raids. The idea of the vigil (as such) came from Occupy Legal, an independent group consisting of lawyers and legal observers that had emerged from Occupy San

Francisco. They saw the vigil as a legally protected form of symbolic protest, with vigils being a constitutionally protected activity in public space that could include tents and people, so long as the people were not "dwelling" (i.e., sleeping, living, permanently staying) in that public space.

The idea of the vigil was approved by the General Assembly on November 23, 2011—with 119 people supporting the proposal, no one objecting, and 11 people abstaining.[4] The proposal stated simply: "We propose holding a 24-hour vigil—it would include tents, library, interaction with the public, activity, etc., but without sleeping. A vigil is completely allowed and would not be interfered with, whereas camping is illegal."[5] The idea to take out a permit for the vigil was not discussed or approved by Occupy Oakland. The first day of the vigil saw an attempt to erect a teepee on the lawn at Oscar Grant Plaza by Zach Running Wolf. When the police physically prevented the erection of the teepee, two members of Occupy Legal, Becca von Behren and Kirk Boyd, entered City Hall to speak with Assistant City Administrator Arturo Sanchez.[6] In that meeting a three-day, renewable permit was negotiated and signed for the vigil that introduced several stipulations on how the vigil could be conducted. It also imposed terms of conduct and obligations for those involved, which would come to encompass the permit holder's effective responsibility for all activity in Frank Ogawa (Oscar Grant) Plaza itself. The terms of the permit outlined that there could be no sleeping and no food storage or cooking in the plaza. The teepee would be the only permitted structure and it could only be erected from 6 A.M. to 10 P.M. The permit also stipulated that there could be no disruptions associated with the vigil, nothing that might constitute the obstruction of "the free enjoyment of the public plaza by other residents."[7]

As discussed in chapter 2, permits are the cornerstone of the negotiated management method of policing protest, a now normative set of imposed requirements and restrictions placed upon free speech and assembly. Permits are used to specify personal

liability for protest activities, to impose self-policing, and to create
a set of broad and vague conditions (i.e., not obstructing others'
enjoyment of the park) that can easily be used to revoke protesters'
ability to lawfully express their views in public space. As we saw at
the beginning of the chapter, Phil Horne of Occupy Legal stated
quite clearly that the vigil idea had originated among that group
of legal observers and lawyers as a means to challenge the city on
the grounds that vigils were constitutionally protected and could
not be evicted by the police. The permit—ironically, introduced
because police would not physically allow the vigil's creation—
would itself become a tool to further repress Occupy Oakland.
The permit, which had to be physically present at all times in the
plaza, was a legal document ostensibly created to protect the vigil,
when in fact it was used (as all permits are) as an intermediary
between protesters and their First Amendment rights, and, in this
case, as a tool for the police to surveil, harass, and repress the vigil
itself. Within a few weeks more than forty people associated with
the vigil were arrested for various, quite loosely defined violations
of the permit, like possessing yoga mats and blankets, which police
said constituted evidence of "dwelling."

Having learned all too well in late October the price of poorly
planned and poorly timed repression, the city and police did not
impose any significant repression in the plaza in the lead-up to the
December 12th West Coast Port Shutdown, which would bring
out more than ten thousand people in Oakland to shut down the
Port of Oakland from 5 A.M. December 12 until 5 A.M. December
13.[8] The police clearly did not want a camp to reemerge before
or on December 12, making violent arrests on Thanksgiving Day
(November 24) to prevent a portable toilet from being delivered,[9]
but otherwise waiting until after December 12 to destroy the vigil.
The police action to seize the Porta-Potty can be read as an act of
necessity from their perspective—and a selective use of repression
in the plaza in the period between the second raid on November
14 and the Port Shutdown December 12—since portable toilets

Image 7   Police preventing the delivery of portable toilets on November 24, 2011, followed by arrests. (Photo by Daniel Arauz)

were an essential component of the camps in a downtown sorely lacking in public restrooms. Outside of the conflict over the Port-a-Potties, the police withheld any major policing operations and arrests until after December 12.

However, within days of the permit's introduction on November 29, the city began using it to police activities in the plaza.[10] The Interfaith Committee's tent, which had stood for two weeks prior, was ordered taken down in keeping with the permit's stipulation that the only permissible structure in the plaza was the teepee.[11] The Interfaith Committee shifted to using a large umbrella, which was tolerated by the police for about two more weeks until after the December 12th Port Shutdown, when more aggressive policing began.[12] The three-day encroachment permit, initially implemented on November 29, was perpetually renewed without incident until a list of violations was issued on December 15, followed by a police raid on December 16.[13]

RACE, CLASS, AND
CRIMINALIZATION: THE STORY
OF MARCEL "KALI" JOHNSON

The Occupy Oakland encampments were perhaps one of the most racially and class-diverse camps in the country. The second camp in particular was largely comprised of people who were houseless, many of whom lived in Oscar Grant Plaza long before it was given that name. As briefly discussed in chapter 3, the camp experience could prove difficult, with dozens of people, most of whom had been strangers to each other weeks earlier, sharing tight living quarters under often stressful conditions. This was also compounded by drug use, interpersonal aggression, and/ or mental difference. In the first encampment Kali Johnson—a black man, understood to be homeless, who was said to be withdrawing from psychiatric medication for a diagnosed major mental illness—had been aggressive and violent with other Occupiers during the first camp. One night during an altercation Kali was knocked out with a two-by-four and removed from the camp. The event highlighted the extent to which things could get out

Image 8   Support for Kali Johnson, May 1, 2012. (Photo by Daniel Arauz)

of control and perhaps also pointed to our collective inexperience mediating serious conflict.

A few weeks later Kali returned to what was now the second encampment. His demeanor was different and he was back on medication. He found himself in the middle of more conflicts within the camp, but in a very different way. Kali showed and proved himself to be adept at intervening in conflicts that arose among different Occupiers. The buzz surrounding his name was now associated with the skill and grace with which he deescalated conflicts and generally improved the overall social life of the second camp. A man who had been a "problem" in the first camp became a solver of problems others could not handle.

During the first vigil raid, on December 16, 2011, dozens of police aggressively entered the plaza. Kali was present and moved to the far edge of the plaza, seated on a bench simply holding a blanket. The police made a point of approaching him, and after running his identification and finding he was on parole, arrested him and two others on an obstruction charge. Kali was held in Santa Rita jail for four days waiting for arraignment and was denied his psychiatric medication while in jail (a common practice in jails). While awaiting the opportunity to be bailed out, an altercation took place between Kali and guards at Santa Rita. Kali was severely beaten and charged with assaulting an officer.[14]

The Anti Repression Committee launched a campaign to help defend Kali in the six months of court battle that would ensue. Kali was held in solitary confinement throughout this entire period. He suffered immensely from this, and it became increasingly unbearable for him as the months dragged on. As a result, he eventually accepted a plea deal that imposed a four-year prison sentence. He explicitly expressed that he took the deal as the only means to get out of solitary confinement. Sentencing would mean being transferred into general population at a state prison, and he felt that even accepting years there would be preferable to another day spent in solitary. He was eventually transferred to San Luis Obispo State Prison where he has remained ever since, serving a four-year sentence for a crime he never committed.[15]

While incarcerated Kali has been subjected to the same denial of medication, solitary confinement, and harassment. He was charged with another assault on a guard in prison, and was pressured into taking another plea deal. He is scheduled to be released in the fall of 2016.[16]

The tragedy of Kali Johnson's story, his targeted and selective punishment connected to his involvement in the movement, carries on long after the movement has ended, draws attention to the differential risk movement participants face depending on the race, class, perceived living situation, psychiatric diagnoses, previous criminal records—and in other examples, gender, sexuality, religion, and resident legal status. The mechanisms of policing (i.e., the vigil raids and gang injunctions discussed here) not only share similarities in terms of logic or practice, but also compound each other. Racial profiling is amplified within social movements, disproportionately targeting activists of color and working-class movement members, while the targeting of people with criminal records will be at the forefront of efforts to preemptively arrest and harass demonstrators. This differential risk that activists face is an inherent part of living in an oppressive and unequal society (Oliver 2008). Occupy Oakland, and the Anti-Repression Committee in particular, did a great deal of work fighting against these policing practices while educating the movement and the public.

Profiling and the Policing of "Public Nuisance"

On December 15, the Oakland police adopted a new stance toward the vigil and began to confiscate anything found on the ground in the plaza and citing anyone who claimed ownership of objects seen lying around. On December 16, the first of three major police raids on the vigil took place. Quickly and without announcement or provocation, dozens of officers in riot gear moved into the park and made arrests for violations of the permit as well as for obstruction when people objected. That night three people were arrested for crimes including sitting on a blanket and taking something out of the trash.[17] During the second raid, on December 30, thirteen people were arrested, this time including several on inflated felonies.[18] The pretense for the raids was that protesters had sleeping bags and food, neither of which were in violation of the permit that specifically prohibited sleeping and cooking. When the police raided that day, they quickly came into the park and started grabbing and arresting people, creating a melee.[19] Two people would face "lynching" charges for allegedly trying to free themselves or others from police custody.[20] Those arrested on the 30th also spent several days in jail unable to be bailed out because the courts were not in session due to the holidays. What quickly became apparent to protesters and later confirmed by police documents was that the police were deliberately targeting specific individuals who had criminal records and were known to congregate at the vigil. Once arrested, these people faced probation holds and more serious legal consequences. Outside of the raids themselves periodic police rounds sent vigilers scrambling to wake up the homeless sleeping on benches or hurrying to make sure that nothing in the park could be construed as a violation of the permit.[21] Police in riot gear raided the plaza on numerous occasions with batons swinging, under the pretenses that homeless people were sleeping in other parts of the plaza or because someone had set their food or backpack down.[22]

The permit was officially revoked on January 3, 2012, because police claimed that the vigil had expanded beyond previously agreed boundaries within the plaza, a claim that is both unprovable and indisputable given the vague terms of the permit and the nature of an open public park. The police conducted a third raid on January 4, arresting twelve, and the next day released a press statement to justify their actions.[23]

That press release echoed the trope of public health and safety that we saw in the federally coordinated November raids, and includes language similar to that of the gang injunctions, which posit "criminal elements" who create a "nuisance which attracts criminal activity." We can see this clearly if we compare city documents from the November raid, the vigil raids, and gang injunctions side by side. In the lead-up to the November raid, a city statement to Occupy Oakland's camp on November 11, 2011, which was burned immediately after it was read, stated in part that:

> The City of Oakland and its police department support and protect the right of all individuals to engage in free speech and their right to assemble. However, *this encampment is a violation of the* **law**. *Your activities are injurious to health, obstruct the free use of property, interfering with the comfortable enjoyment of the Plaza, and unlawfully obstruct the free passage* or use of a public park or square.[24] (emphasis mine)

Less than two months later, we see the same logic of paternalistic governance (governmentality) and language of reluctant enforcement for the sake of the public good employed by the OPD, with regard to alleged violations of the broadly worded vigil permit: "*While the City of Oakland will continue to facilitate expression of First Amendment rights to free speech, in the interest of public health and safety, and the public enjoyment of Frank Ogawa Plaza,* unpermitted and unregulated conditions will not be allowed" (emphasis mine).[25] This same OPD press release and the raids on the vigil to which they are connected parallel the tactics and discourse of spatially criminalizing specific individuals as a threat to social order and a public nuisance, characteristic of the gang injunctions. They are both rooted in the same civil law, quoted below in the city's legal motion for a gang injunction:

The Norteño gang's activities described above *unquestionably constitute a public nuisance under the law*. California law defines a nuisance as:"Anything which is *injurious to health,* including, but not limited to, the illegal sale of controlled substances, or is indecent or offensive to the senses, or an *obstruction to the free use of property,* so as to *interfere with the comfortable enjoyment of life or property, or unlawfully obstructs the free passage or use,* in the customary manner, of any navigable lake, or river, bay, stream, canal, or basin, or any public park, square, street, or highway, is a nuisance."[26] (emphasis mine)

We see here a clear usage of the same code in California civil law to define a group as a public nuisance in a specific area in an effort to legitimate targeted ("problem-oriented") policing in both the gang injunctions and the enforcement/revocation of the permit. Where the injunctions are a court-approved usage of criminal sanctions for violations of a civil legal code (i.e., provisions of the injunction barring wearing certain colors, curfews, limitations on free association, etc.), the permit served as the vehicle to translate violations of the permit (i.e., possessing food, personal property, sleeping) into criminal offenses. Both also entail police profiling of certain types of people—racial profiling in specific neighborhoods in the case of the injunctions, targeting of Occupy protesters in Oscar Grant Plaza, in particular those with police records, in the case of the permit. Alongside a generalized increase in aggressive policing in a clearly defined geographic area, there is also a much more precise targeting of specific criminalized subjects within vulnerable populations. Almost all of those targeted by the gang injunctions had criminal records or were currently on probation or parole, putting them at risk of significant prison time for the most minor offenses (i.e., violations of the provisions of the gang injunction they had been listed on). We saw this process explicitly used in the vigil raids as well.

Police profiling of Occupy drew upon surveillance and intelligence gathering. OPD would regularly walk the park taking photos and notes about those present, and (as we later learned and gained access to) had compiled a photo book of Occupiers, which contained faces and a short criminal history for several members of Occupy Oakland known to congregate in the plaza. Before raids, police were seen with copies of the book as they walked through the park surveying who was present at the vigil at that time, and taking notes. Of the more than forty people arrested in the raids, many were those whose faces and criminal records were contained in this police profile photo book. The fact that they had criminal records helped to legitimate the diagnosis of the vigil (and Occupy Oakland) as a public nuisance. That label of public nuisance in turn served as the precondition to translate minor alleged violations of civil law into arrestable offenses, with bail being denied (at minimum) for anyone still on probation. When applied through aggressive policing, this practice is designed to drive those labeled a nuisance out of specific geographic locations while saturating the area with generalized, aggressive policing under the legitimized auspices of a smart-on-crime, problem-oriented police strategy to protect the public. Speaking about the vigil raids and justifying the arrests made, the Oakland Police Department's public information officer, Johnna Watson, stated: "There's a core group that is part of Occupy, and we're seeing those same people continuing to be involved in the same criminal activity. Smart policing is to identify them. If they feel, in their words only, that they are being targeted—if they continue to participate in illegal activity, then yes, they are going to be arrested."[27] The "criminal activity" here included the alleged and broadly defined violations of the permit: possessing a blanket, food, or a yoga mat, which police interpreted as evidence of "dwelling." Hard police repression had been made possible by criminalizing legal activities through the imposition of the permit. That permit was then used to overtly target people who were legally vulnerable.

STAY-AWAY INJUNCTIONS: THE CITY
AS OCCUPY OAKLAND'S "VICTIM"

Coupled with the raids on the Occupy Oakland vigil in late December 2011 through January 2012 was another tactic of "smart policing" that enhanced the OPD's reclaimed control over Oscar Grant Plaza and further criminalized specific members of the movement, while broadening aggressive policing of the movement as a whole in downtown Oakland. While the permit was revoked as of January 3, 2012, strict enforcement of various municipal codes pertaining to the park was introduced (i.e., the need for permits for amplified sound). With the permit rescinded, the city quickly introduced a new tactic to control certain individuals in specific urban spaces—stay-away orders. A stay-away order is an increasingly common tool, historically used most often in domestic abuse cases against an alleged or convicted abuser, which requires those on parole or probation, and often those simply with pending charges, to stay a certain distance away from the victim.[28] In the case of Occupy Oakland those arrested during the vigil raids and dozens arrested afterward were given stay-away orders as a condition of being released on bail, before any conviction was made (in most cases charges were eventually dropped months later). The stay-away orders made it an arrestable offense for "offenders" to come within 300 yards of the "victim"—Oakland City Hall and the adjacent Oscar Grant Plaza.[29] This barred many members of Occupy Oakland from attending General Assemblies in the plaza. When Occupy Oakland moved one of its (at that time) thrice-weekly General Assemblies to a park outside of the 300-yard perimeter, judges began giving stay-away orders from both parks, despite the fact that many of those given stay-aways after the vigil raids were arrested nowhere near either park. Dozens of Occupiers would be given stay-away orders in the ensuing months.

Legally the stay-aways are an injunction, not unlike the gang injunctions, which also sit within the logic of strategic incapacitation by identifying people determined by city prosecutors

Image 9   Support for immigrants and opposition to stay-away orders, Oscar Grant Plaza, May 1, 2012. (Photo by Daniel Arauz)

to be criminal threats (or as OPD Public Information Officer Johnna Watson calls them with paternalistic affection, "our problem people"), who can be legally barred from being in specific places under threat of criminal prosecution if violated. The vigil raids and the stay-aways both served to criminalize people within the movement and the broader movement said to "harbor" them. These policing tactics, deriving from legal permits and injunctions (whether the permits or stay-aways), served as a pretense to heavily police specific areas and surveil, harass, and aggressively police all protesters in those designated areas. On a level that is much harder to measure, these forms of criminalization, of which there were certainly more, served to limit the movement's growth and active popular support (whether peripheral supporters, people from already criminalized communities, people who were strict adherents to what has become known as "nonviolence," or people who felt intimidated by the threat of police force) (Oliver 2008). These efforts logically decreased the likelihood that new people would join a criminalized and delegitimated movement that was interpellated by a liberal city government and repressed by the notoriously aggressive OPD as an "organized, criminal nuisance" and not a social movement.

OPD Public Information Officer Johnna Watson, again, makes very plain the application of (constitutionally questionable) "smart policing" from OPD's standard repertoire toward Occupy Oakland: "These are some of our problem people and we need to do something to remove them from our streets. This is not something special we are enforcing for protesters, it is something we do and have done in the city for many years."[30] This new penology approach to policing Occupy Oakland does have a long precedent of being used against other criminalized groups and individuals. As Katherine Beckett and Steve Herbert (2010) discuss, this process of criminalization and geographic police control of space has become both heightened and normalized in recent years: "the deployment of new control tools—touted by proponents as alternatives to arrest and punishment—has a 'net widening' effect: it creates crimes and criminal cases that would not exist otherwise. Taken together, these techniques represent a dramatic extension of the state's authority and surveillance capacity throughout urban landscape" (11). The use of stay-away orders in Oakland is common against low-level drug and property crimes—given to people who are simply awaiting trial.[31] As part of a new penology approach of criminalization and preemption, it has become a legally questionable, but nonetheless common, legal technique to criminalize the presence of people in specific areas who have not been convicted of a crime. The strategic incapacitation of protest, as Noakes and Gillham (2006) illustrate, is derived from a broader and more long-standing set of new penology techniques.

The American Civil Liberties Union filed suit against the stay-away orders, challenging the constitutionality of these practices on the grounds that they stifle the assembly and speech rights of those who have not yet been convicted of any crime: "In this country, it is unacceptable to keep demonstrators out of the public square because the government thinks they might engage in illegal conduct in a future demonstration. . . . In this instance, the government has failed to show that the orders are necessary to serve any purpose. The orders are also overly-broad and vague. . . . Seeking to prohibit certain protesters from demonstrating in front of, or coming near, City Hall undermines these rights and values."[32]

The use of legally questionable and aggressive, geographically bounded policing against specific individuals that we see in the policing of Occupy Oakland—the vigil raids targeting profiled individuals and stay-away orders imposed as a condition of bail—requires that the targets first be criminalized, stigmatized, labeled as a threat to the public. The absence of successful criminalization had been key to the great failure of police repression in the movement's first month. This criminalization, a process that is both legal and discursive, is an interpellatory project that utilizes the power of police to define problems and to then devise "problem-oriented solutions" as part of their legitimate realm of authority. By situating these practices within a framework of criminalization, police and city officials crafted legitimacy for their efforts to maintain order, while further delegitimating a mass movement that would soon be subject to the same kind of wanton collective attack that occurred on October 25. And when that attack came, police and city officials would be successful in achieving their goal of demobilization while at the same time mitigating the risk of public sympathy and support. In this, criminalization was the key intervening variable.

Interpellatory Criminalization: From Norteños to Occupiers

Drawing from the City of Oakland's Motion for a Preliminary Injunction against suspected members of the Norteño street gang and from an editorial written by Alameda District Attorney Nancy O'Malley defending the use of stay-away orders against Occupy Oakland, we see a clear parallel process of new penology criminalization and preemption, again, situated in the same civil law. These applications of "problem-oriented policing" are derived from a broken-windows logic of focusing on preempting major crime by criminalizing minor and often otherwise legal or legally unenforced activities associated with disorder. Both of these legal/policing efforts are rooted in the language of abating criminal nuisances through imposing criminal sanctions upon people who have not been convicted of a crime. As a result of questions and contestations over the legality of these policing practices, these efforts are situated in the language of community crisis and the state's paternal obligation to maintain order against a criminal threat that they establish and define.

In her *San Francisco Chronicle* op-ed, Nancy O'Malley lists serious crimes allegedly committed by members of Occupy Oakland to establish a criminal threat and to root strategic incapacitation within the clear criminalization of targets. It should be noted that at this time no Occupier had been convicted of any of these crimes, many of these crimes had not even been charged (but were simply alleged by police), and most charges would later be dropped.

> These protests have devolved into militant operations that call for violence against the police and the city of Oakland. People have attended these marches wearing masks and dark scarves that served to conceal their identities. Their actions were violent, senseless and criminal. . . . To date, my office has filed charges against 65 people alleging criminal behavior ranging from felony assaults on the police, felony vandalism, and resisting arrest to trespassing.[33]

Through labeling Occupy Oakland as a "violent" and "militant operation" driven by motives that are "violent, senseless, and criminal" rather than a social movement, the movement is criminalized and it is explicitly argued that policing should no longer be understood as repressing dissent but, rather, as merely containing crime. This process of criminalization was key to both the stay-aways and the gang injunctions. The same type of laundry list of generalized offenses was used to criminalize those listed on the gang injunctions, to establish the presence of a criminal nuisance, and to build legitimacy for its abatement. The injunction motion follows the same formula of criminalization: "Norteño gang members do, and will continue to, kill, shoot, beat, stab, rob, take over residential and public spaces by force to openly deal and use controlled substances, put up gang graffiti, loiter in public, and treat residents' property as if it were their own—all to instill fear in the community and rival gangs."[34]

After a pattern of criminal history has been presented, and the problem defined by the legal officials of the city, they propose their solutions within the logic of social cohesion and defending the public from criminal threats, based simply on the fact that they were arrested (during Occupy Oakland) or solely on peoples' *past* criminal behavior (in the case of the gang injunctions). O'Malley's editorial and the Preliminary Injunction document both define the interpellated criminal threat as both outside of and a threat to the community, justifying intensified policing within the state's obligation to abate criminal nuisances and protect public health and safety. O'Malley's effort at criminalization is situated in a lineage that harkens back to the Red Scare and Palmer Raids' criminalization of radical politics (Fusfeld [1980] 1992; Goldstein [1978] 2001; Schultz and Schultz 2001). She attempts to draw clear lines between "the movement" and "the community," but also between certain protesters and the movement itself: "Let me be clear: These individuals were not rallying on behalf of Occupy Wall Street, or even the greater Occupy Oakland movement. Rather, they advertise themselves as 'militant, anti-government, anti-police, and anarchists,' with a mission to destroy the community fabric of Oakland through the use of violence."[35]

We saw the same logic earlier in the preliminary injunction where the state situates preemptive policing in its moral obligation to maintain order by eradicating behavior and people it defines as a public nuisance.

"The state has not only a right to 'maintain a decent society,' but an obligation to do so. . . ." The community in the proposed Safety Zone [gang injunction area] deserves to live in a safe neighborhood free from the criminal and nuisance activities of street gangs. The level of violence and threatened violence is too high in the proposed Safety Zone. The People pray this Court issue the proposed injunction, and abate the public nuisance caused by this defendant street gang.[36]

The city and the police are refashioning old tools to new purposes in different contexts. Through the "innovative use" of civil law coupled with improved surveillance to expand policing powers and demonize policing targets, who are framed to the public as imminent violent threats, we see the translation of gang injunction practices and logics to Occupy Oakland.

FROM INJUNCTIONS TO STAY-AWAY ORDERS: OAKLAND'S BROADENING STATE OF EXCEPTION

The paradigm of new penology is situated within an increasingly carceral political culture where the ability to create or posit moral panic allows for the imposition of preemptive tactics against a criminalized and amorphous enemy of the community (Goffman 2014, 8; Rios 2011, 8–23). Within the common sense of law and order, whether it is tough-on-crime or smart-on-crime, the state has assumed a widened purview to criminalize, target, and neutralize different groups of people based on suspicion rather than traditional criminal investigation. The resultant slippage of constitutional rights in relation to one group (alleged gang members) quickly establishes a legal and practical norm through which other groups can be targeted.

This chapter of the struggle between Occupy Oakland and police repression was far less visible than either the less-lethal police aggression of October 25 that almost killed veteran Scott

Olsen, or the tens of thousands who would shutter Oakland's main capital-transmission belt—the Port of Oakland—twice in a six-week period. However, the raids and subsequent stay-away injunctions in the two-month period beginning in late December 2011 were a clear pivot point for Occupy Oakland. Criminalization helped dampen or intimidate public support while driving wedges between "good" protesters and "bad" protesters. Legalistic mechanisms legitimated what would become increasingly aggressive policing against the movement as a whole. Occupy Oakland quickly went from victim of police violence to criminal nuisance.

The movement went from planning massive actions (stretching as wide as the entire West Coast on December 12) to having reactive, small marches against the police whose routes needed to navigate around the 300-yard perimeter of police turf downtown, judicially established by the stay-aways. General Assemblies became smaller, as the discussions shifted from where and how to do community outreach, and what the movement's next big effort should be, to report-backs on police harassment and court dates. Instead of fund-raising to pay for posters, or for the sound trucks, or food necessary for the next mass action, the movement sought bail money for comrades and occupied courtrooms day after day (Earl 2005).

The criminalization initiated in late December and early January was a prelude to the massive coordinated delegitimation and preemptive aggression against several hundred protesters trying to occupy a vacant public building later that month. By situating questionable police tactics socially, politically, and discursively within a framework of justified criminalization, and effectively deploying court injunctions (however constitutionally precarious), city officials and the Oakland Police Department drew from the preexisting tools at hand strategically to incapacitate Occupy Oakland.

CHAPTER 6

The Meshing of Force and Legitimacy in the Repression of Occupy Oakland's Move-In Day

THE STRATEGY OF delegitimating and containing an effort to occupy the vacant Kaiser Convention Center on January 28, 2012, was perhaps the most comprehensive and effective effort by the police and city officials to challenge and disrupt an Occupy Oakland action. Using mutually reinforcing strategies of force and discourse, this strategy coupled aggressive street tactics from police—ranging from extensive intelligence gathering, to excessive use of less-lethal weapons, to tactics of kettling and mass arrest[1]—with comprehensive political discrediting of the movement by the mayor and other city officials, and separately by the mainstream press.

The objective of the action was to seize a vacant building somewhere in or around downtown Oakland, to re-create the camp in a new form. This idea had been percolating within Occupy Oakland, being openly discussed even before the second encampment raid in mid-November. If successful this effort would be a tactical advance in terms of an escalation from the encampments, which also could provide greater movement security over the space as well as protection from the winter

Image 10 Front of the march on January 28, 2012. (Photo by Daniel Arauz)

elements. The motivation and goals for the action were clearly stated before the action:

> It's cold outside.
> Like millions of people in this country,
> Occupy Oakland has no home.
> And yet, all over the city, thousands of buildings stand
> empty.
> On January 28, we're going to occupy one of those build-
> ings and turn it into a social center.
> We're going to fill the space with a kitchen, first aid station,
> sleeping quarters, an assembly area, libraries, free school
> classes, and hundreds of uses yet to be determined.
> Let's establish our new home, defend it, and adapt it to
> Oakland's needs.
> *We get what we can take.*[2]

The planning for the day had taken the form of an open assembly, similar in many respects to the General Assembly but solely focused on this one action, which met for weeks leading up to January 28. Various working groups formed and targets were discussed but not publicly decided upon for logistical and security reasons. In terms of vacant indoor spaces with enough size to fulfill the goals of the action, there were a handful of likely candidates. One that had been openly discussed previously was the city-owned Kaiser Convention Center. Originally opened in 1914 and known as the Oakland Civic Auditorium through most of its existence, the center had been closed since 2006.[3] Sandwiched between Laney College and Lake Merritt, the Kaiser Convention Center was less than a mile and a half from Oscar Grant Plaza where demonstrators would be marching from, attempting to keep their destination hidden until they made their approach. The Oakland Police Department's operations emails for that day,[4] obtained by Berkeley Copwatch, revealed that not only were Homeland Security, the Coast Guard, and Immigration and Customs Enforcement being kept abreast of developments on the street minute by minute, but the OPD had been able to secure a list of Occupy Oakland targets, including the Kaiser Center. Before Move-In Day demonstrators had started assembling in Oscar Grant Plaza, the list of a handful of potential targets had been sent out to every unit commander on the street.[5]

The march began from Oscar Grant Plaza, led by large banners reading "If it's vacant, take it!" and accompanied by dozens of people carrying shields and wearing helmets—to serve as a frontline in the event of the police attacking with rubber bullets, bean-bag munitions, flash-bang grenades, or similar less-lethal weapons. Some shields were made of large rubber garbage receptacles, many others out of large sheets of corrugated metal, while others were made of a variety of materials, mostly wood with replications of various radical books on their faces.[6] There was a children's contingent and a sound truck was blaring, as more than 1,500 people marched southeast, their destination still unstated. The tone for the day was vibrant, but serious, with a high likelihood of police confrontation.

The attempt to occupy and make social use out of a building that had sat vacant for five years—by providing meeting spaces, food, and shelter for the movement and anyone who needed it—was very much in keeping with the core political objectives of Occupy Oakland and the movement as a whole. Although the action ended up being a repeat of the failure of the November 2nd post–Port Shutdown attempt to occupy the Traveler's Aid building—on a much bigger scale, at a time when the movement had lost considerable steam, and with deeper repercussions for the movement's trajectory—the potential of Occupy Oakland creating a large social center was a formidable threat. It was a threat that the mayor and police took very seriously. The social control response was multifaceted, strategic, and, ultimately, effective.

January 28, 2012: The Iron Fist and Velvet Glove Finally Meet

In spite of a massive policing effort (discussed in greater detail below), the central focus of this chapter is the role of political discourse in criminalizing social movements, enabling full strategic incapacitation that is presented as justified, embedded in a Manichean common sense that goes beyond undermining immediate tactical efforts toward undermining the viability and integrity of movements themselves. This chapter is the story of the meeting of the iron fist with the velvet glove, of police aggression activated and legitimized through the political delegitimation and criminalization of Occupy Oakland (Platt et al. 1975, 179).

Pathologizing Dissent, Manufacturing Consent: Oakland's "Violent Sideshow"

It is only through understanding the context of the escalation of social movement tactics and their interpretation by powerful officials that we can make sense of the social control response. While the camps themselves had been defined as a social problem by a range of powerful actors, the movement itself had not been criminalized. The raids on the vigil had been largely invisible to the public and framed in the same parlance of bureaucratic necessity that had underscored the camp raids. The period that led to January 28, 2012 (J28) marked a clear discursive shift on the part of the city. The discourse from city officials moved away from one of depoliticized repression cloaked in the language of amorphous paternalistic obligations to keep the movement safe from itself and to maintain public safety, under a vague logic that presented the movement more as unwieldy and inadvertently burdensome than illegitimate and criminal. In the two months leading up to January 28, the press, city officials, and the police quickly transitioned toward a wide-ranging political criminalization and full-frontal attack on the movement as a whole. In the preceding weeks, the movement itself became the enemy—a depoliticized criminal entity bent on violence and mayhem, an unwelcoming place for respectable people seeking social justice.[7] The city of Oakland press release the day before the action first drew upon a litany of arrests that had taken place recently at "Fuck the Police" marches[8]—a regular series of marches largely responding to the vigil raids and connected to, but not officially called for by, Occupy Oakland. Invoking the "outside agitator" trope often deployed against social movements (King 2010) and recently used in Oakland during the Justice for Oscar Grant movement, the press release would go on to portray Occupy Oakland as primarily orientated toward violence and harboring criminal networks:

> Over the past few weeks, organizers have held marches in downtown Oakland which were billed as anti-police initiatives. During this period, about 15 arrests were made, with approximately 60% of those arrested residing outside the region or the state. Since the first encampment was removed on October 25, 2011, approximately 300 people have been arrested. The Police Department has been successful in obtaining restraining

orders against individuals who repeatedly commit crimes, and are working with the Alameda County District Attorney's Office and Oakland City Attorney's Office to explore felony and enhanced charges for people who criminally plan and/or work in concert to break the law.[9]

Foreshadowing the planned J28 action, the statement went on to cast a negative frame on the movement that sought to criminalize and politically marginalize the movement:

> "The City of Oakland will not be bullied by threats of violence or illegal activity," said City Administrator Deanna Santana. "Breaking into buildings, assaulting police officers, provoking confrontations, and vandalizing property are tactics that are counter-productive and divide our community. They drain scarce City resources away from the neighborhoods in greatest need. Oakland deserves better," she said.[10]

The power to popularly define a phenomenon enables the power to act upon it. Todd Gitlin (2003) borrows from Antonio Gramsci and the framing literature to discuss the role of the media in the New Left of the 1960s, focusing on how the "mass media have become core systems for the distribution of ideology," tracing the effect of media framing both inside and outside the movement (in the general public). Following Gramsci, Gitlin demonstrates the political power that media has through its ability to define, interpret, and morally evaluate social actors in political conflict. This ability to construct what Gramsci calls "common sense" imbues the media with the power to determine and distinguish which movements or actions are "legitimate main acts" and which are "illegitimate sideshows." The aforementioned press release does an exceptional job of this. We will also see this distinction drawn quite clearly in the *San Francisco Chronicle*, as Occupy Oakland is set up as a violent sideshow, a trope the mayor and police would soon extend into a criminal sideshow.

The discourse of the mayor, other city officials, the police, and journalists all coalesced in condemning the militancy of a core segment of the movement, equating a lack of a universal commitment to "nonviolence" with a lack of integrity and legitimacy. Moralistic blame was placed on anarchists, the broader anticapitalism endemic to the movement, and Occupy Oakland as a whole, for its failure to police itself and its militant sectors. The combination of aggressive policing and political discrediting of the movement was successful, if hard to fully measure empirically. Occupy Oakland never saw more than a couple of thousand people in the streets after the December 12th Port Shutdown. The criminalization of the movement played no small role in that. While Occupy Oakland persisted after December 12, as a movement with hundreds of core members, and as it went on to engage in grassroots organizing alongside and within working-class communities and struggles, the movement failed to garner mass, local support after its first two months. William Gamson ([1975] 1990) identifies a dynamic that summarizes the policing of this action, emphasizing how hard repression occurs quite frequently when a movement is both "threatening *and* vulnerable" (82). The tactics used in response to the attempted Kaiser takeover serve as the clearest example of a broad-based strategy of social control, turning one of Occupy Oakland's founding strengths, its militancy, into a liability.

As I discussed in chapter 3, the movement exploited police over-aggressiveness on October 25, 2011, turning the tactical mistakes made by police into their strategic failure, taking the social tensions that social control had produced and creating a lack of social control. In short, Occupy Oakland was willing to challenge the police and endure repression, which created social control mistakes—mistakes the movement took advantage of. The General Strike and West Coast Port Shutdown mobilized broad public sympathy and support into mass direct action. As we approached January 28, 2012, the political and discursive foundation had been laid for effective strategic incapacitation—from the second raid, to the vigil raids and stay-away orders, to widespread demonization of the movement in the press. While Occupy Oakland was ready to exploit police mistakes in October 2011, the police took great care to make sure that January 28, 2012, would be the day that *they* took advantage of the movement's tactical mistakes, and that police violence on J28 would be seen much differently than it was earlier. The police would mass arrest more than 400 people on January 28 and later face a resulting class action lawsuit for unlawful arrest,[11] which was settled nearly three years later for $1.4 million.[12] However, the police's tactical victory on that day, combined with the visuals of a movement detained and contained, coupled with press demonizations of the action[13] and calls for intra-movement denunciations from the mayor, far outweighed the potential legal cost that the lawsuit represented, a lawsuit that was yet to be heard over a year later. Criminalization and legitimated strategic incapacitation created a victory for the forces of social control in the "Battle of J28"—it would also be the beginning of the end of the war with Occupy Oakland.

The street policing of Move-In Day was straightforward strategic incapacitation. The objectives were to prevent members of Occupy Oakland from occupying a vacant building.[14] Mutual aid riot forces were on call and utilized by the end of the day. The use of a full range of tactics, including the application of less-lethal weapons on entire crowds, was available and used, though the command over such orders was reinforced in the planning documents. Kettling and mass arrest tactics were also available for use, despite being generally quite questionable legally. It was clear to the police heading into January 28 that the action could be portrayed as having an inherent criminal nature, and the use of strategic incapacitation would not prove counterproductive so long as officers followed orders and command was clear, keeping the incapacitation strategic.

Definition, Representation, and Force

Holistically, this moment was the confluence of negotiated management (both applied and normative) and strategic incapacitation—mutually constituted, mutually reinforcing, and fully activated. The movement had maintained an advantage from the very start by refusing negotiation but preserving popular support, an advantage compounded by police aggression on October 25, creating the momentum that produced November 2 and December 12. The depoliticized second raid on November 14, stripping the movement of its visibility and its public recognizability, followed by a permit used as a tactical tool legitimating strategic incapacitation under the official parlance of an agreed relationship of cooperation, had begun to turn the tide. Occupy Oakland retained a large militant core, broad networks, and functioning General Assemblies in spite of the shifting waters—but was nonetheless stranded on the edge of the Bay, waiting for a tide of support and broad-based resonance that either evaporated or was rechanneled.

Up until J28, the story of Occupy Oakland's mass mobilizations for city officials and the police was a story of fractured hegemony and policing as a potential political liability. A cornerstone of political sociology, as initially established by Max Weber, is the idea that the state's monopoly over the use of force is rooted in political legitimacy—the consent of the many and the coercion of the few (1946, 78–79). Gramsci expands this basic point into a political framework that takes into account social struggle and contradiction, the ability of that hegemony to be challenged or lost. This is what we had seen in the first few months of Occupy Oakland's existence. In order for (police) force to reestablish its legitimacy and social control function, other powerful actors (most notably elected city officials) needed to provide a different set of definitions about policing and protest, a political frame that defined the "protest/police problem" as one of disreputable protesters, not rogue cops or a brutal, corrupt police force.

Image 11   Police charge Occupy Oakland march at Oak Street on the afternoon of January 28, 2011. (Photo by Daniel Arauz)

As I discussed in chapter 3, there is a zero-sum game between protesters and police in terms of legitimacy, with legitimacy playing a large role in tactical success or failure. Gramsci defines the state (for him a fusion of political society and civil society) as "hegemony armored with coercion." City structures of power were presented with a conundrum after October 25, 2011, when their "armor" was seen as illegitimate and their hegemony in danger of being seriously challenged. Both would be reconstituted by reframing Occupy Oakland not only as a problem, but as a problem that could only be solved by aggressive policing. Later in this chapter, the words of the mayor, city administrator, and city council members illustrate the reconstitution of hegemonic control over Occupy Oakland, exactly as Gramsci describes in the *Prison Notebooks*: (1) speaking for and as "the people" (assertion of hegemony); (2) defining political phenomena, such as Occupy Oakland, the local sociopolitical context, and state alternatives to create justice (role of the state as educator); and (3) assertion and exercise of the legitimate use of coercion in the name of the common good (legitimized police repression). The marginalization and criminalization of Occupy Oakland simultaneously legitimized and activated hard police repression (Starr, Fernandez, and Scholl 2011, 94–96).   •

This process of criminalization is not new and has actually taken on a formulaic expression since the World Trade Organization protests in Seattle in 1999. It is, however, a process that had not been successfully implemented against Occupy Oakland until the lead-up to January 28, 2012. Luis Fernandez quotes a high-ranking member of the Washington, DC, police about the logic and tactics of protester criminalization that speak directly to the same strategies employed by city officials in Oakland immediately before the J28 effort: "We try to get all the information we can to the media so that people know how violent these groups are and the type of things they might do because . . . of course, we need the public support to do what we do. Without it, we can't do our job" (2008, 152). The power of the state to define phenomena as a criminal problem, to forge policing solutions, and to garner both social control and political legitimacy is a basic process of governing, and a cornerstone of repressing unconventional challengers (Foucault 1994, 2007; Gramsci 1971; Simon 2007; Weber 1946). Amory Starr, Luis Fernandez, and Christian Scholl (2011) further outline the contours of the criminalization process: "The state constantly asserts its respect for the rights of 'peaceful,' 'law-abiding' political expression. Those who refuse to follow the rules of protest permits, routes, and styles do not deserve the state's respect. Thus, by definition, all those who disturb in the slightest the channel provided by police are threats, are violent, unpredictable, preternaturally out of control, beyond the bounds of social mores. Political policing cleverly merges social decorum with the architecture of state control" (95).

Criminalization is never a simple assertion of the law, but a reinforcement of the broader norms of which the law is a part (in the context of protest, non-disruption, and cooperation with police) and the marginalization of the transgressor (Durkheim 1979, 66–67). In Oakland, the city press releases would define Occupy Oakland as a simple criminal entity and not a social justice movement, and go so far as to call on other Occupy sites to strip Occupy Oakland of the name "Occupy." The political marginalization and concomitant police repression are fused, and both tied to a moral demonization of the movement as a whole, based on a selective and often exaggerated or fabricated list of "unintelligible acts" by individual protesters. David Graeber (2007) discusses the discrediting and criminalization of protesters through a folklorish listing of offensive and physically violent activities (supposedly) previously committed, ascribed to upcoming protests as a whole:

> During the WTO protests (Seattle, 1999) themselves, I must emphasize, no one, including the Seattle police, had claimed anarchists had done anything more militant than break windows. . . . [L]ess than three months later, a story in the *Boston Herald* reported that, in the weeks before an upcoming biotech conference, officers from Seattle had come to brief the local police on how to deal with "Seattle tactics," such as attacking police with "chunks of concrete, BB guns, wrist rockets, and large capacity squirt guns loaded with bleach and urine" (Martinez 2000). . . . Each time there is a new mobilization, stories invariably surface in local newspapers with the same list of "Seattle tactics"—a list that also appears to have become enshrined in training manuals distributed to street cops. (389)

This same type of laundry list of violent offenses was seen in the OPD operations brief and in its press release, as well as the City of Oakland's press release, and the media coverage of Move-In Day, before and after J28, as part of a broader set of discourses painting Occupy Oakland as nihilistic outsiders and blaming them for everything from lack of city funds to poor police response to crime. It is a mistake to simply reduce these

negative representations of protesters as simply media bias or reliance on state sources for information, or the adherence to their
frames. Marginalization and criminalization are material forces
of repression, on their own, and quite often a necessary precondition for successful hard repression efforts. This criminalization
is itself a form of (soft) repression intertwined with the use of
police force: "Criminalizing a demonstration allows police to
invoke regulatory measures to outlaw, disperse, and assault dissenters" (Starr et al. 2011, 43).

The Anti-Politics of Political Repression

While the policing of the January 28 action was central to
the overall effort to thwart the occupation of the Kaiser Convention Center, they weren't the only forms of repression lev-
ied against the action, nor can the efficacy of the policing of
that day be understood outside of the broader contexts of the
repression deployed. Using police tactics that would later be challenged in court,[15] the public relations aspect of social control
from prominent Oakland politicians saw its clearest, sharpest, and
most forceful application immediately before and after the action.
The words of Mayor Jean Quan and City Administrator Deanna
Santana need to be evaluated as primary forces of social control
and soft repression if we are to understand the social and political
contexts that aided or hindered support for the movement and
that empowered and rationalized the aggressiveness of the police.
Because these political discourses explicitly seek to demobilize
movement supporters while legitimating police aggression, they
are squarely as much of a material force as the batons they enable.
This was a pivotal moment in which the movement was trying
to further its definition of itself as both provocative and socially
responsible, while the city and police sought to frame the movement's efforts as violent and politically directionless (Hall et al.
[1978] 2013, 239–240).

To quickly contextualize the political discourses that sought to delegitimate the January 28 action and steer sympathizers in another direction while legitimating police aggression, the role of city officials as knowledge producers must be accounted for when evaluating protest and policing (Gramsci 1971, 350). In the few days immediately before and after the action, the movement was consistently portrayed as violent, childish, foreign, and apolitical, incurring a major financial burden to the city and a distraction to police who were unable to address the city's immense crime problems. According to the City of Oakland January 27, 2012, press release,[16] the movement was described as pitching a "tantrum" and "using Oakland as their playground," engaging in "violent actions against Oakland" intended "to provoke the police and engage in illegal activity," while it "claim[s] to stand for" addressing issues of social justice. The mayor would go on to offer an alternative to "tactics that are counter-productive and divide our community" with a call to "work together, collectively, productively, and cooperatively"—by giving time and money to a long list of nonprofits outlined at the end of the press release, most of whom would be present for the mayor's Volunteer Fair, traditionally held in the fall, and strategically announced immediately before the action. City Councilman Ignacio de la Fuente, a potential rival for mayor in the next election and aggressive critic of Quan's perceived lenient handling of the Occupy movement, again said that the movement was engaged in "domestic terrorism."[17]

With the movement's social justice aims seriously called into question, to the extent that Mayor Quan repeatedly stated that the movement was using the language of social justice to mask mayhem and criminality, the policing of the movement was about crime prevention and not protest management, enabling hard physical repression of the movement while at the same time depoliticizing it. This power to frame debate and define phenomena, to delegitimate social movements (to even strip them of that title), and to empower police repression as the necessary upholding of law and not the stifling of dissent, is a discursive force with enormous material bearing. The nature of the movement and the police did not dramatically change in the previous three months, nor had their respective tactics—but their meaning and effect surely had. Knowledge producers, such as city officials and the press, have the power to define protesters and police to a large extent, as well as their actions, the meaning and legitimacy of those actions, and the sentiments motivating them. The aims of the movement, to occupy publicly owned space, which had been vacant for years, to provide a location for protest, community, and self-sufficiency had not changed, even if the venue had.[18] The police use of force on January 28 was very similar to October 25; but instead of the onus for the conflict and the direction of public scrutiny being placed on the OPD, it fell squarely on the shoulders of Occupy Oakland, which struggled to carry the load.

The Invocation of the Myth of Nondisruptive Change in the Press

The media play a similar and often complementary role to city administrators in criminalizing, marginalizing, or delegitimizing movements. Though their role is similar to that of city officials in framing and defining protest and protest policing, there are substantive differences in their role in the process of repression, often in the specificity of the audience, as well as the ways in which processes like criminalization take place through the institutions of the mass media. Frequently, when the media focus does not criminalize movements it nonetheless makes them seem politically marginal, or ignores them altogether. The mainstream press coverage of protests is typically very conflict-driven and analytically shallow. The protest is covered as a disruptive, chaotic event, with protesters often portrayed as confused or apolitical and movements themselves as fragmented, juvenile, or disconnected from the concerns of everyday people. Sarah Sobieraj illustrates how movements are either ignored or consistently portrayed as culturally marginal or criminal in her research sample: "For those organizations that did receive coverage . . . [they] were often characterized by trivialization and an emphasis on violence and disorder" (2011, 90). She goes on to articulate a dimension of the negotiated management trap, with actions that went out of their way to police themselves, ensuring "nonviolence," still getting defined by conflict (91). Instead of the press focusing on the issues of the protest, the story became about how orderly the protest was and what the logistics of a peaceful protest look like. The media clearly has a preoccupation with conflict and "violence" and a universal aversion to substantively covering protests as political events, regardless of the adopted tactics. The *San Francisco Chronicle*, the Northern California newspaper of record, latched on to this question of "violence." Emphasizing and compounding movement divisions around tactics while overtly seeking to marginalize Occupy Oakland, the *Chronicle* was able to discursively undermine militant, risky, or otherwise unsanctioned actions in a way, and with a level of detail, that the city or police could never feasibly articulate publicly from their respective platforms.

This question of tactics that fall outside of the parameters of negotiated management—the refusal to coordinate with or defer to the police, and the refusal to adhere to what (in the United States) is contemporarily termed "nonviolence"—had been greatly discussed in the media coverage of Occupy Oakland since the shutting down of the Port of Oakland on November 2. Kevin Fagan, the *San Francisco Chronicle* protest beat writer, was at the forefront of challenging the legitimacy of Occupy Oakland on the terms of its failure to adhere to negotiated management, in a prominently featured series of articles.[19] Key to almost all of Fagan's articles on the movement is the amplification of divisions over questions of tactics and conflicts with the police.

In a skillful and developed way Fagan articulated the "good protester/bad protester" trope (Fernandez 2008, 156–161), finding new ways in almost every article to invoke the idea that protests should not be disruptive, gathering a variety of voices—from city officials to store owners, from police to nonviolence trainers— offering unsolicited advice on how to run a successful movement. In a series of articles that stretched Occupy Oakland's existence, Fagan sought to make Occupy Oakland the "bad protester" articulated against the "good protesters" he calls the "99 percenters"—put forward as kind of a silent majority within the Occupy movement whom he sought to give a voice. The only real conflict that is justified in his articles is the tension between Occupy Oakland and the "99 percenters" whom he interviews in the suburbs and rural areas on the outskirts of the Bay Area, who were consistently portrayed as more respectful and legitimate. None of these other Occupy sites ever formally condemned Occupy Oakland, any of its actions, or any of its tactics, but Fagan's chief concern is with identifying protesters who are primarily focused on not alienating people. This concern about alienating potential supporters is evidenced through these Occupiers not setting up encampments or associating with homeless people,[20] or by Occupiers who feel that the anti-bank message is lost when there are confrontations with police.[21]

Although media articles covering social movements rarely provide any contextual depth or historical perspective (Boykoff 2007a, 33–35), Fagan produced one, but with the clear intention of trying to marginalize Occupy Oakland in a historical perspective. As a media liaison for the December 12th Port Shutdown, I was interviewed by Fagan for this article—an almost ninety-minute conversation. The article, "Protests of Past Hold Lessons for Today" (December 4, 2011),[22] is framed by police expectations, as provided by a former police sergeant, that revolve entirely around the terms of negotiated management as the only form of legitimate protest. It reads as a retort to the long-standing radical refrain that "direct action gets the goods": whereas the article seeks to amplify and reify the notion that "cooperation with the police gets the goods." Fagan's driving concern in this article was how to create better relations between protesters and police, as had existed in the 1960s. He began by (and proceeded to keep) asking me how we could have protests where there were no conflicts between protesters and the police. I explained in various ways how the tension was rooted simply in protesters seeking to disrupt the social order and police trying to maintain it, and how this had less to do with violent versus nonviolent tactics, as the history of the 1960s actually illustrates, and more to do with disruption versus cooperation, and the police violence common in maintaining that order.

The article is designed to make Occupy Oakland seem out of touch, not just with the present but with the past. It is premised around the idea of a bygone era of the 1960s, mythologized as the coexistence of major social change alongside cooperation between protesters and police. In this article history was revised to suit the needs of the present in this framing—the contemporary norms of negotiated management were not hegemonic in the 1960s, and they actually emerged *in response to* the upheaval of that period, as a mitigating force for future crises. Those who chose peaceful tactics in the South during the civil rights movement not only took significant risks, they were violently attacked by police and white vigilantes, regardless of the orientation of their tactics, because they were disruptive and determined to alter the social order that the police were charged to protect. In the article, negotiated management is defended by a former police sergeant and an older pacifist, both harkening back to the days of police–protester cooperation and peace. The veteran activist and nonviolence trainer, invoking norms that are said to stretch from the 1950s through the 1980s, argues that a mutually beneficial relationship of negotiated management between protesters and police has been lost, and should be regained—that people have forgotten the rules. He suggests, "One of those rules is that there would be no surprises. . . . Each side would say, 'This is what we will do,' and, 'This is what the response will be,' and you had monitors trained in the discipline of nonviolence who would keep an eye on everything."[23]

While negotiated management has become normalized, it was not the norm in the 1960s. It emerged after the 1960s; it emerged *because* of the 1960s. It arose because of the crises of that period and a conscious state effort to mitigate similar upheavals in the future. The conflation of pacifism and cooperation with police comes from the history of the post-1960s, when pacifism as such became wedded to negotiated management (and vice versa), losing the disruptive capacity that had made Martin Luther King Jr., SNCC, or the Berrigan brothers the disruptive and effective political forces that they were (Churchill 2003, 48). Civil rights marchers never negotiated that their children would get attacked by dogs or bombarded with water cannons. Father Daniel Berrigan was forced underground and later served years in prison for the nonviolent act of destroying draft files during the Vietnam War, which he certainly did not ask permission to do. Reverend Martin Luther King Jr. wrote one of his most famous essays from a Birmingham jail cell; he was in jail because he did not have a permit to protest. The conflated concern here is not really over tactics, but over a refusal to follow the directives of the police and (their interpretation of) the law (King [1963] 2003).

"Nonviolence" became choreographed and largely stripped of its disruptive capacity by the great extent to which it was incorporated into negotiated management. What is commonly understood as a debate over violent versus nonviolent tactics is completely overdetermined by the (usually unspoken) conflict between disruption and cooperation. Outside of the reach of this chapter, but worth noting, is the extent to which certain protesters are defined as violent (and thus illegitimate) for failing to adhere to negotiated management, even if they have no confrontation with police or any living thing. Wearing a mask or a helmet and breaking windows is understood as violent under the contemporary

understanding of protest, even if there is no harm or even engagement with police. The simple wearing of masks is illegal in many
major US cities (or criminalized in media discussing protests)—as
this logic is extended from what is violent (disruptive) to what is
provocative (potentially disruptive) (Starr 2006, 71). An effort was
made in Oakland to make the possession of shields or poles illegal after January 28.[24] It is evident here, in just a small sample of
prominent articles in a major paper, how negotiated management
is embedded in dominant discourse and the social imaginary, how
movements are evaluated and historically situated in the press to
create a common sense around dissent, even if history itself needs
to be massaged to fit the new norm.

STRATEGIC INCAPACITATION IN THE "WAR ROOM"

Despite the soft repression efforts of city politicians and the
press, the police still had challenges and put forward a multifaceted effort to address the J28 action. The police committed
hundreds of officers in riot gear—as well as twenty officers, captains, and sergeants solely committed to intelligence/undercover
work—to their effort to thwart the taking of an indoor space by
Occupy Oakland. Internal OPD documents make clear that it
would use all the means at its disposal to prevent the takeover of
a vacant indoor space. The goals of the action were illegal (breaking and entering, trespassing, etc.) and the police planning was
framed quite simply as the prevention of illegal action. Occupy
Oakland was also labeled as inherently violent and criminal. The
first page of the OPD Operations Plan for January 28 states
that Occupy Oakland is "openly hostile toward law enforcement, including several physical assaults."[25] The next paragraph
lists various (alleged) offenses of Occupiers against police specifically—mostly various forms of assault on an officer, resisting
arrest, and de-arresting fellow protesters. The Operations Plan
ends with sixteen pages of legal codes for crimes ranging from

graffiti to assaulting an officer with a firearm, and from resisting arrest to rioting and arson. While the various tactical operations plans and OPD briefings clearly state that the use of force
should be measured and that less-lethal weapons be deployed
only by OPD (and not from mutual aid forces), the planning
documents make clear that aggressive policing was going to be
the order of the day. The OPD tactics on January 28 encompass
all the aspects of strategic incapacitation—criminalization, preemption, less-lethal weapons, the control of urban space, and the
use of surveillance and intelligence. The most pronounced and
enhanced aspect of the OPD's response to J28, in spite of the
tactical victory on the street all day and the tactical advancement
in terms of the use of kettling, was their extensive use of surveillance—immediately before, during, and after the demonstration
on January 28.

In protest situations surveillance is only useful if it can be
quickly compiled; intelligence gathered has little value to police
during a protest unless it can also be effectively disseminated.
Oakland's Emergency Operations Center, located just north of
downtown, was preexisting and had been used on November 2
and December 12, 2011, and previously during the Justice for
Oscar Grant movement. Beginning January 28, 2012 and going
forward, it would be emphasized as a high-tech center for police
command and control. The center is the hub for police coordination; information from numerous sources is received and
analyzed and useful information is presented to commanders
for timely police response. Within the command center at least
three officers monitor Twitter and other social media; other officers receive reports from undercover officers within the protest;
updates are received from various uniformed police units; live-
streaming (real-time video posted to the web by people embedded with the protest) is monitored; reports from the media are
utilized; the OPD email tip line is watched, among other likely
information sources.[26] The emergency operations center is a

highly rationalized surveillance network designed to provide the police with real-time knowledge to enhance the effectiveness of their efforts. The application of this set of tools to preempt and neutralize protest shares several similarities with both stakeouts and modern military combat (Eisenstadt 2012, 134; Haggerty and Ericson 2001, 43–64). Despite questions that have been raised by civil libertarians, as the *San Francisco Chronicle* reports in an article framing the center as a tool of officer safety, the "Oakland police's war room [is] the new normal."[27]

Emanating from this war room, besides direct communication with commanders, was a series of emails to a wide range of agencies. A selection of these emails was acquired via the Freedom of Information Act and posted on the Internet.[28] These documents show the types of information the OPD was receiving, who it was shared with, and how it was put to use. While most of the email addresses receiving updates from the Command Center on January 28 were OPD sergeants, lieutenants, and captains, or elected officials and officials in the Oakland Fire Department, the emails also went to ICE (Immigration and Customs Enforcement) as well as the Coast Guard command center and several officers. The emails sent early in the day, before the march took place, had a range of information that was available on the Internet, such as rally times, the rules of conduct for the space after it was taken, and so forth.[29] There was also some information that was not publicly available, specifically a Word document listing the potential targets for the day, a list police were fully aware of before the protesters even congregated. As people began assembling in Oscar Grant Plaza, there were reports from undercover officers about the number of people and when and where equipment (i.e., shields and banners) was being delivered. The email list was used during the march to report what other officers were being confronted with and doing as well as to provide reports from heavy monitoring of Twitter, live-streaming, websites, unidentified "Internet chatter," and mainstream news reports.

CONTAINMENT, KETTLING, AND
THE CLOSURE OF MOVE-IN DAY

The police used a range of less-lethal weapons throughout the day on a crowd of approximately 1,500 that was led by protesters with large shields and helmets. The planning and coordination of the movement's action left much to be desired:[30] The Kaiser Center had no Occupiers already inside for the street protesters to support and the area around the building made it difficult for large crowds to easily access it, allowing the OPD to simply follow and attack the march as necessary. Much of the afternoon was filled with protesters trying to outmaneuver police, often in a very unwelcoming geography that was filled with construction sites, fences, and highways.

Between 2 and 3 P.M. the march made its way in and through Laney College, which sits directly south of the convention center. Through a maze of construction zones, and somewhat surreally over a narrow foot bridge that stretches over a channel connected to Lake Merritt, the march sought to evade police as it made its way toward the target. As protesters approached the Kaiser Convention Center, it was surrounded by a phalanx of riot police who stood behind a large drainage ditch, like soldiers in front of a dry moat, protecting an empty, dusty castle. At one point, projectiles were lobbed over a fence at police who responded with beanbag and rubber bullet munitions. Orders to disperse were given, followed by rubber bullets and tear gas, and the march retreated from the area back to Oscar Grant Plaza.

After an hour of rest, a second march left, attempting to claim a different space. It was surrounded by police but was able to escape by tearing down a fence. The bulk of those still out on the street were eventually kettled in front of the YMCA a few blocks from Oscar Grant Plaza—more than 350 were mass-arrested without being given a dispersal order, including six journalists, bringing the total number of arrests for the day over 400.

While the OPD would face an unlawful arrest lawsuit due to this mass arrest, their primary objective of blocking Occupy Oakland's effort to physically reestablish itself was a major victory for the movement's opposition. Many people spent three days in Santa Rita jail, with the failed action not only taking a political toll but also an emotional and psychological one for hundreds of active people in the movement. The coalescing of City Hall's political delegitimation of the movement, the aggressive tactics of the police, and the movement's failure to meet its objectives on January 28 marked the clear beginning of the movement's decline. It also makes clear the initiation of a coherent and effective strategy of social control that is rooted around the mutually reinforcing set of political tactics that seeks to delegitimate and criminalize the movement alongside evolving aggressive, but strategic, policing techniques.

THREE DAYS IN SANTA RITA: HARASSMENT, INTIMIDATION, AND BIOMETRICS

Most of the 408 arrestees were transported to Santa Rita County Jail, where most stayed for three days on misdemeanor charges. Occupy arrestees were subjected to various forms of harassment and intimidation outlined in the class action suit.[31] The holding cells were overcrowded, were cooled (in winter conditions), and lacked beds. Arrestees with medical conditions like multiple sclerosis and HIV were denied medications, menstruating women were denied tampons, and broken bones were left unset.[32] When arrestees were transferred to general population the sheriff's staff informed other inmates that the protesters were the reason for deprivations experienced in the last day, to incite hostility and violence.[33] Jeb Purucker, a January 28th arrestee, reflected on and contextualized the experience shortly after his release:

The focus within the movement over the past week has increasingly been on the brutality that we experienced in jail. We were denied food and necessary medication, leading to seizures; we were abused both physically and verbally; we were crammed into overcrowded and inadequately ventilated cells in which the tear gas that still clung to our clothes made breathing unbearable. . . . To focus on the brutality of the experience as though this is somehow exceptional is to misunderstand the basic function of jails and police forces in society. The violence that we came up against on Saturday is the violence that is required daily to maintain and reproduce society as it is presently constituted. What we experienced for a few nights, while awful, is simply daily life for the unpaid prison laborers who cleaned out our cells when we went home.[34]

Of the more than 400 arrested, only 12 were charged with a crime—8 misdemeanors and 4 felonies.[35] Beyond this treatment, those arrested on felonies (at least eight people) were told they needed to provide DNA samples in order to be eligible for bail. According to the lawsuit, buccal swab samples were taken (from the inside of the cheek). Arrestees also had hair samples taken for DNA and their irises scanned (a common personal identifier, with similar uses as fingerprinting).[36] On top of the harassment and intimidation in jail, the unlawful collection and retention of DNA materials has a chilling effect on protest, particularly in a context of widespread criminalization and surveillance. The subsequent introduction of further biometric technologies by the OPD in the following days would compound both the level of surveillance and criminalization (Starr et al. 2008, 260).

Three days after Move-In Day, the OPD received an early Valentine's gift from software developer Cognitech, Inc.[37]—a donation of its biometric, video-enhancing software system, Tri-Suite 11. The software (which was solicited by OPD and donated by Cognitech) enhances video to improve quality, zoom while preserving quality, and also allows for biometric measurement of subjects captured on video. Cognitech's press release, announcing the gift to the OPD, explains how the biometric imaging works:

> Cognitech's AutoMeasure tool-set is the world's only automatic forensic photogrammetry software that allows the user to perform accurate biometric measurements of a suspect's dimensions (e.g. height, width, area), including crime and accident scene measurements from video surveillance and photographs. This software is important to the work of police departments as it allows the user to know the suspect's biometric measurements based on the AutoMeasure calculations which in turn helps the user eliminate and narrow down individuals who might have been considered suspects.[38]

The reception in the official Bay Area political discourse was that this was a novel way to identify "masked anarchists," to enhance video surveillance from past protests, and perhaps identify and bring charges against Occupy protesters from months earlier. The fact that there are more than 250 known security cameras in downtown Oakland alone,[39] along with numerous police on the ground committed to video surveillance at major actions, makes the acquisition of this software compound the chilling effects of the DNA sampling and iris-scanning that took place in jail. Within a context of recent tactical defeat in the street and the now-unavoidable feeling that the movement may be starting to wane, and in light of the recent individualized targeting, which took place in the previous weeks in the vigil raids, the movement and many individuals within it felt increasingly under siege. Again, this is a furthering of the reach and scope of surveillance under the guise of necessity amid a declared social emergency, more specifically a handful of broken windows.

January 28 was a victory for the enemies and critics of the movement on many fronts. On January 29, Occupy Oakland found 400 members being harassed and intimidated in jail for days, the movement thoroughly criminalized for its militancy and defeated in spite of it. The OPD gained back the ability to use strategic incapacitation tactics against Occupy Oakland, made possible by the demonization of the movement by city administrators, the press, and others—a demonization that was compounded after J28. The tactical dialectic of legitimacy and successful street tactics now belonged to the police, a position reclaimed on January 28 and never surrendered back to Occupy Oakland.

NEGOTIATED MANAGEMENT AS
NORMATIVE SOCIAL CONTROL

While the hard repression was successful, with the Kaiser building remaining just as empty on January 29 as it was on the morning of January 28, Occupy Oakland was not able to escape the logic of negotiated management by refusing to abide by it. It was imposed by city officials, the mainstream press, and the police as a reasonable and normative expectation. Once that expectation was not met, J28 was not only demonized in press releases and articles, but also ceased to be considered protest at all. By falling outside of the normative expectations of negotiated management, the goals of the movement became delegitimated, the movement itself turned into a criminal enterprise, and the tactics interpellated as terroristic.

Negotiated management, after becoming normalized, is not simply about whether protesters get a piece of paper from City Hall or have coffee with the police before an action. After the permitting of protest becomes normal, the traditional terms contained within the permit become the definition of what (legitimate) protest is, and the rubric through which to measure what forms of protest are not acceptable. While the physical permit is a means to an end (public order), the state's concern is with that end, not the means. Wearing body armor in expectation of police aggression, physically confronting police officers, refusing to obey police orders, and seizing abandoned property are criminalized actions because they are not permitted (the formal means). They are not permitted because they are disruptive, a (potentially) viable threat to social order (the unintelligible ends of the movement). The state's goal is not simply to prevent specific instances of disruption, but to make disruption unintelligible as a means to social justice, to negate it as a realm of possibility. In the absence of the permit as a legal document, it remains a moral code of expected behavior, enforced directly by the police. This enforcement is consciously portrayed as taking place outside of what is accepted as "protest"—the enforcement is simply a matter of crime and law, since the tactics chosen have negated the legibility of those in the streets as "protesters." As the history of Occupy Oakland has demonstrated, the acceptance of these criminalization techniques by (potential) supporters is not a given. As further elaborated in chapter 8, movements finding more effective ways to pressure bases of potential support, and viable channels for the movement to define its own politics and draw its own distinctions around tactics and strategies (under terms that the movement creates, that are to a great extent insulated from outside pressures) is essential to moving past this set of social control traps.

The normalization of negotiated management helps to legitimate police violence against dissenters who do not abide by its rules. The police violence of October 25 that elicited mass support for the movement—where riot police attacked a peaceful crowd with less-lethal weapons for hours—and the police violence of January 28 were similar. Both days featured the same riot squad and the same use of tear gas and rubber bullets on a crowd who had done nothing besides assemble in the street. However, what the violence meant, the definition of those subjected to it, and whether or not it should be considered illegitimate repression of protest or the legitimate enforcement of law hinged largely upon the logic of negotiated management and the moral understandings of tactics that fell outside of its norms.

The mayor and the mass media quite explicitly defined this effort (before and after January 28) as criminal, as apolitical, as violent, as illegitimate. While these discursive techniques do not necessarily create tensions within movements, they do utilize existing tensions to splinter movements and maintain social order.

Fagan did not conjure up the "99 percenters," even if he had to literally seek them out ninety minutes outside of Oakland. While social movements are a struggle for political hegemony, there are also struggles within movements over tactics and strategy, which occur organically but are also exploitable by forces of social control. Fagan's series of articles and the city's press release exacerbated those tensions, bestowing legitimacy on the permitted and the "peaceful," and activating and justifying forces of repression that neutralized the current threat. Beyond the maintenance of social order in that moment, this entire normative system of negotiated management threatens all who might protest outside of the bounds of negotiated management in the future, offering legitimacy and protection to those who choose sanctioned, nondisruptive protest while shunning those who refuse it. Through the state and media inserting themselves into tactical movement debates, both sides of the debate (which is often called "nonviolence" vs. "diversity of tactics") are galvanized and the opposing side morally delegitimated—one for "assuming the responsibilities of the state," the other for its "irresponsibility." Preexisting political differences become unbreachable chasms, as repression raises the stakes of movement differences. Social movement actors embodying "good protester"/"bad protester" dualisms sever whatever trust and collaboration could be established.

The first camp saw a police force more than willing to turn a blind eye to petty criminality and violations, because of the movement's aims and the public perception of those aims. Less than four months from the first pitched tent in Oakland, the political ambitions of the movement had been discursively erased, the movement's base divided over tactics, and the 1,500 people in the street (including a fair number of children) interpellated as simple criminals rather than social justice demonstrators. It was the city's ability to demonize the movement's militancy that put police violence in a more socially acceptable context. The state's power to define what is "protest" and what is "criminal" (or "violent" and hence illegitimate) is largely connected not only to their position as elected officials, but to the normative power of negotiated management as a force of social control, regardless of whether it is chosen or imposed as a normative structure. However, this criminalization is only effective if it resonates in the minds and demobilizes the bodies of those who had previously supported the movement. Protests that have politics or utilize tactics that fall outside of the realm of the reasonable, cooperative, predictable, and containable cease to be considered protest at all. The extent to which many supporters of social justice support this logic amplifies its effectiveness.

When Occupy Oakland did not take negotiated management's bait, they got caught in the normative net. These relationships and processes are hegemonic, whether social movements like them or not, whether they are inherently repressive or not, whether they are constitutional or not. As they swim forward, movements will need to either foster widespread delegitimation of the net or formulate viable strategies for cutting its strings, because the dialectics of "behaving"/"misbehaving" (or debates that counterpose "diversity of tactics" and "nonviolence") constitute swimming in circles.

Negotiated management is a form of knowledge-power that defines the common understandings of protest and deploys techniques of social control to serve its own ends. Even when negotiated management is vehemently rejected by a group of protesters, it is used to criminalize those protesters and subject them to physical repression, reinforcing the norm of negotiated management and the threat of police force contained therein, while morally and politically empowering those who wish to embrace it. The conundrum this presents is that even tactics that deviate from the norm of negotiated management end up reinforcing it, as it is both a micro-power technique of repression and a macro-power technique of knowledge that utilizes transgressions to reinforce the norm (Foucault 2007, 358). This was the social control net that was set for Move-In Day, a web in which the movement was mired as it struggled on in the following months.

CHAPTER 7

Poison in the Garden

A SPRING OF SEEDS
THAT NEVER GREW

AFTER THE MILITANT but ultimately unsuc-
cessful effort to make social use out of the long-shuttered Kaiser
Convention Center, and the arrest of 408 people, most of whom
were ensnared in a mass arrest that evening, the movement had
been dealt a serious blow in terms of hard repression: tactical defeat
on the street, pending legal charges, and a slew of new stay-away
orders. The movement had also been smeared in the press, with its
legitimacy being challenged both locally and nationally by the liberal political establishment of the city. The failure to claim a vacant
building amid police repression—to reconstitute a camp indoors
and establish a tactical innovation for the rest of the occupy movement nationally (most of which were facing more serious weather
restrictions to creating or maintaining camps outdoors)—compounded the declining energy and momentum of Occupy Oakland as a mass movement in the Bay Area. By the time most people
were out of jail it was early February, and although most committees were still functioning and the General Assembly continued to
meet and make decisions, Occupy Oakland was at a crossroads trying to figure out exactly who and what it was, with the camps gone
and the ability to pull off successful mass marches waning amid
evaporating public support and increased hard and soft repression.

The camps had, themselves, been contradictory—on the one hand, an autonomous space in the center of downtown, a prefigurative project of direct democracy, the Oakland Commune; on the other hand, the camps had experienced instances of sexual assaults, other forms of interpersonal violence, and hard drug use, problems the movement did not have many resources to effectively address. They also had only limited time to develop a functional model to adequately solve these issues under the watchful eye of a hostile media and political establishment. As discussed in chapter 4, after the second raid the movement had almost universally given up on reconstituting another camp in Oscar Grant Plaza. Nonetheless the camps were a, if not the, defining characteristic of this movement nationally, with numerous cities and towns still maintaining their camps through the winter.

As Oakland had put the originating idea of the camps behind them, and an effort to occupy a building recently failing despite a degree of preliminary planning, mass demonstrations themselves were clearly another defining aspect of Occupy Oakland. It is easy to see January 28 as a turning point, Occupy Oakland's most major defeat. After January 28, there was a palpable feeling that the movement had got the wind knocked out of it. However, Occupy Oakland's ability to draw out tens of thousands of people happened only once, on November 2, 2011. In the aftermath of the first encampment raid, the publicly visible police violence used to prevent the construction of a new camp, and a large (mostly self-mobilized) base of supporters, more than fifty thousand people came out on November 2 for a day of action culminating in the shutdown of the Port of Oakland, which was situated in and around the newly built second encampment. People wanted to get that back, that energy, the feeling, the sight of an overwhelming mass of humanity clogging the downtown of the city. January 28 was much smaller, but also of a different nature—explicitly stated to occupy a building with the predetermined knowledge that the march would be physically attacked by the police. But even before the roughly two thousand people set out with shields and helmets on January 28, 2012, Occupy Oakland's ability to draw large numbers of people into the streets had already been waning.

In Oakland, the December 12th West Coast Port Shutdown successfully kept the Port of Oakland closed for over twenty-four hours, but the total number of people who came out to make that victory happen was a fraction of the number of people who came out on November 2. Roughly ten thousand people participated over the course of the December 12th Port Shutdown in Oakland, with about five hundred people shutting down a shift the evening of the 12th and about one hundred people shutting down a shift in the middle of that night, in the wee hours of the 13th.[1] It was a victory, it met its local objectives of shutting down the Port, but it was evident that support was waning, especially when the amount of outreach is taken into consideration. The December 12 action had several weeks of intensive outreach by a few hundred people all over Oakland and the Bay Area, whereas November 2 had had a few harried days of largely uncoordinated outreach. The decline of the movement in terms of mass demonstrations was apparent long before January 28.

POISONING THE GARDEN: LEGAL HARASSMENT, SMEAR CAMPAIGNS, AND MANUFACTURED CONFLICT

From February through April 2012, there was a tremendous amount of activity, with a range of projects: organizing with non-union and union workers (Occupy AC-Transit; organizing in solidarity with wrongfully terminated immigrant steelworkers and striking licorice workers; a workers' assembly); a planned caravan to Longview, Washington, to support locked-out longshore workers that was cancelled when a labor contract was signed; a

Image 12   Occupy4Prisoners action at the gates of San Quentin Prison, February 20, 2012. (Photo by Daniel Arauz)

large and vibrant demonstration at San Quentin prison; innovative foreclosure defense work; the occupation of a vacant lot and its transformation into a large, functioning urban farm; as well as hosting regular barbeques all over the city. Although no mass marches were attempted between January 28 and May 1, there were numerous and varied repression efforts. The hard and soft forms of repression discussed in this section should be instructive for future movements that have an initial wave of success and then start to find themselves mired in intimidation, smear campaigns, rumors, and deliberately instigated internal division, which ultimately leave movement participants tired, jaded, and less engaged. These repression efforts, in Oakland, included the formation of an anti-Occupy, pro-police "community group"; the bringing of baseless hate crime charges against three Occupiers; a group insinuating that a prominent Occupy Oakland writer and organizer was a terrorist; the spreading of rumors that the anti-repression committee and the finance committee were embezzling money;

and a variety of interpersonal threats of violence, as the functionaries of the Democratic Party were attempting to coopt the movement at the national level, under the pretense that Occupy had become too focused on the police and repression. These efforts, mixed with the usual tensions and conflict that arise when decentralized movements do not know what to do next, would lead to most longtime Occupy Oakland participants abandoning the movement after a lackluster May Day demonstration in 2012. In its first few months, Occupy Oakland had the wind at its sails in open water, weathering the currents of hard repression without being blown off course. From February 2012 on, the movement found itself rowing through the reeds—trying to establish a stronger working-class base as well as remobilize the broader Bay Area Left—as various and perpetual repression efforts sapped the movement's already declining strength.

Soft repression efforts from the mass media and city officials followed a similar track as was discussed in the last chapter, one of overt criminalization and delegitimation of the movement as a whole. The small-scale hard repression of harassment arrests that took place in this period were intertwined with this criminalization. The soft repression of "Stand for Oakland" provided contrived traction for the media pretenses about an Oakland community tired of Occupy. Unprincipled behavior from within Occupy Oakland in the form of deliberate attacks on prominent participants and the sowing of suspicions and divisions served to preoccupy a movement searching for a cohesiveness and energy that was being torn apart from multiple directions. Occupy Oakland had got up from being knocked down on January 28, and took these months of body blows with a tucked chin, waiting for their opening to strike back with a mass action on May Day. However, May 1 would see the OPD deliver the knockout blow, set up by the wearying array of shots taken by the movement in the months prior.

COVERT TEA PARTY ACTIVISTS
TAKE A "STAND FOR OAKLAND":
REPRESSION, ANTI-REPRESSION,
ANTI-ANTI-REPRESSION
(AND MORE REPRESSION)

Eight days after the January 28, 2012, action, Occupy Oakland called for a "Day of Action against Police Repression" on Monday, February 6, when many J28 arrestees were being arraigned and defense lawyers would be making their first efforts to challenge stay-away orders in court. At this event a number of those arrested spoke to the two hundred or so people gathered at the noon rally at Oscar Grant Plaza about the inhumane conditions to which they had been subjected at Santa Rita jail after being arrested on January 28. The *Daily Kos* published a quote from one of those held at Santa Rita after January 28: "Just got out of Santa Rita Jail last night the prisoners from the Oakland Commune were being denied medications (some had seizures) while the guards said they didn't care if they died. Some people were brutally beaten. They put tear gas in the vents of my cell twice. They were keeping people without restrooms forcing them to shit and piss themselves or puke all over and stay in the same area."[2]

Taking advantage of the momentum they had gained on January 28, the police rushed the sound equipment at the anti-repression speakout at Oscar Grant Plaza, and eventually wrestled it away from Occupiers who had encircled it and attempted to ward off the police seizure. Occupy Oakland never had taken out a permit for amplified sound (and never would)—despite the use of sound equipment being common for outdoor meetings over the past four months, which regularly numbered in excess of two hundred people. Of the dozens of times Occupy Oakland had used sound equipment, it had never been seized by the police and no citations for failing to obtain a sound permit were issued. In spite of the irony of riot police attacking a small rally that had gathered to listen to the experiences of those recently abused in

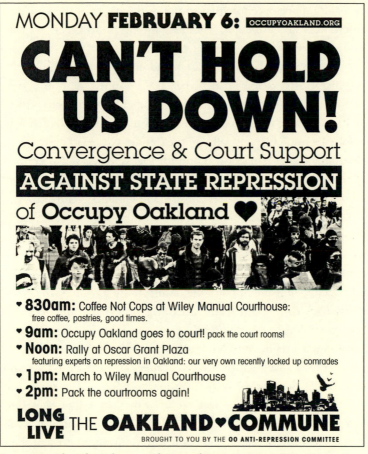

MONDAY **FEBRUARY 6:** `OCCUPYOAKLAND.ORG`

CAN'T HOLD US DOWN!

Convergence & Court Support

AGAINST STATE REPRESSION

of **Occupy Oakland** ♥

- **830am:** Coffee Not Cops at Wiley Manual Courthouse: free coffee, pastries, good times.
- **9am:** Occupy Oakland goes to court! pack the court rooms!
- **Noon:** Rally at Oscar Grant Plaza featuring experts on repression in Oakland: our very own recently locked up comrades
- **1pm:** March to Wiley Manual Courthouse
- **2pm:** Pack the courtrooms again!

LONG LIVE THE **OAKLAND ♥ COMMUNE**

BROUGHT TO YOU BY THE **OO ANTI-REPRESSION COMMITTEE**

Image 13   Flyer for February 6th Day of Action against State Repression.

jail, an irony lost on the range of corporate media reporters present for the event, the police confiscated the public address system. This police action against the anti-repression rally dampened the day and frustrated those present; it also temporarily seized the voice of the General Assembly, while flaunting the OPD's newly gained upper hand. The small-scale hard repression of Occupy Oakland's rally, cloaked (again) in the language of permits, is, however, not the main story from that day. It was complemented by a soft repression effort that spoke in the name of the Oakland community and presented itself as standing up to Occupy Oakland's "angry, loud disrespectful, thugs."[3]

A group called Stand for Oakland emerged after January 28 and had its first action on February 6—a counter-demonstration against Occupy Oakland's anti-repression rally. Numbering thirty or forty people, the Stand for Oakland group assembled shortly before the noon Occupy rally on the steps of City Hall, across from where the camps had stood. Stand for Oakland was self-described as being "formed of area business owners and concerned citizens" whose "concern is for the recent surge in violence, vandalism, and loss of business in the downtown and western regions of Oakland, issues that are said to have cost the city an estimated $5 million in security and lost revenue."[4] Despite representing themselves as community members "who support some of the core premises of the Occupy movement [and who want] to help bring some credibility back to it,"[5] some quick investigation would uncover that the group was much differently comprised, although the mainstream media representation would take them at their word.[6]

A quick investigation of the leaders of Stand for Oakland reveals that they were not just ordinary concerned citizens, and that their personal politics were actually diametrically opposed to Occupy Oakland.[7] This front group was able to fashion itself as part of the movement and part of the community, to present their members as disaffected liberals, echoing many of the tropes forwarded by Kevin Fagan of the *San Francisco Chronicle* (discussed further in chapter 6)—a myopic fixation with a divided Occupy movement. Stand for Oakland was very much a reformulation of this contrived conflict over movement legitimacy, forged by the corporate media and echoed by (what was really) a police front group whose spokespeople's political history stands in clear opposition to the movement they claim to be trying to save.

The pamphlet "Who Is Stand for Oakland?" examines the backgrounds of Stand for Oakland's more vocal members, to identify their actual political histories: "'Stand for Oakland' is likely the production of a handful of relatively conservative Oakland political activists, and several members of the Oakland business lobby. They have, however, tapped a genuine frustration among many centrist liberals who for a variety of reasons feel alienated from Occupy Oakland, and who have been swayed by the now predominant framing—spread now incessantly by most major newspapers and TV stations—of the movement as causing 'violence.'"[8] Delving into the personal political careers of those who spoke to the press as Stand for Oakland's concerned citizens, one finds: Marilyn Singleton, a Tea Party candidate running against Congresswoman Barbara Lee; Nancy Sidebotham, the chair of the Oakland Police–funded Neighborhood Crime Prevention Council; Paul Junge, the Oakland Chamber of Commerce's public policy director; and Phil Tagami, a major Oakland real estate developer, who "achieved notoriety during earlier protests when he patrolled the Rotunda Building [adjacent to Oscar Grant Plaza], which he owns, with a shotgun, threatening to murder protesters."[9] Amid this small gathering of counter-protesters standing in front of a "Stand for Oakland" banner was a man carrying a picket sign that read "The Real 99%," with an arrow pointing down to him. Although this front group did seem to mobilize a small amount of organic community frustration with Occupy Oakland, it remained, as one nearby Occupier noted in a video of the protest,[10] an "Astroturf movement"—a fake grassroots movement.

Stand for Oakland's own website states quite explicitly that it saw its role as one of soft repression and infiltration. In an article posted to the moderated Stand for Oakland website, Stand for Oakland is conceiving of itself as an ancillary of the Oakland Police Department and an explicit effort to publicly discredit Occupy Oakland:

Lately I have been reading several arguments that the Oakland Police Department needs to take an even more aggressive stance against Occupy Oakland. The purpose of "Stand For Oakland" should be to get the community active in opposing the destructive behavior of Occupy Oakland without relying on the police and placing the burden on them. While it may be easy to sit back and let the police deal with them, doing so only makes us part of the problem. . . . The only court which is going to keep Occupy Oakland in check is the court of public opinion.[11]

The article goes on to highlight a weakness of Occupy Oakland that the writer felt should be exploited, the open and democratic General Assembly process, where the construction of committees and the endorsement of all Occupy Oakland actions takes place, necessitating that more than 90 percent of those present at a General Assembly meeting approve of the proposal being put forth. Stand for Oakland was explicitly calling on people hostile to the movement to infiltrate it with the intention of neutralizing its decision-making process.[12] Stand for Oakland's call to action for those seeking to infiltrate and disrupt Occupy Oakland was entitled "Occupy Occupy Oakland GA"—making clear their intentions and political positionality:

This may be an opportunity for those of you who support some of the core premises of the Occupy movement to help bring some credibility back to it. For those of you who feel that Occupy Oakland is irredeemable, now is your chance to put them to task and prove it. Can you think of any other group you have opposed that has afforded you this level of input into their internal processes? We'd be foolish not to take advantage of this opportunity. . . . In order to keep our participation above board we would need to keep our own behavior in check.[13]

The months that would follow without a General Assembly meeting being stacked with political opponents perhaps

highlights Stand for Oakland's own contradictions as a fake organization when their efforts to "Occupy the General Assembly"
failed to materialize. Although their orientation and politics were
clear to anyone who bothered to go to their website or to web
search their spokespeople's names, their intention to discredit and
delegitimize Occupy Oakland found an ample sounding board
in the local press.

All of the local major television and newspaper media outlets, as well as the *Huffington Post*, the *National Review*, and others,[14] covered the Stand for Oakland protests, describing them
based on their own press release, as concerned citizens, against
the backdrop of the January 28 failure that had left the movement's militancy easily called into question. For a (by any definition) small, one-time, counter-demonstration made up of people
largely connected to local elites whom the movement was challenging, Stand for Oakland easily garnered media attention while
Occupy Oakland press releases connected to actual grassroots
efforts across Oakland were almost entirely ignored. Whether one
attributes Stand for Oakland's easily courted corporate media
attention to political bias or to a media fixation on drama and
conflict, the coverage dovetailed nicely into the political divisions journalists like Kevin Fagan had been disproportionately
highlighting for months. The *San Francisco Chronicle* reported the
events of February 6, 2012, as an incoherent movement at war
with itself, "with both sides accusing each other of missing the
point of the Occupy movement."[15] The *Chronicle* article used the
opportunity to echo (yet again) their emphasis that Occupy Oakland was apolitical, directionless, violent, and marginal. By ignoring the political reality of who Stand for Oakland was, a group
led by business elites, far-Right politicians, and pro-police groups,
and by legitimating what was essentially a police front group as
a dissident wing of the movement mobilizing fed-up residents,
the movement was delegitimated as the police repressed an anti-
police repression, gathering and confiscating sound equipment

that had been central to the General Assembly's functioning since October 2011.

THE "ICE CREAM 3":
POLITICAL SMEARS THROUGH
THE COURT SYSTEM

Stand for Oakland would not be the only time in this period where counter-protesters and police would combine to discredit Occupy Oakland and attempt to drive wedges into the movement from the outside. The case of the "Ice Cream 3" illustrates the ways in which criminal charges, which were baseless and ultimately dismissed, can serve to smear social movements. In this case the movement was presented as comprised of violent, thieving, homophobes in a case that would ultimately be dismissed by a judge, but only after two and a half months of Occupy Oakland's name being associated with pending hate crime charges. These hate crime charges were brought against three Occupiers, to be thrown out in late May 2012—at a moment when the repression and delegitimation of the movement was a moot point, as many in Occupy Oakland were declaring the movement dead.

The case stems from an altercation that took place at a bank protest, on February 22, 2012, in Piedmont—a wealthy town that sits within the city of Oakland that surrounds it, located about two miles north of downtown Oakland. A woman, Kelly Stowers, got into an argument with three Occupiers as the three were leaving Fenton's Creamery (an ice cream store), en route to the protest. After Stowers had allegedly said that they didn't belong in that neighborhood and were "acting like niggers," one of the three allegedly called her a "dyke bitch."[16] A witness reported that the alleged victim, Stowers, had insulted and punched one of the defendants and was baiting them to fight.[17] It was also alleged that Stowers had been robbed by one of the three. The allegedly robbery, along with the alleged slur about her perceived sexuality, were combined by the police and district attorney to be charged as a hate crime. Initial bail for each of the three was set at $100,000 bond; two of the defendants remained in jail for weeks awaiting trial. Despite the fact that the alleged victim had given an initial report that named a man, who was not arrested, as the one who stole her wallet, followed by two very different accounts of what had happened, a trial date was set, though the charges were eventually thrown out by the judge in late May. The Ice Cream 3, as the defendants had become known, were free, but only after their mug shots had been tagged, alongside Occupy Oakland's name, with antigay hate crime charges in dozens of mainstream media articles.

Despite the fact that prosecutors must have known that the charges they were bringing would never stick, the association of hate crimes with a beleaguered movement served to smear not just the accused, but the movement as a whole (Boykoff 2007a, 143–144; Earl 2005, 118). The district attorney, Nancy O'Malley, who had taken the lead in pursuing stay-away orders for Occupiers, in spite of the clear likelihood that they could be overturned, also had no reservations about bringing an objectively tenuous set of hate crime charges against members of Occupy Oakland, with the OPD releasing a lurid press release. As with many smear efforts, those doing the smearing (whether state or nonstate actors) often have little to lose in making public or even legal accusations against movement participants, especially in the short run. The charges would be dropped, but the association of Occupy Oakland with antigay bigotry would hang in the air for months, in a Bay Area where LGBTQ liberation is an intrinsic part of the broader Left that Occupy was trying to mobilize for May 1. The nature of any smear campaign is to raise suspicions, breed doubt and distrust within the movement, forge political camps around contrived controversies if possible, to manufacture stress and anxiety, to facilitate burnout among movement members, to drive away supporters, demobilize more loosely involved participants, and generally to delegitimate and destroy the movement as a whole. These baseless hate-crime charges were but one of many smear campaigns directed at individuals, committees, and the entire movement in the spring of 2012.

HELLA UNPRINCIPLED BEHAVIOR: SMEAR CAMPAIGNS, RACIST INSINUATIONS, AND DIVISIVENESS

Four days after the events that would have three members of Occupy Oakland brought up on hate crime charges, a member of the Occupy Oakland Media Committee posted an article that insinuated that Jaime Omar Yassin, quite arguably the movement's best reporter and blogger, was an international terrorist, a drug smuggler, and potentially an FBI informant. The article featured an image of a man alleged by the US Department of Defense to be a terror suspect, and spoke in hypotheticals that Occupy Oakland's Jaime Omar Yassin *may be* the pictured Jaime Yassine Uribe. The article surfaced, ironically enough, on the same day the Anti-Repression Committee brought, and the General Assembly passed, principles of solidarity against police repression that included not providing information to the police and not "post[ing] potentially incriminating information about our comrades on the internet and social media (This includes any forms of information posted on Facebook, Twitter, blogs, email, etc.)."[18] The article in question that attempted to link a prominent member of Occupy Oakland with the individual on the Department of Defense website presented its accusations as hypothetical questions, attacking and demanding the release of legally sensitive material and invading the privacy of, and attempting to tarnish the reputation of, movement members. These baseless questions about the integrity of a key Occupy Oakland participant were cloaked as well-meaning inquisitiveness—in the name of transparency and accountability. The article in question included the following:

We are not making any accusations, and we are not suggesting any specific action be taken. However, together we decided that others should be made aware of this information because those involved with the Occupy Movement have a right to know with whom they may be associating themselves, especially if there is the potential that this person may be infiltrating the movement for the purpose of harming it.

This potential needs to be taken seriously, given the history of federal infiltration of protest movements, and, if we remember the case of Brandon Darby, it wouldn't be the first time in recent years. We believe first and foremost in transparency, accountability, and the freedom of information.[19]

This post was extremely racist, unprincipled, and unfounded. At the General Assembly that same day, this understandably became the exclusive focus, as some members of the Media Committee tried to justify the post by further bad-mouthing Yassin. Those at the General Assembly did not share the speculative worries that some in the media collective were spreading on Occupy Oakland's website (the post was quickly taken down) and were outraged at this racist, slanderous attack. A resolution that the entire Media Committee be completely disbanded passed the next week and a new Media Committee was created. That resolution read, in part:

Last Saturday, an offensive, irresponsible, and dangerous article titled "Occupational Awareness" was posted on the OO Media website. Occupy Oakland denounces the article. The article contains personal attacks on an individual in Occupy Oakland that are untrue and unsubstantiated, and that are extremely dangerous to him and to the movement. The article appeals and legitimates a fantasy of "terrorist threat" that has consistently been used by the state to repress and silence protest, and to create false "enemies," and uses classic racist

tactics of racial profiling to do so. This article is not only a
serious danger to the person attacked, it is a danger to our
movement and it requires immediate action.[20]

These accusations were made and supported by a small
group of people from within Occupy Oakland's Media Committee.[21] The effort was combined with personal attacks on him and
conflicts he had had with some of these members. The charges
made against Yassin, or, as they would insist, questions about him
that demanded further consideration, were met with an almost
universal dismissal and resounding outrage.

The movement spent two General Assemblies and plenty of
time in between dealing with this smear. Movements have a need
to respond to repression, whether hard repression from police and
courts or soft repression, especially from within their own ranks.
Time spent rooting out and dealing with repression or extremely
unprincipled behavior is not time wasted, but it is time spent.
Movements often find themselves mired in (quite often manufactured) controversies, internal conflicts, and rumors that hope
to latch onto already existing political differences, political camps,
identity groups, and interpersonal jealousies or hostilities.

This effort to smear a prominent member of the movement along with Occupy Oakland more broadly, on the movement's own website, needed to be dealt with, and was dealt with
clearly and effectively. At a time when Occupy Oakland needed
to be branching out, it was forced into insularity by what were
completely necessary steps to expunge (unelected) committee
members who did not represent the interests of the movement.
Occupy Oakland's effort to cut a cancer out of its own body
proved successful but left it weakened and tense. People who had
associated with the guilty parties were looked on with suspicion,
and understandably major internal transgressions like this elicit
increased scrutiny of others in and around the movement. Similar smear efforts by some of the same participants in this attack

would reemerge in the coming weeks and months, trying to utilize fabricated controversy to pressure individuals and committees to disclose legally sensitive material.

UNACCOUNTABLE, NONTRANSPARENT DEMANDS FOR ACCOUNTABLE TRANSPARENCY

Led primarily by Shake Anderson, a member of the Media
Committee who had been part of the smear campaign against
Jaime Omar Yassin, a wave of persistent insinuations of misconduct, fraud, and embezzlement were brought against members
of both the Finance and Anti-Repression Committees and the
committees themselves. Once again cloaked in the language of
accountability and transparency, speculative rumors were repeatedly posed as hypothetical realities, through questions harped on
by a small number of persistent people from within the ranks
of an open Occupy movement. Starting in April and May of
2012 and intensifying in June, these efforts mirrored the attack
on Jaime Omar Yassin in their groundlessness, their personally
invasive nature, their presentation as reasonable inquiry, and their
ability to effectively smear Occupy Oakland by simply (and persistently) making vague accusations. Despite the public posting
of the accounting for both committees, rumors associated with
Occupy Oakland's finances (totaling less than $30,000) were
combined with related intimidation and threats of violence from
others, which would persist into the fall of 2012.

The insinuations were that members of the Anti-Repression
Committee were embezzling money for their own personal use,
and that certain people were bailed out of jail based on personal ties to people in Anti-Repression while others were not.
According to people in both committees, Anderson was also
requesting information as to whose names were on the respective bank accounts and the names of those who had donated
money to Occupy Oakland—information that was private for

reasons of personal security. The modus operandi was again to make vague, unsubstantiated claims and then demand the release of sensitive information while preoccupying committees with double-checking their accounting (which was sound) and compounding the emotional exhaustion that many committed members, involved in a range of Occupy Oakland activities, were navigating during this period.

In both vague and specific terms, personal threats of violence were made to members of both committees as well as other prominent members of Occupy Oakland, in person, online, and through rumors. The chair of the finance committee, which was a thankless and difficult job, eventually stepped down after publishing flawless accounting books with no gaps or discrepancies. She had been repeatedly harassed and threatened with violence. After disclosing their own equally sound accounting, the Anti-Repression Committee released a lengthy statement that addressed these attacks in the context of repression. As with many forms of soft repression, the line between suspicious or unprincipled behavior (spreading rumors, threats, interpersonal violence, intimidation, disruption, etc.) and state covert operations is rarely clear (Boykoff 2007a, 123–124; Glick 1989, 18). The Anti-Repression Committee's statement speaks clearly to these behaviors in the context of ongoing repression:

> We feel that as a community we need to shift our thinking about repression, to recognize the subtler more insidious forms that it takes and the ways that it targets our sources of strength and plays on existing conflicts and divisions in an attempt to weaken, distract, and consume us. This does not mean that we should become mired in trying to identify state infiltrators and agents. We may never know who the infiltrators are, and ultimately, whether individuals are directly working for the state when they engage in disruptive and divisive behaviors is not the point. We need to instead

focus on behaviors. If behaviors support and consolidate state campaigns of repression—then they do the state's work of repression.[22]

On the question of violence and intimidation, in this context of disruptive behavior that had admittedly unclear intentions, the Anti-Repression Committee added the following:

> What we as a community cannot accept is threats, intimidation, and acts of violence directed against one another. In recent weeks a number of individuals have been subject to different forms of threats and intimidation. Some have received threatening personal messages. Some have been harassed and made to feel unsafe on the streets. That such behavior coming from people who identify as part of Occupy Oakland is entirely unacceptable should go without saying. But we draw attention to these recent threats because we need to recognize the way that they further the state's goal of repression, regardless of who is behind them, by making us more insular (turning inward to the safety of a small group of loved ones and trusted comrades) and cautious (afraid to reach out and take the risks necessary to make the changes we desire).[23]

During this campaign the question of accountability and transparency was repeatedly situated in the logic of movement health and growth (i.e., who would want to be part of a cliquish, secretive, and crooked movement?). This series of accusations—the drama, the threats of violence, and the disruptions at committee meetings and General Assemblies—all served to dwindle the movement's numbers. People found excuses not to come to meetings or simply drifted away; others coming around to a General Assembly for the first time as the weather started to turn warm and dry found more tension than cohesion, amid conflicts that would be difficult for an outsider to understand, if they were so inclined to try. For those in the movement who were fully committed, they found themselves having far more conversations (inside and outside of formal committee and GA meetings) about how to deal with the drama of the week rather than trying to mobilize for actions that were, despite all of this tumult, constant and ongoing throughout this period—the largest of which being the May Day mobilization.

WITH FRIENDS LIKE THESE . . . : THE 99% SPRING BRINGS COOPTATION IN FULL BLOOM

As the Occupy movement attempted to expand and reinvent itself across the country in the spring of 2012, several weeds sprouted up in the prefigurative garden. Not least of these was the "99% Spring" campaign, later called "99% Power," led and funded by Left-leaning civil society institutions (Moveon.org, trade unions, nonprofits) concerned with inequality, but very distant from anything resembling an anticapitalist politics. They trained thousands in a set of narrow and symbolic nonviolent tactics, disrupted shareholder meetings, and sent symbolic tax bills to banks. Ilyse Hogue, the campaign director at MoveOn.org, a key organization in the 99% Spring, wrote in *The Nation* in mid-March 2012 that "Occupy Is Dead"[24] and that the 99% Spring would succeed where Occupy had failed—while mimicking Occupy's slogans. Hogue argued that the movement had failed to continue to address economic inequality and had become "preoccupied" with responding to police repression. She states, "With a spirit of inclusiveness that mimics the slogan ["We are the 99 percent"], established institutions from MoveOn to National People's Action to the United Auto Workers are investing collective resources into The 99% Spring."[25] The spirit of inclusiveness projected onto the movement was supported by Hogue's claims that several groups had already been using Occupy in their names that have no direct relationship to the movement or General Assembly decision-making bodies, failing to mention that

these efforts had been previous cooptation efforts primarily created and supported by the same people behind the 99% Spring.

The organizations that comprised this effort at coopting the
Occupy movement and imposing a very limited and limiting set
of tactics with no clear strategy or vision (radical or otherwise)
were a litany of individual trade unions, both major US trade
federations, environmental groups, and a range of nonprofits.
There likely was no unified intent on behalf of every actor in
this campaign. In Oakland, some local groups doing the nonviolent direct action trainings had serious reservations about the
effort, but participated in it nonetheless. Beyond questions of
organizational intent, what mattered was the effect of this effort
in the existing political context of broad-based repression, the
dismissive, patronizing, and divisive terms in which this effort had
been put,[26] and the timing—right before the 2012 presidential
election. If successful, this would have undoubtedly served as a
wedge over tactics (intentionally or not), exacerbating the "good
protester" / "bad protester" trope that is always used, and that was
steadily deployed in Oakland that spring, and nationally, from
liberal mayors to Fox News and everywhere in between. In its
failure, the 99% Spring helped suck energy out of the movement
at a time when it was trying to regroup itself. People who may
have helped mobilize for May Day actions or signed up to help
staff picket lines attended nonviolence trainings before signing a
petition chastising Bank of America for not paying more taxes,
doing it directly at corporate shareholder meetings as part of the
"Shareholder Spring,"[27] or now had a legitimized excuse to simply stay home.

This attempt overtly tried to bring powerful, institutionally embedded organizations into the process of reformulating
the radical, populist politics that the national Occupy movement
started, striving to wrestle legitimacy from a popular, radical, and
disruptive movement, and channel its message and energy into
political groups that are reformist at best, wholly complicit with

the current political economic order at worst. The plans for this effort also predated the formation of the Occupy movement in the United States.[28] The original goal likely was to generate systemically nonthreatening actions to draw attention to inequality and injustice—not to stop it, but to gather votes for Democrats, who, ostensibly, address those issues. The entrance of these powerful actors of the institutional Left shifted the discursive terms of debate away from a radical analysis, presenting a more palatable alternative, in terms of tactics and demands, that could be used as a responsible foil against the Occupy movement.

Articulating a radical politics in an effort to construct a new common sense that resonates with a broad swath of society presents a tension that must be reconciled between a clear radical vision/strategy and social resonance. This process is made all the more difficult by forces like progressive mayors or the media who are commonly seen, accurately or not, as being on the Left/progressive spectrum of politics, who nominally sympathize with the message of the movement but demonize any tactic that may help the movement's vision materialize. While the Occupy movement tried to articulate counter-hegemonic political ideas and put them into action, the 99% Spring was designed to translate the Occupy movement back into the existing common sense.

May Day 2012: The Synergistic Culmination of Policing and Social Control

In spite of all the challenges that Occupy Oakland had faced in the months leading up to May 1, 2012—from the January 28 letdown to the city's legal harassment and the movement's own internal conflicts, through national efforts to kill the movement so as to use its corpse for compost material—the day offered a chance to create a new footing for the movement. Many in Occupy Oakland invested a great deal of hope in May Day 2012, seeking another big action like November 2, December 12, or

January 28, to revive the movement through a display of vibrant and disruptive mass action. For various reasons this would not be the case: poor outreach, organizing conflicts, new and more effective police tactics, and the overall wane of the movement. In the weeks leading up to May 1 there was insufficient outreach done and a vague plan for what the day's activities would be—despite weeks of meetings stretching back to early March exclusively planning for that day. A conflict between some within Occupy Oakland and some within the Dignity and Resistance March (the separate May 1 immigrants' rights march), over a permit for Oscar Grant Plaza, preoccupied much of Occupy Oakland's planning. Morning actions targeting gentrification near downtown and the Department of Youth Services, as well as Child Protective Services, which had recently taken away custody of an Occupier's children for bringing them to an Occupy Oakland barbeque,[29] and an action at City Hall against gang injunctions and stay-away orders, were highlights of the day, but were small—with only a few hundred participants each.

In the early afternoon police used new crowd-control tactics, examined below, that successfully frustrated mass assembly in the streets. The late afternoon Dignity and Resistance March, which most people from Occupy Oakland met and joined, was a success, with approximately five thousand people in the streets.[30] Later that evening the police deployed their new dispersal tactics again, quite effectively, and the day whimpered to a close. The effectiveness of the police action compounded the meagerness of Occupy Oakland's efforts, with many in OO feeling that the strength of the movement lay solely in its ability to consistently demonstrate its power through mass mobilization. The smallness of the crowd coupled with the tactical outmaneuvering by the OPD led many prominent voices in and around the movement to declare Occupy Oakland dead.[31]

The stated police objectives for the day were to maintain order by selectively targeting people witnessed to have engaged in criminal activity while allowing for "peaceful expressions of free speech."[32] This stated objective is no different from operations plans for past actions; however, what this meant in application was a new strategy and a new set of tactics. At this point in the spring, the OPD was awaiting the public release of the independent Frazier Report,[33] which would come out a few weeks later and detail the dozens of violations and necessary reforms stemming from police conduct in relation to Occupy Oakland the previous fall. The Frazier Report came in a context of upcoming federal receivership hearings and ACLU complaints, which would culminate in class action lawsuits about the use of mass arrests and the arrests of credentialed journalists on January 28. The police would embed mainstream media behind police forces on May 1, while reportedly being very aggressive with other credentialed journalists who were in the protest.[34] Press releases from City Hall and statements from OPD brass drew upon tactics that had worked in the past, criminalization of segments and individuals in the movement and the clear articulation of a good protester/ bad protester trope, similar to January 28, evolving police tactics to more effectively neutralize Occupy crowds, while mitigating public sympathy and legal repercussions. The city's press release leading into May Day equated Occupy Oakland's failure to procure a permit with the potential for violence and inconveniences to the public:

> The City of Oakland is aware of a number of marches, protests, and activities planned in downtown Oakland and throughout the City next Tuesday May 1st; some of the organizers have secured permits, and others have not. . . . As we've stated many times before, the City of Oakland is committed to facilitating peaceful expressions of free speech rights, and protecting personal safety and property. We will not tolerate destruction or violence. We are asking the community to come together, look out for one another, and stay safe. . . .

We have planned to facilitate permitted marches to minimize traffic disruption along permitted routes; pedestrian
and vehicular safety will be maintained by OPD. However,
additional traffic congestion or delays could occur all day and
into the evening as a result of marches or activities that are
organized without a permit.[35]

The Oakland Police Department's use of snatch squads on
the street (discussed below) maintained control over space and
limited the capacity for disruption and mass action on the part of
the movement (Starr, Fernandez, and Scholl 2011, 43). The OPD's
snatch squad tactic targeted individuals while simultaneously
splintering and neutralizing crowds, rather than targeting crowds
as a whole with violence (as on October 25) or mass arrests (as
on January 28). In reality, the police honed their aggressiveness on
the street, rather than restraining it or selectively applying it (as
they would successfully portray in the mainstream press), pointing to various, vague reforms they had undergone and pointing
to the low arrest numbers and few instances of property destruction as a rebranding of Oakland Police crowd control—as not
only effective, but lawful.[36]

In the weeks leading up to May Day, a wanted list of people from Occupy Oakland had been posted, showing names and
information of people who had warrants or were suspected by
OPD to be "known to incite, lynch, or fight police."[37] This list
was probably drawn from the profile book the police used during the December and January raids on the plaza. This compounded a completely separate tension in the planning of May 1.
The two main material concerns that people from Occupy Oakland had about some members of the Dignity and Resistance
Coalition taking a permit out for their rally at Oscar Grant Plaza
was that the permit would be used by the city to draw a "good,
responsible, permit-taking protester" versus "bad, violent, and
criminal protester" dichotomy, and that it would be used as a

weapon against people from Occupy who would be at the plaza and downtown, before and after the permitted portion on May 1, and beyond. We saw the former very clearly in terms of City Hall discourse before May 1. In a lengthy press release from City Hall, the issue of permits and their absence was bolded, with Occupy Oakland's actions portrayed as unsafe and disruptive to citizens, and the Dignity and Resistance March portrayed as least disruptive as possible to the people of the city, sanctioned, and safe.[38] The city and OPD had had little opportunity to make use of tangible examples of negotiated management to discredit Occupy Oakland. When they were presented with the opportunity they seized upon it. The valid concern from the Dignity and Resistance planners was for the safety of many undocumented participants in their march. The Oakland police simply exploited the contradiction between the two different orientations in relation to negotiated management.

The Legalisms and Politics of Protest Policing Tactics on May 1

The primary objectives and concerns of the city and police were the need to prevent the reemergence of an encampment in Oscar Grant Plaza and the need to contain the movement and control space without egregious claims of police misconduct. The city issued a press release solely devoted to outlining the enforcement of no camping and other codes in the plaza on May 1, as well as the requirement of a permit for groups larger than fifty people.[39] Occupy Oakland also saw a more stringent application of the right to assemble on May 1 than it had previously, with the exception of October 25. As discussed in greater detail below, around noon, a crowd of about one thousand was attacked for simply congregating in the intersection at Fourteenth and Broadway, a traditional point of assembly downtown, right off of Oscar Grant Plaza. While people were allowed to congregate in the plaza in order to lessen the number in the streets during the day, after the Dignity and Resistance program concluded the police quickly cleared the park. Later that evening, after the permit had expired and most people had left or were leaving, protesters in the same area and in Oscar Grant Plaza were attacked and divided into a handful of small groups cordoned by several large and coordinated police skirmish lines, similar to the afternoon's crowd-control tactic. The police had demonstrated their ability to disrupt Occupy Oakland crowds of 500–2,000 over the course of the day, and had also stifled whatever possibility may have existed in disruptive mass action that evening, including reestablishing an encampment, which had been discussed but not actively planned.

The OPD was able to review the findings of the Frazier Report in April, while the report was not made public until mid-June. The delay of the public release of the Frazier Report until after May 1 was strategic. It allowed the OPD to claim that it had successfully begun a process of reform while pointing to a police success on May 1 as proof of substantive adjustments. A release of the report before May 1 would have attracted media attention, put the OPD on the defensive before the day of protest, and portrayed the movement as a victim, garnering potential public support for the movement and scrutiny of the police and potentially swelling the numbers participating in May 1 activities. With the Frazier Report findings known to the OPD and not the public before May 1, the police adopted very vague and generalized reforms in their handling of protesters, while adopting new tactics that worked against a somewhat discredited and declining movement.

The OPD still found itself facing various structural constraints before May 1, stuck in a legal Catch-22 while also having to choose between a lesser of evils in terms of public relations. If OPD did not announce a new crowd-control policy, its previous misconduct would either have to have been the direct application of the old policy or an admitted violation of that policy. By announcing a new crowd-control policy shortly before the release of the Frazier Report, the OPD was able to create a clean slate for itself. While demonstrating the extent to which it had reformed the force before the scathing report was released, the OPD and city somewhat mitigated its negative political and legal impact.

In the course of this graceful navigating of the report and reforms, the OPD had to violate a federal court mandate in the process. As the ACLU quickly pointed out on April 24, 2012, the day after the OPD protest policy change was announced, the Oakland police did not have autonomy over their crowd control policy, since a major instance of police brutality against anti-war protesters on the Port of Oakland in 2003 led to a federal judge having oversight of the OPD's crowd-control policies. The new crowd-control policy that OPD had announced was vague: It simply referenced adherence to the Police Officer Standards and Training (POST), the basic standards of crowd control for California police, with OPD Chief Jordan adding five key, but general, points that would all be spelled out in greater detail in the Frazier Report.[40] After the ACLU's public announcement that the OPD was violating the mandate of the federal court by announcing this new policy, police spokespeople vacillated as to whether there was a new policy or not.[41] On May 1 it was clear that there was a new policy, and the tactic of snatch squads was at its forefront.

ORGANIZED CHAOS POLICING: SNATCH SQUADS AND THE SPLINTERING OF PUBLIC ASSEMBLY

On May 1, the same day that a federal judge issued a mandate to the Oakland Police to review the more than one thousand existing complaints against it from Occupy Oakland participants within the next week or face daily or weekly fines, the OPD introduced its new tactic of snatch squads, coupled with a clear attempt to intimidate protesters with military weaponry. The city, which had told the judge it did not have the resources to deal with the complaints, unleashed the new, armored personnel carrier it bought from Blackwater Security (also known as Xe, and later Academi) in a no-bid contract for more than $300,000, ultimately paid for by Homeland Security.[42] At least one officer was seen multiple times carrying an M-4 assault rifle throughout the day. The implicit logic of intimidating many protesters with military weaponry, while selectively (or not so selectively) targeting protesters, was successful against a crowd that was small for a major Occupy Oakland action.

The OPD's new crowd control tactics were largely successful at dealing with the relatively small crowd. To avoid the use of kettling large groups of protesters, the OPD used undercover agents and uniformed snatch squads to target people ostensibly thought to be key to Occupy tactical teams, and divide groups of protesters from the inside out. Officers would target an individual, inside, but near the edge of the crowd, aggressively arrest that individual with four to six officers, using another formation of officers to use the disruption to form skirmish lines within the crowd, splitting it. Snatch squads are typically initiated unexpectedly, with a small group of police arresting a single individual, often tackling and encircling that person, then using the physical act of that arrest to drive a wedge and split the crowd. This tactic created confusion and disorganization among protesters. As some fled the immediate area where the snatch took place, others would step forward to verbally or otherwise challenge the police, leading to more arrests or physical confrontations between police and protesters, along with the deployment of batons, flash bang grenades, and pepper spray being used with the intention of further splintering and dispersing the crowd.[43] The police used this tactic of snatch squads midday in a geographic area where they could be most effective, inside of the block between Fourteenth and Fifteenth Streets on Broadway, with officers on both sides of the street as support for those who formed the wedges in the middle of the street. The use of flash bang grenades and stinging gas/smoke bombs complemented the snatch squads, dispersing people just as effectively. The whole effort utilized the geography of the street—inside a long city block, using the buildings on either side of the street with police at the end of both blocks to allow a loose kettle to be created, with the ability for people to leave but not to march as a crowd.

It was clear at the noon skirmish at Fourteenth and Broadway that the new counter-protest formation that the OPD was using was not something the officers were well trained in. When snatches took place and when commands were given to shift formation, the police did not move in a uniform or fluid way. Instead, officers looked puzzled and kept checking with the officers around them before getting back in formation. Nonetheless, the snatch squads, along with flash bang grenades and stinging gas projectiles, were effective at arresting (mostly) people who had committed no crimes, while creating chaos on the street—a chaos initiated and controlled by the police. Chemical weapons were used mostly against individuals who were confrontational, loud, did not obey officers' verbal commands, or were simply near the new police formations or arrests in progress, and not directed at the crowd as a whole. Importantly, less-lethal weapons were deployed from inside of the crowd at targets, rather than from outside of the crowd from a police skirmish line. This tactic splinters crowds, dispersing people in multiple directions in small groups rather than in a single direction as a whole group. This tactic also does not create a visual image where police as a distinct group are firing less-lethal weapons at a crowd, which suggests that police are attacking indiscriminately. Despite the fact that many of the snatches were clearly indiscriminate, as online videos suggest as well, the snatch squads were tactically effective, while shielding the police from mass arrest lawsuits and potential public opinion blowback against police violence. In the evening the police used similar tactics to successfully split protesters into several small groups downtown, a dispersion that largely mitigated militant action after dark.

Instead of being able to use May Day as a springboard for a summer of major actions, Occupy Oakland whimpered into the summer months licking its wounds, while intermittently declaring itself dead. The General Assembly would only have the 100-person quorum to make official decisions twice more, despite a handful of vibrant, but small, grassroots efforts. By July, quorum was lost for good. The police had surely won the day, successfully navigating the precariousness brought on by their past abuses, forthcoming scathing reports of police conduct, and federal oversight hearings. The small May Day crowd was met with more effective street policing tactics, the aggressiveness of which was tempered by the visually less egregious nature of attacking from the inside out, and dividing rather than containing. This OPD tactical evolution, coupled with the discursive criminalization that preceded it, produced little measurable blowback for the police politically, legally, or in terms of public opinion. Instead of attacking a peaceful crowd wantonly from the outside, or mass-arresting a similar group, the police had a small number of arrests, maintained control of the streets, and not only saved face, but successfully came out as a force that had learned its lessons on crowd control.

CHAPTER 8

Beyond Control

FOSTERING LEGITIMATE COUNTER-CONDUCT

> The police are not monolithic or invincible. We should be careful not to feed into this illusion, as it encourages cynicism and defeatism. We cannot afford to pretend that militant popular struggles can proceed unopposed by the police. At the same time, however, it is an error to think that repression makes organizing futile. In spite of waves of nearly complete suppression of democratic rights in the United States, police repression has never been able to stop the struggles of the American people for very long, partly because new forms of organized resistance have evolved alongside of and at times ahead of police practices.
>
> —Platt et al. 1975, 196

THIS BOOK HAS illustrated an evolution of policing and broader social control tactics that were propelled by the contextual forces at play at different moments. Over time, the policing of major protest actions became more effective at disrupting the movement, particularly large militant actions, while adopting strategies that were increasingly effective at eroding the political legitimacy of the movement, or certain sectors of it, by representing the movement as inherently criminal and a social problem. While physical repression was never taken off of the table, it became one tool amid a much more developed strategy, an evolution that was largely driven by the failure of brute force alone early in the movement.

PUTTING VELVET ON THE
HAMMER AFTER A SERIES
OF REPRESSION MISTAKES

From its point of formation, Occupy Oakland deliberately rejected negotiation with city officials and police and instead sought, and for a short period created, autonomous space in the heart of downtown. The rushed and poorly coordinated police raid and subsequent defense of the first evicted encampment, compounded by the willingness of those assembled on the evening of October 25 to withstand police violence, forged massive public support and a political opportunity that was quickly exploited with the call for a November 2nd General Strike. The following eviction would be part of a broader, coordinated, national raid in eighteen cities. With input from a variety of federal agencies (Homeland Security and Federal Bureau of Investigation) as well as private think tanks (the Police Executive Research Forum), the second encampment raid in Oakland was very different from the first. The strategy nationally was to mitigate potential political blowback as a result of police repression that could further movement mobilization. This was done largely by repeatedly emphasizing the necessity of eviction due to threats to public health and safety. Beyond supporting physical repression, a key element of this discourse of health and safety sought to make the idea of long-term occupations of public space infeasible, irresponsible, and unimaginable.

Occupy Oakland then saw numerous applications of various urban police tactics: The translation of various anti-gang techniques against the movement in the vigil raids and stay-away orders painted the movement as criminal, and the frequent arrests in the plaza served to heighten concerns of potential supporters. This criminalization was made all the more elaborate and stark in the weeks that led into the January 28, 2012, effort to occupy a vacant publicly owned building. Further efforts to divide the movement's base and smear Occupy Oakland continued through the winter and spring while unprincipled behavior within the movement pushed a now-shrinking movement to look inward, as it tried to hold on for a May 1 mass action that proved too small and fragmented for the movement to persist much beyond that point. The hasty but effective introduction of police training in more evolved crowd-control tactics on May 1 was perhaps more symbolic than necessary. Analogous to the general refashioning of social control against Occupy Oakland, on that day the movement was surrounded in a process of criminal quarantine, delegitimated by its failure to police itself through permits, and subsequently splintered and whittled down by police repression that divided and dispersed what was left of the movement. Overall, the repression of Occupy Oakland was enacted in such a way, and entwined with various efforts at criminalization, that to the passive observer it may have simply looked like an unintelligible melee.

Rather than portraying an all-powerful police force enacting a grand strategy from a master playbook, we see in this story several trials, errors, and outright failure—with varying political, legal, and financial costs for the city and police. The process of this evolution was sparked by the initial public backlash against police brutality, a factor that must be integrated into our understanding of social movements and their policing. The story of both the rise and fall of Occupy Oakland hinged upon a balance of legitimacy that sits within the dialectical relationship between policing tactics and protest tactics. There is never a situation, no matter how it may look and feel on the street, where demonstrations simply involve the police and the protesters. The two main trajectories in the story of Occupy Oakland—first, how the movement initially side-stepped the tacit repression of negotiation and was bolstered by subsequent hard repression after the first encampment raid; and later, how social control was regained through a deliberative and integrated mixture of hard and soft repression—both largely revolve around public support. It is important to understand how and why repression works, but it is equally important to look at the reasons why and how it can fail.

A core theme of this book has been the interrelation between movement tactics and policing tactics, how both seek to build off of their own previous successes, and how they both try to exploit political opportunities forged by the others' mistakes, weaknesses, or temporary inabilities. The policing and social control techniques applied to Occupy Oakland were a mixture of proactive and reactive responses to movement tactics—responses that, on the whole, became more effective over time against a waning movement. To understand this interrelationship of tactics and strategy we have to look at the broader social contexts in which they exist. For instance, Occupy Oakland, from its inception, was largely populated by seasoned militant activists who had prior experience in conflict with the OPD. In a different vein, the OPD and city officials' experience with gang injunctions allowed them to be able to functionally translate them to the challenges that Occupy presented. Successful movement activity is premised upon public support for the movement, whether this takes an active form of participation, more passive forms of voicing support in a conversation among coworkers or broaching the subject at dinner, or it may mean quietly donating to the bail fund online. The presence of support can ward off future repression, as it did in the weeks after October 25, while a lack of public support can leave the movement vulnerable to attack, as we saw on January 28. Whether in trying to understand the success of social movements or the triumph of repression, public support and the imparting of legitimacy to either forces of social control or the social movements trying to move through and beyond them are an essential, if complicated, variable that requires further examination.

LEGITIMACY AND SOCIAL CHANGE

What the history of Occupy Oakland highlights is that police repression does not operate in a social vacuum, and more importantly, hard repression does not always succeed. It is easy to conflate the process of police repression with its form—heavily weaponized and armored police in military formation determined to contain dissent and to incapacitate disruption and disorder. Repression is only successful if it succeeds at disrupting, dividing, and demobilizing movements—riot policing is only one facet of this. Public support and legitimacy are crucial to whether police repression is successful or not.

Both the success of protest, and alternately the policing of protest, hinge upon questions of tactics, strategies, and goals. As Lesley Wood notes, "Protesters, like police, struggle with questions of strategy and tactics, jockey for legitimacy and influence, and are constrained by their internalized logic, and the ongoing and shifting structure of the activist field" (2014, 43). Put very simply, social movement success is derived from disrupting the normal functioning of power and the modes of daily life that sustain and reproduce them (Piven 2006; Piven and Cloward 1977); the success of policing (broadly defined) involves the preservation of the existing order and its supporting sets of normative relations, obligations, and roles. A central component of either successful disruption or social control is popular support and legitimacy. Social movement legitimacy is quite different, often directly opposed, to that of the state or official institutions of existing power. Intrinsic to the process of substantial social change is a shift in what is seen as right, and who has the right to act and exert power in the social world. Part of the process of social movements and social change entails redefining roles and relationship—reconceptualizations of power that are inherently a redefinition of right and wrong. Legitimacy, ultimately, is about people choosing sides—whether they do that actively or passively, whether it is a determination made consciously or unconsciously, or whether the existing state of affairs is tacitly supported by apathy. The public's choice to support the goals and ambitions of the police, city administrators, or the press—or to side with the movement—is an often unstated but essential ingredient in the success of either social movements or repression efforts.

Legitimacy is not about pursuing a political or tactical lowest common denominator, where disruptiveness becomes vulgar and impolite. Legitimacy is also not about remaining mired in the politics of respectability—where powerful actors paternalistically define appropriate modes of conduct and speech by retaining a phalanx of riot police for those that lack the appropriate self-control. First among themselves, and then to the public, movements must begin to redefine the moral grounds upon which protest and repression take place. Protest is too often defined by the script of negotiated management provided by a velvet glove, promulgating a tired theatrical performance, while the riot cops clench the hook of strategic incapacitation with an iron fist, lingering behind the curtain for anyone who sings out of tune or goes off script.

Significant social change intrinsically involves the reordering or dismantling of dominant social structures, relations, and associated roles toward the formation of new political and economic arrangements, with accompanying new ways of relating to each other. In Gramscian terms, this is the pursuit of a new hegemony—a new set of dominant ideas and social practices derived from a new political, economic, and cultural order. If non-reformist movements are to be successful they need to delegitimate the structures and relations they seek to change and those that defend them, while bolstering their own power and bases of support and growth.

The Paradox of Social Control and the Conundrum of Movement Disruptiveness

The Paradox of Social Control

Every movement and specific protest is different; one should be wary of theoretical models presented as immutable, or the reduction of complex social change processes to basic physics equations. Nevertheless, there exist persistent tensions within protest policing (as well as protest itself) that can momentarily or periodically foster opportunities for social movements. The paradox of social control, put most simply, is that physical repression (state violence) against social movements can (and in the case of Occupy Oakland did) lead to popular blowback and the further mobilization of the movement, rather than the intended containment and demobilization. Quite often, repression needs to not only "work" tactically, but it needs to be seen as something other than repression. The 1960s-era crisis of legitimacy ushered in an era of cooptive negotiation and prompted more strategic and better-trained and -equipped policing, if and when they became necessary. Both of these changes were prompted by movement militancy and a crisis of legitimacy that highlighted the endemic, if usually latent, risks involved in the use of violence against social movements.

A central element in the refashioning of repression by city officials, the mainstream press, and the police in Oakland from November 2011 to May 2012 was in successfully portraying repression as something other than what it was—the protection of public health and safety, an obligation to maintain public order, or the simple policing of depoliticized criminal conduct. By making the camps seem dirty and dangerous, by highlighting Occupiers who had previous criminal records, or through generally portraying Occupy Oakland as the "bad seed" of the Occupy movement, the movement ceased to be a movement, and political repression became simple law enforcement. Basically, effective repression legitimates itself while delegitimating its target. In relation to the public and legitimacy, this is connected to broader forms of governmentality and discipline through which these soft repression efforts resonate and persuade. The criminalization of disruption as a threat to security, health, safety, and profits is perhaps more of an effective barrier to social change than the most militarized and surveillance-savvy policing that could be developed. This is the object of soft repression—to produce manageable forms of dissent so that force is not needed.

The Conundrum of Movement Disruptiveness

The disruptiveness that is both essential to social change and largely shunned and demonized by people not only outside, but often inside, social movements is another inherent tension in relation to protest and social control. Normative negotiated management, which includes, but goes beyond, the formal negotiation of permits between protesters and police, has instilled the idea that protest should be predictable, polite, and respectable to those being protested against. It would be a mistake to trace the genealogy of this tendency to the formation of the negotiation model in the 1970s (Mitchell 2003), but the expectation of negotiation has certainly been furthered and legitimated by the decades in which it was dominant, shaping the past (the "myth of non-disruptive change" from chapter 6) but also the present, and potentially the future. Colloquially, this takes the form of debates over "violence"—which itself is usually referring to property destruction or failure to obey police commands. Despite the very debatable (and highly debated) conceptualization of what constitutes violence, this narrowing of the terms and scope of the discussion obscures more than it illuminates. It is not so much violence but disruption that produces either external criminalization (in terms of soft repression) or internal divisions within movements over tactics. Although disruption includes physical confrontations between protesters and police and between protesters and inanimate objects such as windows and dumpsters, it is obviously broader than that. Disruption is defined by Francis Fox Piven (2006) as, simply: "the activation of interdependent power," adding that "protest movements are significant because they mobilize disruptive power" (20). Disruption always involves bodily risk because it disturbs the existing social arrangements

and orders, relationships that the police are charged with preserving—quite often through force. It is commonly the case that
the argument used against street militants is that they prompt
(and are therefore directly responsible for) movement repression.[1]
This begins a circular argument of who and what causes violence—protesters or police—while it is quite often the case that
the parties involved are still debating the definition of violence
itself. Questions of strategy, already complex and muddled by
the nature of largely open mass movements, are rarely addressed
within these conversations overshadowed by the threat of police
force and expectations of protest comportment instilled by (the
legacy of) negotiation. Impression management and concerns
with public perception and legitimacy should not be (allowed to
be) excuses for the avoidance of risk in this process of pursuing
disruption and change.

COUNTER-CONDUCT:
BEYOND MISBEHAVING

The story told in this text has drawn extensively on Michel
Foucault's concept of governmentality because it provides a
framework for understanding repression that provides sufficient
scope, depth, and specificity. The distinction between hard and
soft repression has also been used throughout, though I have
hoped to illustrate how the two are mutually constituted—that
every expression of soft repression carries with it the threat
of physical force, while every act of hard repression is imbued
with normative definitions of justice and right. While the story
of Occupy Oakland presents a vibrant reminder that repression
does not always work, that the overwhelming advantages the state
holds in relation to the deployment of brute force can also serve
to its detriment, the narrative of this movement also outlines in
developed (though not exhaustive) fashion the breadth of social
control and the range of forces and factors that serve to contain,
discredit, divide, and disrupt social movements.

Going back to Max Weber's conceptualization of power (1946, 77–90), or even further back to Niccolo Machiavelli's (1961, 67–76) understanding of politics, or to Sun Tzu (1971, 64), there has been a clear appreciation that political power was premised upon a combination of force and persuasion (or coercion), with persuasion being a more stable form of control than brute force. Following from this, the extent to which institutions and social orders can be made to seem natural and legitimate will provide for even more stable social relations. Foucault, probably more persistently than any other theorist, emphasized that power in the contemporary world is embodied and exercised in what people do (human activity), rather than just in institutionalized structures of unidirectional coercion and domination. Analogous to Karl Marx's demystification of the economy, illustrating how economic power (wealth) did not derive from money or machines or the abstract magic of market exchanges, but from human activity, human labor, so too does Foucault's conception of power seek to demystify social relations and social order, and thus also highlight how social order can be unmade or reconstituted.

The factors that determine the transformative potential of movements, and the actors who comprise them, should be seen in light of (and in spite of) the full spectrum of repressive forces seeking to undermine movements, including the conceptions movement actors may carry in their own heads: "The strategic adversary is fascism . . . the fascism in us all, in our heads and in our everyday behavior, the fascism that causes us to love power, to desire the very thing that dominates and exploits us" (Foucault, quoted in Rimke 2011, 201). Understanding that people are products of their environment and lived experiences—subject to the persistence of hegemonic ideas and values, rules and roles—the unmaking of the existing social order toward a dramatically different world can seem daunting, if not impossible. Occupy was one of many recent movements struggling to put into practice and advance a new society forged from below rather than imposed from above. This arduous process will need to be informed by a broader and adequately expansive definition of repression and power—both in terms of overcoming the efforts of dominant social groups to dismantle movements and in reconceiving power in order to effectively constitute it in a new society.

Truly successful movements, movements that can withstand the broad spectrum of repressive mechanisms (partially) outlined in the previous pages, are those that go beyond objecting to or revolting against power, but are fundamentally orientated toward becoming their own power. Movements engaged in counterconduct do not act against existing power, but are actively expressing their own power—surely encountering confrontations, but confrontations in which the terms of the conflict are not constrained within existing relationships and forms of governmentality—of regulated and structured modes of behavior and conduct. Conflicts waged on the terrain and within the logic of governmentality invariably validate the authority the movements seek to challenge (i.e., negotiating with a police force actively threatening to physically harm you; heeding to political arguments about the economic costs being incurred by the movement on neoliberal city governments or capital). "Politics is no more or less than that which is born with resistance to governmentality, the first uprising, the first confrontation" (Foucault 2007, 390).

THE TENTS ARE GONE, BUT THE STAKES REMAIN LAID

Perhaps what the Occupy Oakland camps provided, even more so than any mass protest or street militancy, was a living, functioning community of rebellion that went beyond demanding redress for grievances but proactively defined itself as its own authority and conceived itself as a springboard for solutions. Geographically situated at the intersection of commerce and government, the camps were emblematic of more than protest against certain social outcomes, but a refusal to participate in the dominant social orders. Occupy Oakland put forward a prefigurative politics in practice, inside and beyond the camps, not a commune seeking to avoid power somewhere in the California redwoods, but to militantly confront it while attempting to construct its own. As Foucault put it, this is a process of political contestation, social transformation, and deliberative action: "There must be a moment when, breaking all the bonds of obedience, the population will really have the right, not in juridical terms, but in terms of essential and fundamental rights, to break any bonds of obedience it has with the state and, rising up against it, to say: My law, the law of my own requirements, the law of my very nature as population, the law of my basic needs, must replace the rules of obedience" (Foucault 2007, 356).

Ultimately, the ability to move beyond the various barriers of repression and social control lies neither in finding a more palatable way to object to the foot on your neck, nor in a process of becoming more of a "bad" protester. It ultimately lies in movements having the collective power, themselves, to define "good" and "bad"—the power to articulate their own vision of a social order (or at least the nature of social relationships) and determine who and what is a transgressive against the new norms and orders that movement is in the process of building. Occupy Oakland, and the Occupy movement generally, attempted this, if only in a fragmented way and for a brief period of time. Withstanding and overcoming the existing interconnected mechanisms of hard and soft repression, of which police repression is only the clearest and most pronounced example, will not be an easy or straightforward process. Why would it be otherwise?

Notes

Chapter 1   The Commune by the Bay

1. "Bay of Rage: Anticut #2 Mobile Disruption for Libraries, Oakland, 6/17/11: photos, 1 of 2," *IndyBay*, June 18, 2011, http://www.indybay.org/newsitems/2011/06/18/18682186.php.
2. Jane Hamsher, "List of Active Occupy Encampments Across the Country—Now at 61," *Firedoglake*, December 20, 2011, http://fdlaction.firedoglake.com/2011/12/20/list-of-active-occupy-encampments-across-the-country-now-at-61/.
3. Occupy Oakland General Assembly, "General Assembly Resolutions (Oct 10–Nov 16 Summary)," October 10, 2011, https://occupyoakland.org/2011/11/general-assembly-resolutions/.
4. These initial decisions and similar decisions not to negotiate with the city or police passed with more than 90% support at General Assemblies. The experiences of many Oakland Occupiers in the recent student Occupation movements in the University of California system as well as in the Justice for Oscar Grant Movement provided a widespread though not universal common sense against negotiating with city officials or the police, discussed further in chapter 2.
5. Mayer Zald defines social control as "the process by which individuals, groups, and organizations attempt to make performance, the behavior and operation of other groups, organizations, and individuals, conform to standards of behavior or normative preferences" (in Boykoff 2007a, 12). In this book, social control is the objective of various forms of repression and is a general category that can take very different forms.
6. Jesse McKinley and Malia Wollan, "Outrage Over Veteran Injured at 'Occupy' Protest," *New York Times*, October 27, 2011, http://www.nytimes.com/2011/10/28/us/veterans-injury-at-occupy-protest-prompts-outrage.html?_r=0.
7. Emergency Operations Center, "OPD Enforces 'Notice of Violations and Demand to Cease Violations' in Frank Ogawa Plaza," October 25, 2011, www2.Oaklandnet.com/oakca/groups/ceda/documents/.../oak031901.pdf.

8. "Occupy Oakland Burns the Mayor's Demands," *not yet dead nyc*,
    https://readthenothing.wordpress.com/tag/occupy-oakland-burn
    -mayors-letter/.
9. The Riders were a group of Oakland police officers who were found
    to have kidnapped, planted evidence on, and beaten city residents
    in custody. Henry Lee, "'Riders Lied, Brutalized Man, Ex-Rookie
    Testifies / Whistle-Blower Says He Feared Losing Job by Coming
    Forward," *San Francisco Chronicle*, December 14, 2004, http://www
    .sfgate.com/bayarea/article/OAKLAND-Riders-lied-brutalized
    -man-2629441.php.
10. Source: declassified email exchanges between city officials and OPD.
    Daniel Willis and Thomas Peele, "In Their Own Words: Occupy
    Oakland According to City Officials—Part 1," *Oakland Tribune*,
    February 25, 2012, http://www.mercurynews.com/top-stories/ci
    _20030387.
11. Marcus Wohlsen, "Occupy Oakland Raided by Police," *Huffington
    Post*, October 25, 2011, http://www.huffingtonpost.com/2011/10
    /25/occupy-oakland-raided-by-police_n_1030603.html.
12. Ibid.
13. "Mutual aid" refers to the process by which a city requests and
    receives officers from surrounding jurisdictions for a specific time
    and purpose. In Oakland, this meant that on some occasions (such as
    October 25), the riot police on the street came from OPD but also
    from surrounding cities and towns, area colleges, and the California
    Highway Patrol.
14. Matthai Kuruvila, Justin Berton, and Demian Bulwa, "Police Tear
    Gas Occupy Oakland Protesters," *San Francisco Chronicle*, October
    25, 2011, http://www.sfgate.com/bayarea/article/Police-tear-gas
    -Occupy-Oakland-protesters-2325544.php.
15. Frazier Group LLC, "Independent Investigation: Occupy Oakland
    Response (October 25, 2011)," June 14, 2012, www2.Oaklandnet
    .com/oakca1/groups/.../documents/.../oak036236.pdf.
16. Jesse McKinley and Malia Wollan, "Outrage Over Veteran Injured at
    'Occupy' Protest," *New York Times*, October 27, 2011, http://www
    .nytimes.com/2011/10/28/us/veterans-injury-at-occupy-protest
    -prompts-outrage.html?_r=0.
17. Ishaan Tharoor, "Straight Out of Cairo: Tahrir Square Shows Solidar-
    ity with Occupy Oakland," *Time*, October 28, 2011, http://world
    .time.com/2011/10/28/straight-out-of-cairo-tahrir-square-shows
    -solidarity-with-occupy-oakland/.
18. Jason Kessler, "Occupy Oakland's General Strike Call: 'Shut Down
    the 1%,'" *CNN*, November 1, 2011, http://money.cnn.com/2011/11
    /01/news/economy/occupy_oakland_general_strike/index.htm.
19. Associated Press, "Oakland Police Arrest about 300 Occupy Protest-
    ers," *USA Today*, January 28, 2012, http://usatoday30.usatoday.com

/news/nation/story/2012–01–28/occupy-oakland-protests
/52852280/1. Overall, 408 people were arrested that day.Yael
Chanoff,"Hearing Today on Bizarre Occupy Oakland Stay-Away
Order Case," *San Francisco Bay Guardian*, February 10, 2012, http://
www.sfbg.com/politics/2012/02/10/hearing-today-bizarre-occupy
-oakland-stay-away-order-case.

20. In this context, criminalization refers to the ability of repressive
actors to define and portray groups or entire social movements as
primarily a criminal threat to be contained, usually through force.
See Starr, Fernandez, and Scholl 2011, 94–96.

21. Interpellation refers to the process through which state ideologies
and definitions are materialized through the discrete practices of
state subjects in relation to subaltern bodies. See Althusser 2001,
117–120.

Chapter 2   From Permits to Storm Troopers

Direct quotes as well as the logic of this argument were previously published in the following article: Mike King,"Disruption Is Not Permitted:
The Policing and Social Control of Occupy Oakland," *Critical Criminology*
21, 4 (2013b): 463–475.

1. While there are several potential problems with the data, such as
underreporting of aggressive policing in later years as well as changes
in the nature of protests (as Soule and Davenport 2009 note), or the
social status of those protesting or various forms of oversight over
police abuse, the basic shift in policing that McPhail, Schweingruber,
and McCarthy 1998 outline is accurate.

2. Tikkun Daily,"Oakland Police Trained Alongside Bahrain Military
and Israeli Forces Prior to Violent Occupy Oakland Raid," *Alternet*,
December 4, 2011, http://www.alternet.org/speakeasy/2011/12
/04/prior-to-violent-occupy-oakland-raid-opd-trained-alongside
-bahrain-military-and-israeli-border-forces.

3. (1) Police control of physical space. (2) Preemptive and aggressive
policing. (3) Targeted arrests and use of less than lethal weapons.
(4) Surveillance.

4. To say that repression is "normalized" is to say that it is rooted in
social relationships and roles that are taken for granted, rarely ques-
tioned, and viewed as natural or at least difficult to alter. Durkheim's
discussion of how social norms affect behavior helps clarify:"Thus
the necessity with which the categories press themselves upon us is
not merely the effect of habits whose yoke we could slip with little
effort; nor is that necessity a habit or a physical or metaphysical need,
since the categories change with place and time; it is a special sort of
moral necessity that is to intellectual life what obligation is to will"
([1912] 1995, 17).

CHAPTER 3   THE OAKLAND COMMUNE,
POLICE VIOLENCE, AND POLITICAL OPPORTUNITY

1. In many cities, such as Las Vegas, Seattle, and Detroit, permits were taken out for their camps at one point in time.
2. Occupy Oakland, "General Assembly Resolutions (October 10–November 16 Summary)," November 17, 2011, https://occupyoakland.org/2011/11/general-assembly-resolutions/.
3. Earlier US movements that utilized occupation as a tactic are varied: the Flint Sit Down Strike of 1936–37; the student occupations at NYU in 1968; the American Indian Movement occupation of Alcatraz from 1969 to 1971; and more recent student occupations at the New School in NYC, UC Berkeley, and UC Santa Cruz.
4. An email conversation between various Oakland city officials, the mayor's office, and police officials (made available through a Freedom of Information Act request) reveals how various key state decision makers made sense of the first Occupy Oakland encampment. Daniel Willis and Thomas Peele, "In Their Own Words: Occupy Oakland According to City Officials—Part 1," *Oakland Tribune*, February 25, 2012, http://www.mercurynews.com/top-stories/ci_20030387.
5. Ibid.
6. Ibid.
7. Many of the political issues raised by Occupy were similar to the Alterglobalization movement, which had grown to be a mass movement in North America with the Seattle World Trade Organization protests in 1999 and persisted strongly until 2003. Both movements shared a general rejection of neoliberal governance and the social inequality that it perpetuated, along with an understanding that these politics and policies were endemic to contemporary governance across political parties. However, the tactics and focus were quite different. Where the Alterglobalization movement revolved around economic summits and annual meetings of organizations like the World Bank and International Monetary Fund, spending months before it planning for a major convergence that would be over in a few days, with little ongoing local organizing taking place in many locations. A slogan of that movement had been "think globally, act locally," but for many involved we felt as though we were chasing the global elite around the world where they met behind walls of steel and phalanxes of riot police. Protests against trade agreements like NAFTA or organizations like the World Trade Organization or International Monetary Fund could have had a broader public resonance, but the public remained largely ignorant of even the most general of trends and issues related to globalization—with multinational trade agreements and economic policies largely shrouded in the simple and misleading generalizations offered by politicians and the media. The movement in the United States was largely subsumed by the

Anti–Iraq War movement, which began in the fall of 2003, before the war had begun.

8. Matt Bieber, "Harvard Kennedy School's Marshall Ganz Talks About Occupy Wall Street," *The Citizen*, November 18, 2011, http://www .hks.harvard.edu/news-events/news/articles/ganz-interview. Also see Maeckelbergh 2012; Sitrin 2006; and also the critique and contextual discussion of horizontalism in Ciccariello-Maher 2013.

9. Matthew Cooper, "Poll: Most Americans Support Occupy Wall Street," *The Atlantic*, October 19, 2011, http://www.theatlantic.com /politics/archive/2011/10/poll-most-americans-support-occupy -wall-street/246963/.

10. Source: declassified email exchanges between city officials and OPD. Daniel Willis and Thomas Peele, "In Their Own Words: Occupy Oakland According to City Officials—Part 1," *Oakland Tribune*, February 25, 2012, http://www.mercurynews.com/top-stories/ci _20030387.

11. Ibid.

12. Phillip Matier and Andrew Ross, "Jean Quan, Oakland's New Mayor, Gets Car Booted," *San Francisco Chronicle*, November 24, 2010, http://www.sfgate.com/bayarea/matier-ross/article/Jean-Quan -Oakland-s-new-mayor-gets-car-booted-3164530.php.

13. Source: declassified email exchanges between city officials and OPD. Willis and Peele, "In Their Own Words."

14. Ibid.

15. Ibid.

16. Ibid.

17. Ibid.

18. Ibid.

19. Matthai Kuruvila, "Occupy Oakland: Jean Quan 'I Don't Know Everything,'" *San Francisco Chronicle*, October 26, 2011, http://www .sfgate.com/bayarea/article/Occupy-Oakland-Jean-Quan-I-don-t -know-2325178.php#photo-1832226.

20. There were cases of sexual assault, an instance where an occupier fell and hurt himself, and one case of a dog biting a member of the media who had been accused of filming inside people's tents and had been asked to leave.

21. Willis and Peele, "In Their Own Words."

22. Chip Johnson, "Occupy Oakland Demonstration Has Taken Ugly Turn," *San Francisco Chronicle*, October 21, 2011, http://www.sfgate .com/bayarea/johnson/article/Occupy-Oakland-demonstration-has -taken-ugly-turn-2326629.php.

23. Oakland Police Department Briefing, "Occupy Oakland—Frank Ogawa Plaza BF01–2011–0007," October 25, 2011 [copy in author's possession].

24. Emergency Operations Center, "OPD Enforces 'Notice of Violations and Demand to Cease Violations' in Frank Ogawa Plaza," *City of*

Oakland, October 25, 2011, www2.Oaklandnet.com/oakca/groups /ceda/documents/…/oak031901.pdf.

25. Oakland Police Department Briefing, "Occupy Oakland—Frank Ogawa Plaza BF01–2011–0007," *City of Oakland*, October 25, 2011 [copy in author's possession]; Oakland Police Department Operations Plan, "Occupy Oakland—Phase 1 BF01-XX," October 25, 2011 (declassified document) [copy in author's possession]; Oakland Police Department Operations Plan. "Occupy Oakland—Phase 2 BF01-XX," October 25, 2011 (declassified document) [copy in author's possession].

26. City of Oakland—City Administrator's Office, "Attention to Persons Staying Overnight in Frank Ogawa Plaza (Date: October 21, 2011)—Notice of Violations and Demand to Cease Violations," October 21, 2011, https://www.indybay.org/uploads/2011/10/21 /occupyoakland_arrestwarning_oak031873.pdf.

27. Kevin Fagan and Matthai Kuruvila, "Oakland Council Acts to Sink Occupy Port Blockades," *San Francisco Chronicle*, December 20, 2011, http://www.sfgate.com/bayarea/article/Oakland-council-acts-to -sink-Occupy-port-blockades-2413201.php.

28. Aaron Sankin, "Oakland Police Only Weeks Away from Being Placed into Federal Receivership," *Huffington Post*, January 27, 2012, http:// www.huffingtonpost.com/2012/01/27/oakland-police-department _n_1237785.html.

29. Ibid.

30. Lee Romney and Maria L. La Ganga, "Occupy Oakland: Thousands of Protesters Rally at Port," *Los Angeles Times*, November 2, 2011, http://articles.latimes.com/2011/nov/02/local/la-mew-occupy -oakland-march-to-port-mobile.

31. Oakland Police Department, "Occupy Oakland General Strike: BF01–2011–0009," November 2, 2011 [copy in author's possession].

32. Gavin Aronsen, "Report: Aggressive Police Response to Occupy Oakland Was 'Flawed,'" *Mother Jones*, June 15, 2012, http://www .motherjones.com/mojo/2012/06/occupy-oakland-police-response -report.

CHAPTER 4   LEGITIMATING REPRESSION
THROUGH DEPOLITICIZING IT

1. City of Oakland Press Release, October 27, 2011 [copy in author's possession].

2. Leo Romney and Associated Press Business Staff, "Patience Tested Over Waste, Crime at Wall Street Protest Sites," Associated Press, October 25, 2011, http://www.cleveland.com/business/index.ssf /2011/10/patience_tested_over_waste_cri.html; CNN News-wire, "Cities Struggle to Deal with Occupy Movement," CNN,

November 15, 2011, http://www.cnn.com/2011/11/14/us/occupy
-movement.

3. Source: declassified email exchanges between city officials and OPD.
    Daniel Willis and Thomas Peele, "In Their Own Words: Occupy
    Oakland According to City Officials—Part 1," *Oakland Tribune*, Feb-
    ruary 25, 2012.

4. Ian Oxnevad, "The Occupy Movement: Rising Anarchy," *Home-
    land Security Today*, April 3, 2012, http://www.hstoday.us/columns
    /guest-commentaries/blog/the-occupy-movement-rising-anarchy
    /3a87bb57b44e5779f7d087472df92af2.html.

5. Willis and Peele, "In Their Own Words." Romney and Associated
    Press Business Staff, "Patience Tested Over Waste, Crime at Wall
    Street Protest Sites."

6. Willis and Peele, "In Their Own Words."

7. The only major police action on the day of the November 2 Gen-
    eral Strike was that evening when Occupy Oakland participants
    temporarily occupied a shuttered homeless services building around
    the corner from the camp. "'Occupy Oakland' Protesters, Police
    Standoff," ABC News, November 3, 2011, http://abclocal.go.com
    /kgo/story?section=news/local/east_bay&id=8415827.

8. Matthew Cooper, "Poll: Most Americans Support Occupy Wall
    Street," *The Atlantic*, October 19, 2011, http://www.theatlantic.com
    /politics/archive/2011/10/poll-most-americans-support-occupy
    -wall-street/246963/.

9. While some Occupy sites took out permits (i.e., Las Vegas, Seattle,
    and Detroit) or otherwise engaged in tactics of negotiated manage-
    ment with police and city officials, for the most part the camps were
    not negotiated, presenting problems for forces of social control. Oak-
    land, probably more than any other site, was defined by a hegemonic
    revolutionary, anticapitalist politics and had a clear rejection of nego-
    tiated management (no permits, no negotiation with city officials, no
    police allowed in the camp, etc.).

10. Rina Palta, "Q&A: Mayor Quan Talks about Occupy Oakland
    Sweep," The Informant—KALW News, November 15, 2011, http://
    informant.kalwnews.org/2011/11/qa-mayor-quan-talks-about
    -occupy-oakland-sweep/.

11. Associated Press, "Mayors Talk Strategy on Occupy Protests," CBS
    News, November 15, 2011, http://www.washingtonsblog.com/2011
    /11/department-of-homeland-security-adviser-helped-coordinate
    -police-crackdowns-on-protests-in-18-cities.html; Rick Ellis,
    "Update: 'Occupy' Crackdowns Coordinated with Federal Law
    Enforcement Officials," *Minneapolis Examiner*, November 15, 2011,
    http://www.examiner.com/article/update-occupy-crackdowns
    -coordinated-with-federal-law-enforcement-officials; "Depart-
    ment of Homeland Security Adviser Helped Coordinate Police

Crackdowns on Protest in 18 Cities," *Washington's Blog*, November 29, 2011, http://www.washingtonsblog.com/2011/11/department -of-homeland-security-adviser-helped-coordinate-police -crackdowns-on-protests-in-18-cities.html.

12. Dominic Rushe, "Occupy Wall Street: NYPD Attempt Media Blackout at Zuccotti Park," *The Guardian*, November 15, 2011, http:// www.theguardian.com/world/2011/nov/15/occupy-journalists -media-blackout; Elizabeth Flocke, "At Occupy L.A. Eviction, Police Restrict Media Coverage," *Washington Post*, November 30, 2011, http://www.washingtonpost.com/blogs/blogpost/post/at -occupy-la-eviction-police-restrict-media-coverage/2011/11/30 /gIQAlWqGDO_blog.html.

13. Simone Wilson, "Occupy L.A. Eviction: Is LAPD Restricting Coverage with Last-Minute 'Pool Media'?" *L.A. Weekly*, November 30, 2011, http://blogs.laweekly.com/informer/2011/11/occupy_la _eviction_lapd_pool_media.php.

14. Christopher Robins, "Justice Dept: Homeland Security Advised Raids On Occupy Wall Street Camps," *Gothamist*, November 16, 2011, http://gothamist.com/2011/11/16/justice_dept_official_raids _of_occu.php.

15. Shawn Gaynor, "The Cop Group Coordinating the Occupy Crackdowns," *San Francisco Bay Guardian*, November 19, 2011, http://www .sfbg.com/politics/2011/11/18/cop-group-coordinating-occupy -crackdowns.

16. Democracy Now! "Former Seattle Police Chief Norm Stamper on Paramilitary Policing from WTO to Occupy Wall Street," *Democracy Now!* November 17, 2011, http://www.democracynow.org/2011/11 /17/paramilitary_policing_of_occupy_wall_street.

17. Jess Bidgood, Dan Frosch, and Malia Wollan, "Other Occupy Sites Hope N.Y. Raid Energizes Movement," *New York Times*, November 15, 2011, http://www.nytimes.com/2011/11/16/us/other-occupy -sites-hope-ny-raid-energizes-movement.html?_r=2&pagewanted= all?src=tp&.

18. Jason Cherkis, "Occupy Wall Street Monitored by U.S. Conference of Mayors, Emails Show," *Huffington Post*, January 25, 2012, http://www .huffingtonpost.com/2012/01/25/occupy-wall-street-us-conference -of-mayors_n_1232080.html.

19. Ibid.

20. Jason Leopold, "DHS Turns Over Occupy Wall Street Documents to Truthout," *Truthout.org*, March 20, 2012, http://truth-out.org/news /item/8012-dhs-turns-over-occupy-wall-street-documents-to-truthout.

21. Ibid.

22. Rina Palta, "Mayor Quan Talks about Occupy Oakland Sweep," The Informant/KALW News, November 15, 2011, http://informant .kalwnews.org/tag/jean-quan/.

23. Bidgood, Frosch, and Wollan, "Other Occupy Sites Hope N.Y. Raid Energizes Movement."

24. Associated Press, "Occupy Protests Face New Issue in Deaths," *USA Today*, November 12, 2011, http://usatoday30.usatoday.com/news /nation/story/2011–11–11/occupy-deaths/51164980/1.

25. Camps persisted into December and beyond in cities such as Atlanta, Miami, Providence, Madison, Pittsburgh, San Jose, and Houston. Jane Hamsher, "List of Active Occupy Encampments Across the Country—Now at 61," Firedoglake, December 20, 2011, http://fdlaction .firedoglake.com/2011/12/20/list-of-active-occupy-encampments -across-the-country-now-at-61/.

26. Ilyse Hogue, "Occupy Is Dead! Long Live Occupy!" *The Nation*, March 14, 2012, http://www.thenation.com/article/166826/occupy -dead-long-live-occupy#.

27. "Shooting Victim Is Tied to Occupy Oakland," *Los Angeles Times*, November 13, 2011, http://latimesblogs.latimes.com/lanow/2011 /11/shooting-victim-tied-to-occupy-oakland.html.

28. Amanda Stupi, "Oakland Mayor Jean Quan on Crime, Occupy an A's Stadium . . . and More Crime," KQED News, March 18, 2014, http://ww2.kqed.org/news/2014/03/18/oakland-mayor-jean-quan -on-crime-occupy-an-as-stadium-and-more-crime.

29. CNN Newswire, "Cities Struggle to Deal with Occupy Movement," CNN, November 14, 2011, http://www.cnn.com/2011/11/14/us /occupy-movement.

30. Ibid.

31. John Ingold, "Suit Accuses Denver Officials of Violating Occupy Protesters' Rights," *Denver Post*, November 23, 2011, http://www .denverpost.com/portal/commented/ci_19395849?source= commented-&_loopback=1.

32. James Barron and Colin Moynihan, "City Reopens Park After Protesters Are Evicted," *New York Times*, November 15, 2011, http:// www.nytimes.com/2011/11/16/nyregion/police-begin-clearing -zuccotti-park-of-protesters.html?_r=0.

33. Associated Press, "NYC Police Clear 'Occupy Wall St.' Camp," CBS News, November 15, 2011, http://www.cbsnews.com/news/nyc -police-clear-occupy-wall-st-camp/.

34. Natalie DiBlasio, "'Occupy' Camps in NYC, Elsewhere Face Public-Safety Closures," *USA Today*, November 15, 2011, http:// usatoday30.usatoday.com/news/nation/story/2011–11–14/ occupy-protest-public-safety/51202232/1.

35. Hogue, "Occupy Is Dead! Long Live Occupy!"; Media Matters Staff, "Bill O'Reilly: The Occupy Movement Is 'a Failure,' 'Dead,' 'Finished,'" *Media Matters*, November 16, 2011, http://mediamatters .org/video/2011/11/16/bill-oreilly-the-occupy-movement-is-a -failure-d/183935.

36. George Avalos, "Oakland Merchants Say Sales Slump by Half Amid Occupy Protests," *Oakland Tribune*, November 8, 2011, http://www .mercurynews.com/real-estate/ci_19292499?sour.

37. Ibid.

38. David Chang, "Tensions Grow at Occupy Philly Camp," NBC 10 Philadelphia, November 14, 2011, http://www.nbcphiladelphia.com/ news/local/Nutter-Occupy-Philly-Has-Changed—133772833.html.

39. Weeks after Quan's condemnation of Occupy's supposed effect on jobs in the city, the City of Oakland gave layoff notices to 2,500 city workers. Jennifer Inez Ward, "Oakland Hands Out Layoff Notices to 2500 City Workers," *Oakland Local*, January 19, 2012, http:// oaklandlocal.com/article/oakland-hands-out-layoff-notices-2500 -city-workers.

   In Philadelphia, the same holds true, with the Philadelphia School District announcing the elimination of almost 4,000 jobs just months before Occupy started. Teresa Masterson, "Philly School District Plans 3,820 Job Cuts," NBC 10 Philadelphia, June 3, 2011, http:// www.nbcphiladelphia.com/news/local/Philly-School-District-Plans -3820-Job-Cuts-120809839.html.

40. City of Oakland—Office of the City Administrator, "City of Oakland Releases Preliminary Cost Estimates for Occupy Oakland Response," November 4, 2011, http://www2.0aklandnet.com/oakca /groups/cityadministrator/documents/pressrelease/oak032069.pdf.

41. Noel Randewich and Dan Levine, "Police Clear Out Occupy Oakland Protest Camp," Reuters, November 14, 2011, http:// www.reuters.com/article/2011/11/14/us-protests-oakland -idUSTRE7AD14Q20111114.

42. "Emails between Oakland Officials Reveal Tensions During Occupy," KTVU, January 13, 2011.

43. Jonathan Simon, "Governing the Occupy Movement Through Crime," *Berkeley Blog*, November 15, 2011, http://blogs.berkeley.edu /2011/11/15/governing-the-occupy-movement-through-crime/.

44. Dakota Smith, "City of L.A. May Be Liable for Occupy Camp," *Los Angeles Times*, November 9, 2011, http://www.contracostatimes.com /california/ci_19294569.

45. Matt Flegenheimer, "A Petri Dish of Activism, and Germs," *New York Times*, November 10, 2011, http://www.nytimes.com/2011/11 /11/nyregion/for-occupy-wall-street-health-is-a-growing-concern .html?_r=0.

46. Sean Maher, "Rats and Drugs Mar Occupy Oakland Tent City, Officials Say," *Oakland Tribune*, October 18, 2011, http://www .mercurynews.com/bay-area-news/ci_19139574.

47. Will Cane, "Public Health Says Occupy SF Camp Is Dirty, Unsafe," *San Francisco Chronicle*, October 26, 2011, http://blog.sfgate.com /cityinsider/2011/10/26/public-health-officials-say-occupy-sf-camp -is-dirty-unsafe/?tsp=1.

48. James Barron and Colin Moynihan, "Police Oust Occupy Wall Street Protesters at Zuccotti Park," *New York Times*, November 15, 2011, http://www.nytimes.com/2011/11/16/nyregion/police-begin -clearing-zuccotti-park-of-protesters.html?pagewanted=all&_r=0.

49. Kacey Montoya, "Health Concerns Growing at Occupy Portland," KOIN Local 6 (TV), November 1, 2011, http://www.koinloca16 .com/news/local/story/Health-concerns-growing-at-Occupy -Portland/m18kBVlXRUSqFP8N00qC3g.cspx.

50. Ateqah Khaki, "Yesterday's Occupy Wall Street Evacuation: Protecting Public Health or Endangering It?" American Civil Liberties Union, November 16, 2011, http://www.aclu.org/blog/free-speech /yesterdays-occupy-wall-street-evacuation-protecting-public-health -or-endangering-it.

51. Washington, DC's Department of Health director said the following about the Occupy DC camp: "'Going down to these camps, it's no different than refugee camps,' Akhter said. 'People are living in very primitive conditions and they're doing it by choice. They are very brave and thoughtful people, but my concern is that they should also take care of themselves. When the weather goes bad suddenly we're watching a tragedy unfold in the middle of Washington, D.C.'" Martin Austermuhle, "D.C. Health Director Compares Occupy D.C. to Refugee Camp," *DCist*, January 9, 2012, http://dcist.com/2012 /01/dc_health_director_compares_occupy.php.

52. The Oakland Coliseum has recently announced plans to install facial recognition cameras for major events. Ali Winston, "Sheriff Sought Controversial Surveillance Software," *East Bay Express*, March 6, 2013, http://www.eastbayexpress.com/oakland/sheriff-sought -controversial-surveillance-software/Content?oid=3480918.

53. City of Oakland, City Administrator's Office, "Notice of Violations and Demand to Cease Violations," November 11, 2011.

54. Police officers' Bills of Rights (in states like California) and the persistent power of police unions shield officers from accountability and help police departments command a greater share of city budgets.

CHAPTER 5   PUTTING THE
OCCUPY OAKLAND VIGIL TO SLEEP

1. Omar Yasssin, "Interview with Phil Horne," November 29, 2011, http://hyphyoo.wordpress.com/category/october-december-2011/.

2. Oakland City Attorney, "Fruitvale Anti-Gang Injunction: Oakland Sues Norteños Street Gang, Seeks Targeted Injunction to Protect Fruitvale Community," February 21, 2012, http://www .oaklandcityattorney.org/Notable/Norteños%20injunction.html.

3. Jill Tucker, "Oakland to Drop Controversial Gang Injunctions," *San Francisco Chronicle*, March 5, 2015, http://www.sfgate.com/crime

/article/Oakland-to-drop-controversial-gang-injunctions-6118233
.php.

4. Occupy Oakland, "G.A. Minutes. 11.23.11," https://occupyoakland
.org/2011/11/ga-minutes-11–23–11/.

5. Ibid.

6. Chris Colin, "A Teepee Grows in Oakland," *Salon*, November 30,
2011, http://www.salon.com/2011/11/30/a_teepee_grows_in
_oakland/.

7. City of Oakland, "City of Oakland Issues Permit for Symbolic
Teepee on Plaza and Reinforces Ground Rules for Peaceful and
Safe Demonstrations," November 29, 2011, www2.Oaklandnet.com
/oakca/groups/cityadministrator/.../oak032357.pdf.

8. Gavin Aronsen, "Occupy Shuts Down West Coast Ports," *Mother
Jones*, December 12, 2011, http://www.motherjones.com/mojo
/2011/12/occupy-oakland-longview-west-coast-port-shut-down.

9. Jaime Omar Yassin, "Serious Questions About OPD's Ability to
Oversee Freedom of Speech Events," November 24, 2011, http://
hyphyoo.wordpress.com/category/october-december-2011/.

10. Jaime Omar Yassin, "Mystery Canopies Appear Through Time and
Space at OGP, Despite Being Banned by City of Oakland," December 3, 2011, http://hyphyoo.wordpress.com/category/october
-december-2011/.

11. City of Oakland, Office of the Mayor and City Administrator
Press Release, "City of Oakland Issues Permit for Symbolic Tee-
pee on Plaza and Reinforces Ground Rules for Peaceful and Safe
Demonstrations."

12. Jaime Omar Yassin, "City's Increased Repression of Oscar Grant Plaza
Vigils Producing Ironic Results," January 3, 2012, http://hyphyoo
.wordpress.com/category/october-december-2011/.

13. John Osborn, "Over the Last Two Weeks, 40 Arrests, and Rising Tensions between City Officials and Occupy Protesters," *Oakland North*,
January 11, 2012, http://oaklandnorth.net/2012/01/06/over-last
-two-weeks-40-arrests-and-rising-tensions-between-city-officials
-and-occupy-protesters/.

14. Bay Area Anti-Repression Committee, "In Solidarity with Kali,"
December 23, 2014, https://antirepressionbayarea.com/in-solidarity
-with-kali/.

15. Ibid.

16. Ibid.

17. Jaime Omar Yassin, "Police Harassment of Occupy Oakland Members Continues in Oscar Grant/Frank Ogawa Plaza," December 16,
2011, http://hyphyoo.wordpress.com/category/october-december
-2011/.

18. Yael Chanoff, "Obstructions of Justice: Controversial Arrests of
Occupy Oakland Participants Raise Civil Liberties Concerns," *San*

Francisco Bay Guardian, January 13, 2012, http://cgi.sfbg.com/2012 /01/10/obstructions-justice.

19. Yassin, "City's Increased Repression of Oscar Grant Plaza Vigils Producing Ironic Results."

20. Susie Cagle, "OPD Arrests Protesters for 'Lynching,'" *East Bay Express*, January 11, 2012, http://www.eastbayexpress.com/oakland /opd-arrests-protesters-for-lynching/Content?oid=3096451. Osborn, "Over the Last Two Weeks."

21. Jaime Omar Yassin, "More Arrests at OGP," December 30, 2011, http://hyphyoo.wordpress.com/category/october-december-2011/.

22. Yassin, "City's Increased Repression of Oscar Grant Plaza Vigils Producing Ironic Results."

23. Oakland Police Department Press Release, "Arrests at Frank Ogawa Plaza," January 5, 2012, www2.Oaklandnet.com/oakca/groups /police/documents/.../oak032791.pdf.

24. City of Oakland, City Administrator's Office, "Notice of Violations and Demand to Cease Violations," November 11, 2011, https://info .publicintelligence.net/OccupyOaklandEviction.pdf.

25. City of Oakland, "City of Oakland Revokes and Denies Permit for Teepee on Frank Ogawa Plaza," January 3, 2012 [copy in author's possession].

26. *California v. Norteños*, December 17, 2010. Court documents available at: https://www.aclunc.org/cases/other_legal_advocacy/people_of _the_state_of_california_vs._nortentilde;o.shtml.

27. Susie Cagle, "Stung by Bad PR, City Officials Adopting Tactics to Suppress Occupy Oakland," *Alternet*, January 24, 2012, http:// www.alternet.org/story/153871/stung_by_bad_pr,_city_officials _adopting_new_tactics_to_suppress_occupy_oakland.

28. Superior Court of California: County of San Francisco, "Civil Harassment Restraining Orders," http://www.sfsuperiorcourt.org /self-help/harassment.

29. Michael Risher, "Stay-Away Orders against Protesters Are Unconstitutional," *ACLU of Northern California*, March 8, 2012, https://www .aclunc.org/issues/freedom_of_press_and_speech/stay_away_orders _against_protesters_are_unconstitutional.shtml; Nancy O'Malley, "Occupy Oakland Tamed with Stay-Away Orders," *San Francisco Chronicle*, February 19, 2012, http://www.sfgate.com/opinion/article /Occupy-Oakland-tamed-with-stay-away-orders-3341492.php.

30. Cagle, "Stung by Bad PR, City Officials Adopting Tactics to Suppress Occupy Oakland."

31. While sitting in court during arraignment for Occupy Oakland arrestees, I witnessed a man not connected with Occupy Oakland receive a stay-away order from a Trader Joe's grocery store as he awaited trial for allegedly stealing a six-pack of beer.

32. Risher, "Stay-Away Orders against Protesters Are Unconstitutional."

33. Nancy O'Malley, "Occupy Oakland Tamed with Stay-Away Orders," *San Francisco Chronicle*, 2/19/12. http://www.sfgate.com/opinion /article/Occupy-Oakland-tamed-with-stay-away-orders-3341492.php.

34. *California v. Norteños*, December 17, 2010. Court documents available at: https://www.aclunc.org/cases/other_legal_advocacy/people_of _the_state_of_california_vs._nortentilde;o.shtml.

35. O'Malley, "Occupy Oakland Tamed with Stay Away Orders."

36. *California v. Norteños*.

CHAPTER 6   THE MESHING OF FORCE AND LEGITIMACY IN THE REPRESSION OF OCCUPY OAKLAND'S MOVE-IN DAY

1. Kettling is a police tactic defined by police encircling protesters, detaining them as a group, and either letting them slowly disperse or subjecting the whole group to mass arrest. The logic is to frustrate the movement of crowds and disperse or arrest them, usually without the widespread use of less-lethal weapons. The tactic has been used frequently in the era of strategic incapacitation, and despite numerous legal challenges, is still a highly used and effective police tactic. See Wood (2014, 37–38). More information on this tactic is available from NetPol (Network for Police Monitoring), http:// networkforpolicemonitoring.org.uk/?page_id=227.

2. A flyer for Move-In Day lays out public objectives of the action: http://occupyoakland.org/wp-content/uploads/2012/01/move-in .png.

3. Ryan Phillips, "Once the Center of Civic Life, Former Oakland Auditorium Now Vacant with Future Still Uncertain," *Oakland North*, February 13, 2012, https://oaklandnorth.net/2012/02/13 /once-the-center-of-civic-life-former-oakland-auditorium-now -vacant-with-future-still-uncertain/.

4. "OPD Operations Emails Move-In Day 28 January 2012." Made available by Berkeley Copwatch, http://www.scribd.com/doc /86830594/OPD-Operations-Emails-Move-In-Day-28-January -2012#scribd.

5. Ibid.

6. The "book bloc" had first appeared in Oakland in the summer of 2011, during the Anti-Cut demonstrations. See Wojtek, "A Book Bloc's Genealogy," *Libcom*, November 21, 2012, https://libcom.org /library/book-bloc%E2%80%99s-genealogy.

7. This was the gist of a press release from the city of Oakland just before Move-In Day. City of Oakland, "City Prepared for Occupy Oakland Protest Saturday: City Leaders Call on Community to Get Involved in Productive Programs to Address Social Needs; OPD Prepared to Deter Unlawful Activity," January 27, 2012, http://www2 .Oaklandnet.com/oakca1/groups/cityadministrator/documents /pressrelease/oak033073.pdf.

8. Oakland Commune, "Fuck the Police, Long Live the Commune," *Bay of Rage,* January 11, 2012, http://www.bayofrage.com/from-the -bay/fuck-the-police-long-live-the-commune/.

9. Ibid.

10. Ibid.

11. *Steven Angell, et al. v. City of Oakland, et al.* United States District Court, Northern District of California (Case # C13–0190).

12. Shelby Sebens, "Occupy Protesters Arrested in Oakland to Share $1.4 Million Settlement," *Reuters,* January 16, 2015, http://www .reuters.com/article/2015/01/16/us-usa-occupy-california -idUSKBN0KP0BK20150116.

13. Kevin Fagan, "Occupy Oakland Protesters Split Over Violence," *San Francisco Chronicle,* January 31, 2012, http://www.sfgate.com/bayarea /article/Occupy-Oakland-protesters-split-over-violence-2852332 .php; Chip Johnson, "Occupy Oakland's Assaults Endanger Public Safety," *San Francisco Chronicle,* January 31, 2012, http://www.sfgate .com/bayarea/johnson/article/Occupy-Oakland-s-assaults-endanger -public-safety-2857872.php.

14. Oakland Police Department, "Operations Plan, 28–29 January 12, BF01 -2012–0005," January 27, 2012, http://www.scribd.com/doc /85134645/Oakland-Police-Department-s-Operations-Plan-for -Occupy-Oakland-Move-In-Day-January-28–29–2012#scribd.

15. *Steven Angell, et al. v. City of Oakland, et al.*

16. City of Oakland, "City Prepared for Occupy Oakland Protest Satur- day: City Leaders Call on Community to Get Involved in Productive Programs to Address Social Needs; OPD Prepared to Deter Unlawful Activity," January 27, 2012, http://www2.Oaklandnet.com/oakca1 /groups/cityadministrator/documents/pressrelease/oak033073.pdf.

17. "Oakland Police Arrest about 300 Occupy Protesters," *USA Today,* January 28 2012; http://usatoday30.usatoday.com/news/nation/story /2012–01–28/occupy-oakland-protests/52852280/1.

18. Move-In Day flyer: http://occupyoakland.org/wp-content/uploads /2012/01/move-in.png.

19. Demian Bulwa, Matthai Kuruvila, and Kevin Fagan, "Occupy Oak- land Throng Closes Down Port," *San Francisco Chronicle,* November 2, 2011; http://www.sfgate.com/bayarea/article/Occupy-Oakland -throng-closes-down-port-2324685.php. Kevin Fagan, "Occupy- Labor Alliance Seen as Increasingly Unlikely," *San Francisco Chronicle,* November 6, 2011, http://www.sfgate.com/news/article/Occupy -labor-alliance-seen-as-increasingly-likely-2324191.php#photo -1830229. Kevin Fagan, "Mellower Occupy Movement Grows in the Suburbs," *San Francisco Chronicle,* November 20, 2011; http://www .sfgate.com/bayarea/article/Mellower-Occupy-movement-grows -in-the-suburbs-2288741.php. Kevin Fagan, "Protests of Past Hold Lessons for Today," *San Francisco Chronicle,* December 4, 2011, http:// www.sfgate.com/news/article/Protests-of-past-hold-lessons-for

-today-2345207.php. Kevin Fagan, "Opposition Grows to Occupy's Port Shutdown Plan," *San Francisco Chronicle*, December 11, 2011, http://www.sfgate.com/news/article/Opposition-grows-to-Occupy -s-port-shutdown-plan-2395227.php. Kevin Fagan, "Occupy Oakland Looking Beyond Port Blockades," *San Francisco Chronicle*, December 14, 2011, http://www.sfgate.com/bayarea/article/Occupy -Oakland-looking-beyond-port-blockades-2400246.php. Kevin Fagan, "Occupy Oakland Protesters Split Over Violence," *San Francisco Chronicle*, January 31, 2012, http://www.sfgate.com/bayarea /article/Occupy-Oakland-protesters-split-over-violence-2852332 .php.

20. Fagan, "Mellower Occupy Movement Grows in the Suburbs."
21. Fagan, "Occupy Oakland Protesters Split Over Violence."
22. Fagan, "Protests of Past Hold Lessons for Today."
23. Ibid.
24. Matthai Kuruvila, "Oakland Panel Weighs Ban on Protesters' 'Tools,'" *San Francisco Chronicle*, May 20, 2012, http://www.sfgate.com /bayarea/article/Oakland-panel-weighs-ban-on-protesters-tools -3571353.php; Matthai Kuruvila, "Unruly Oakland Meeting over Occupy, 'Violence,'" *San Francisco Chronicle*, May 26, 2012, http:// www.sfgate.com/bayarea/article/Unruly-Oakland-meeting-over -Occupy-violence-3588894.php.
25. Oakland Police Department, "Operations Plan, 28–29 January 12, BF01–2012–0005," January 27, 2012, http://www.scribd.com/doc /85134645/Oakland-Police-Department-s-Operations-Plan-for -Occupy-Oakland-Move-In-Day-January-28–29–2012#scribd.
26. Matthai Kuruvila, "Oakland Police's War Room the New Normal," *San Francisco Chronicle*, October 28, 2012, http://www.sfgate.com /bayarea/article/Oakland-police-s-war-room-the-new-normal -3988921.php.
27. Ibid.
28. "OPD Operations Emails Move-In Day 28 January 2012."
29. Ibid.
30. Politically, the press conference before the action threatened to shut down the Oakland Airport (and included other threats) if the police prevented protesters from occupying a public space. Tactically, the convention center had not been accessed ahead of time to increase the likelihood of the march getting into the space. There was also poor leadership of the march, and no secondary target was seriously attempted.
31. *Steven Angell, et al. v. City of Oakland, et al.*
32. Jason Cherkis, "Occupy Oakland Activists Report Inhumane Conditions in Santa Rita, Glenn Dyer Jails," *Huffington Post*, February 4, 2012, http://www.huffingtonpost.com/2012/02/03/occupy -oakland-activists-_n_1253651.html.
33. *Steven Angell, et al. v. City of Oakland, et al.*

34. Jeb Purucker, "Santa Rita, I Hate Every Inch of You," *Viewpoint Magazine*, February 6, 2012, https://viewpointmag.com/2012/02/06 /santa-rita-i-hate-every-inch-of-you/.

35. "Charges Dropped against Many Occupy Protesters Arrested in Oakland," *CBS San Francisco*, February 1, 2012, http://sanfrancisco .cbslocal.com/2012/02/01/charges-dropped-against-many-occupy -protesters-arrested-in-oakland/.

36. Based on interview with J28 arrestees.

37. Cognitech was founded in 1988 and made its name initially by developing video software to help identify the men who beat Reginald Denny during the LA riots in 1992.

38. Cognitech, Inc., "Cognitech, Inc. Announces Donation of Software to the Oakland Police Department: Cognitech, Inc. Donates Their Forensic Video Enhancement Software to the Oakland Police Department in Order to Assist the Oakland Community at Large with Numerous Video Footage from the Occupy Oakland Protests," January 31, 2012, http://www.prweb.com/releases/2012/1 /prweb9156548.htm.

39. Somini Sengupta, "Privacy Fears Grow as Cities Increase Surveillance," *New York Times*, October 13, 2013, http://www.nytimes .com/interactive/2013/10/13/technology/surveillance-cameras-in -downtown-oakland.html.

CHAPTER 7   POISON IN THE GARDEN

1. Gavin Aronsen, "Occupy Shuts Down West Coast Ports," *Mother Jones*, December 12, 2011, http://www.motherjones.com/mojo /2011/12/occupy-oakland-longview-west-coast-port-shut-down.

2. AoT, "Breaking: Oakland Arrestees Tortured. Updated," *Daily Kos*, January 31, 2012, http://www.dailykos.com/story/2012/01/31 /1060354/-Breaking-Oakland-Arrestees-Tortured-UPDATED#.

3. Stand for Oakland, "View of Counter-Protest from Above," February 7, 2012, http://standforoakland.blogspot.com/2012/02/view-of -counter-protest-from-above.html.

4. Ibid.

5. Ibid.

6. "Counter-Protestors Criticize Occupy Oakland Tactics," *CBS San Francisco*, February 6, 2012, http://sanfrancisco.cbslocal.com/2012 /02/06/occupy-oakland-protesters-counter-protesters-gather-at -city-hall/. Laura Anthony and Alan Wang, "'Stand Up for Oakland' Group Denounces Occupy Violence," *ABC*, February 6, 2012, http:// abc7news.com/archive/8533839/.

7. "Who Is Stand for Oakland?" pamphlet, https://www.indybay.org /newsitems/2012/02/07/18706824.php.

8. Ibid.

9. Ibid.

10. Tom Vee, "'Stand with Oakland' Astroturf Movement?" YouTube, February 18, 2012, https://www.youtube.com/watch?v=j2gw0ZYBSzY.

11. Kevin Townsend, "Occupy Occupy Oakland GA," *Stand for Oakland*, February 23, 2012, http://standforoakland.blogspot.com/2012/02/lately-i-have-been-reading-several.html.

12. This limitation of open, directly democratic decision-making processes is desirable in many ways, but contains this serious and potentially debilitating intrinsic vulnerability.

13. Townsend, "Occupy Occupy Oakland GA."

14. "Occupy Oakland Clashes with Stand for Oakland, Police (VIDEO)," *Huffington Post*, February 6, 2012, http://www.huffingtonpost.com/2012/02/06/occupy-oakland-stand-for-oakland_n_1258663.html; Patrick Brennan, "Self-Occupied Oakland," National Review, March 5, 2012, https://www.nationalreview.com/nrd/articles/293370/self-occupied-oakland.

15. Justin Berton, Demian Bulwa, and Kevin Fagan, "Occupy Oakland Is Target of Protest," *San Francisco Chronicle*, February 7, 2012, http://www.sfgate.com/bayarea/article/Occupy-Oakland-is-target-of-protest-3082041.php#photo-2281247.

16. Demian Bulwa, "Occupy Oakland Protesters Face Hate-Crime Charges," *San Francisco Chronicle*, March 21, 2012, http://www.sfgate.com/crime/article/Occupy-Oakland-protesters-face-hate-crime-trial-3422406.php.

17. Ibid.

18. Occupy Oakland General Assembly Resolutions, "[Passed at 2/26/12 GA] Proposal for Principle of Solidarity Against Police Repression," https://occupyoakland.org/2012/02/1-for-22612-ga-proposal-for-principle-of-solidarity-against-police-repression/.

19. Cami Graves, "Occupational Awareness," *Occupy Oakland Media*, February 26, 2012, www.hellaoccupyoakland.org/occupational-awareness-alert/. (Screenshot saved at: https://electronicintifada.net/sites/electronicintifada.net/files/occupational_awareness_occupyoakland_media_1.pdf.)

20. Occupy Oakland General Assembly Resolutions, "[Passed at 3/4/12 GA] Proposal to Disband the Media Committee," https://occupyoakland.org/2012/03/1-for-3412-ga-proposal-to-denounce-people-who-tweet-a-shit-storm/.

21. Jaime Omar Yassin, "Why Did a Rogue Group of Occupy Activists Smear Me with 'Terror' Claim?" *Electronic Intifada*, January 16, 2013, https://electronicintifada.net/content/why-did-rogue-group-occupy-activists-smear-me-terror-claim/12099.

22. Occupy Oakland Anti-Repression Committee, "Confronting the Many Faces of Repression," https://occupyoakland.org/2012/10/facesofrepression/.

23. Ibid.

24. Ilyse Hogue, "Occupy Is Dead, Long Live Occupy," *The Nation*, March 14, 2012, http://www.thenation.com/article/166826/occupy -dead-long-live-occupy.

25. Ibid.

26. These powerful actors chose to declare Occupy dead, discredit it, and offer an alternative, rather than to help those who had been organizing or to rejuvenate Occupy as independent outsiders.

27. Maine People's Alliance, "Economic Justice: Bank of America and the 99% Spring," July 11, 2012, https://www.mainepeoplesalliance.org /content/economic-justice-bank-america-and-99-spring.

28. Jake Olzen, "The '99% Spring' Movement to Train 100,000 Activists: Co-Opting Occupy or Helping Spread Its Message?" *Alternet*, March 26, 2012, http://www.alternet.org/story/154706/the_%2299_spring %22_movement_to_train_100,000_activists%3A_co-opting_occupy _or_helping_spread_its_message.

29. Staci Everheart, "Occupy CPS on May Day with Occupy Oakland Patriarchy," *Feministing*, April 23, 2012, http://feministing.com /2012/04/23/occupy-cps-on-may-day-with-oakland-occupy -patriarchy/.

30. Matthai Kuruvila, Demian Bulwa, Carolyn Jones, and Kevin Fagan, "Thousands March in Oakland in May Day Protest: May Day Actions / Peace Meets Violence Many Protesters Came Ready for Confrontation—Others Threw Flowers," *San Francisco Chronicle*, May 2, 2012, http://www.sfgate.com/bayarea/article/Thousands-march -in-Oakland-in-May-Day-protest-3524772.php.

31. Oakland Commune, "Occupy Oakland Is Dead, Long Live the Oakland Commune," *Bay of Rage*, May 16, 2012, http://www.bayofrage .com/featured-articles/occupy-oakland-is-dead/; Advance the Struggle, "Occupy Oakland Post–May Day: Strengths, Limits, and Futures," May 20, 2012, http://advancethestruggle.wordpress.com/2012/05 /20/occupy-oakland-post-may-day/.

32. City of Oakland, "City of Oakland Prepared for Today's Marches, Protests, and Activities: Marches, Protests, and Activities—Some with City Permits Others Without—Planned Throughout Day and Throughout City," May 1, 2012, http://www2.Oaklandnet .com/oakca1/groups/cityadministrator/documents/pressrelease /oak034721.pdf.

33. The "Frazier Report" on the policing on October 25: Frazier Group, LLC, "Independent Investigation: Occupy Oakland Response October 25, 2011," *City of Oakland*, June 14, 2012, http://www2 .Oaklandnet.com/oakca1/groups/cityadministrator/documents /webcontent/oak036236.pdf.

34. Eric Arnold, "Was Oakland PD's Proposed Crowd Control Policy Illegal?" *New American Media*, May 25, 2012, http://newamericamedia.org /2012/05/was-oakland-pds-proposed-crowd-control-policy-illegal .php.

35. City of Oakland, "City of Oakland Prepared for Today's Marches, Protests, and Activities."

36. Ryan Phillips, "OPD Changing Its Crowd Control Policy," *Oakland North*, April 23, 2012, https://oaklandnorth.net/2012/04/23/opd -changing-its-crowd-control-policy/.

37. Dave Id, "Oakland Police January 28th Hit List. Who Is on the OPD List for May Day?" May 1, 2012, https://www.indybay.org /newsitems/2012/05/01/18712503.php.

38. City of Oakland, "City of Oakland Prepared for Today's Marches, Protests and Activities."

39. City of Oakland, City Administrator's Office, "The City of Oakland Is Committed to Facilitating Peaceful Forms of Expression and Free Speech Rights, and Protecting Personal Safety and Property," April 30, 2012 [copy in author's possession].

40. The five keys were: Crowd Management Training, Community Involvement, Media and First Amendment Rights, Use of Force Investigations, and Use of Mutual Aid.

41. American Civil Liberties Union, "ACLU and NLG Ask Oakland Police Department If It Seeks to Abandon Key Protections for Demonstrators," American Civil Liberties Union of Northern California, April 24, 2012, https://www.aclunc.org/news/aclu-and-nlg-ask -oakland-police-department-if-it-seeks-abandon-key-protections -demonstrators.

42. Zunguzungu, "A Snapshot of Your Security-Industrial Complex," May 1, 2012, https://zunguzungu.wordpress.com/2012/05/01/a -snapshot-of-your-security-industrial-complex/.

43. Despite the fact that police had argued that the snatch squads would target people who were known to have committed crimes, this did not appear to be the case given whom I saw arrested or what the video evidence shows. See: Jacob Crawford, "Oakland Police Use Snatch Squads and Flash Bang Grenades on May Day 2012," YouTube, May 1, 2012, http://www.youtube.com/watch?v= z4kfOATzPMk.

CHAPTER 8   BEYOND CONTROL

1. Chris Hedges, "The Cancer in Occupy," *TruthDig*, February 6, 2012, http://www.truthdig.com/report/item/the_cancer_of_occupy _20120206.

References

Agamben, Giorgio. 2005. *State of Exception*. Chicago: University of Chicago Press.

Aksyutina, Olga. 2012. "Protest as 'Extremism': The Criminalization of Dissent within Dutch Immigration Policy." In *Protest and Punishment: The Repression of Resistance in the Era of Neoliberal Globalization*, edited by Jeff Shantz, 167–192. Durham, NC: Carolina Academic Press.

Althusser, Louis. 1970. *For Marx*. New York: Vintage.

———. 2001. *Lenin and Philosophy and Other Essays*. New York: Monthly Review Press.

American Civil Liberties Union. 2014. *War Comes Home: The Excessive Militarization of American Policing*. New York: ACLU Foundation.

Balbus, Isaac. 1973. *The Dialectics of Legal Repression: Black Rebels before the American Criminal Courts*. New York: Russell Sage.

Balko, Radley. 2013. *Rise of the Warrior Cop: The Militarization of America's Police Forces*. New York: Public Affairs.

Beckett, Katherine, and Steve Herbert. 2010. *Banished: New Social Control in Urban America*. New York: Oxford University Press.

Berlant, Lauren. 1997. *The Queen of America Goes to Washington City*. Durham, NC: Duke University Press.

Bloom, Joshua, and Waldo Martin Jr. 2013. *Black against Empire: The History and Politics of the Black Panther Party*. Berkeley: University of California Press.

Boykoff, Jules. 2007a. *Beyond Bullets: The Suppression of Dissent in the United States*. Oakland, CA: AK Press.

———. 2007b. "Limiting Dissent: The Mechanisms of State Repression in the USA." *Social Movement Studies* 6, no. 3: 281–310.

Breines, Wini. 1989. *Community and Organization in the New Left, 1962–1968: The Great Refusal*. New Brunswick, NJ: Rutgers University Press.

Brissette, Emily. 2013. "Prefiguring the Realm of Freedom at Occupy Oakland." *Rethinking Marxism* 25, no. 2: 218–227.

Chambliss, William. 2001. *Power, Politics, and Crime*. Boulder, CO: Westview Press.

Chimurenga, Thandisizwe. 2014. *No Doubt: The Murder(s) of Oscar Grant.* Los Angeles: Ida B. Wells Institute.

Churchill, Ward. 2003. *Pacifism as Pathology: Reflections on the Role of Armed Struggle in North America.* Winnipeg: Arbeiter Ring.

Churchill, Ward, and Jim Vander Wall. 1988. *Agents of Repression: The FBI's Secret Wars against the Black Panther Party and the American Indian Movement.* Boston: South End Press.

————. 1990. *The COINTELPRO Papers: Documents from the FBI's Secret Wars against Dissent in the United States.* Boston: South End Press.

Ciccariello-Maher, George. 2013. *We Created Chavez: A People's History of the Venezuelan Revolution.* Durham, NC: Duke University Press.

Cornell, Andrew. 2012. "Consensus: What It Is, What It Isn't, Where It Comes from, and Where It Must Go." In *We Are Many: Reflections on Movement Strategy from Occupation to Liberation,* edited by Kate Khatib, Margaret Killjoy, and Mike McGuire, 163–173. Oakland, CA: AK Press.

Critical Resistance. 2011. *Betraying the Model City: How Gang Injunctions Fail Oakland.* Oakland, CA: Critical Resistance.

Curtis, Adam. 2004. *Power of Nightmares: The Rise of the Politics of Fear.* Documentary. Directed by Adam Curtis. London: British Broadcasting Company.

Datta, Ronjon Paul. 2011. "Security and the Void: Aleatory Materialism contra Governmentality." In *Anti-Security,* edited by Mark Neocleous and George Rigakos, 217–242. Ottawa: Red Quill Books.

Davenport, Christian. 2010. *Media Bias, Perspective, and State Repression: The Black Panther Party.* New York: Cambridge University Press.

Davis, Mike. 1990. *City of Quartz: Excavating the Future in Los Angeles.* New York: Verso.

Dhaliwal, Puneet. 2012. "Public Squares and Resistance: The Politics of Space in the Indignados Movement." *Interface* 4, no. 1: 251–273.

Drummond-Cole, Adrian, and Darwin Bond-Graham. 2012. "Disneyfication of Downtown Oakland." *New Political Spaces* 19, no. 1. Accessed August 9, 2015, http://urbanhabitat.org/19-1/drummond-cole-bond-graham.

Durkheim, Emile. [1912] 1995. *The Elementary Forms of Religious Life.* New York: Free Press.

————. 1979. "The Normal and the Pathological." In *Classics of Criminology,* edited by Joseph Jacoby, 64–67. Oak Park, IL: Moore Publishing.

Earl, Jennifer. 2005. "'You Can Beat the Rap, But You Can't Beat the Ride': Bringing Arrests Back into Research on Repression." *Research in Social Movements, Conflicts, and Change* 26: 101–139.

————. 2011. "Political Repression: Iron Fists, Velvet Gloves, and Diffuse Control." *Annual Review of Sociology* 37: 261–284.

Eisenstadt, Nathan. 2012. "Policing the 'Summer of Rage': Maintaining Post-Politics against the Specter of Dissensus." In *Protest and Punishment: The Repression of Resistance in the Era of Neoliberal Globalization*, edited by Jeff Shantz, 131–166. Durham, NC: Carolina Academic Press.

Eliasoph, Nina. 1998. *Avoiding Politics: How Americans Produce Apathy in Everyday Life*. New York: Cambridge University Press.

Federici, Silvia, and George Caffentzis. 2004. "Genoa and the Antiglobalization Movement." In *Confronting Capitalism: Dispatches from a Global Movement*, edited by Eddie Yuen, Daniel Burton-Rose, and George Katsiaficas, 142–153. Brooklyn, NY: Soft Skull Press.

Feeley, Malcolm, and Jonathan Simon. 1992. "The New Penology: Notes on the Emerging Strategy of Corrections and Its Implications." *Criminology* 30, no. 4: 449–474.

Fernandez, Luis. 2008. *Policing Dissent: Social Control and the Anti-Globalization Movement*. New Brunswick, NJ: Rutgers University Press.

Foucault, Michel. 1990. *The History of Sexuality: An Introduction—Volume 1*. New York: Vintage Books.

———. 1991. "Governmentality." In *The Foucault Effect: Studies in Governmentality*, edited by Graham Burchell, Colin Gordon, and Peter Miller, 87–104. Chicago: University of Chicago Press.

———. 1994. *Power*. New York: New Press.

———. 2007. *Security, Territory, Population*. New York: Palgrave Macmillan.

Freeman, Jo. 1972. "The Tyranny of Structurelessness." *Berkeley Journal of Sociology* 17: 151–165.

Fusfeld, Daniel. [1980] 1992. *The Rise and Repression of Radical Labor*. Chicago: Kerr Publishing.

Gamson, William. [1975] 1990. *The Strategy of Social Protest*. Belmont, CA: Wadsworth Publishing.

Garces, Chris. 2013. "People's Mic and 'Leaderful' Charisma." Cultural Anthropology (online), last modified February 14, 2013, http://www.culanth.org/fieldsights/65-people-s-mic-and-leaderful-charisma.

Garland, Christian. 2012. "Illuminated in Its Lurid Light: Criminalization, Political Repression, and Dissent in the UK." In *Protest and Punishment: The Repression of Resistance in the Era of Neoliberal Globalization*, edited by Jeff Shantz, 29–48. Durham, NC: Carolina Academic Press.

Gerstyle, Gary. 2004. "The Immigrant as Threat to American Security: A Historical Perspective." In *The Maze of Fear: Security and Immigration after 9/11*, edited by John Tirman, 87–108. New York: New Press.

Gillham, Patrick, Bob Edwards, and John Noakes. 2013. "Strategic Incapacitation and the Policing of Occupy Wall Street Protests in New York City, 2011." *Policing & Society* 23, no. 1: 81–102.

Gillham, Patrick, and John Noakes. 2007. "'More Than a March in a Circle': Transgressive Protests and the Limits of Negotiated Management." *Mobilization* 12, no. 4: 341–357.

Gitlin, Todd. 2003. *The Whole World Is Watching: Mass Media in the Making and Unmaking of the New Left*. Berkeley: University of California Press.

Glick, Brian. 1989. *War at Home: Covert Action against U.S. Activists and What We Can Do About It*. Boston: South End Press.

Goffman, Alice. 2014. *On the Run: Fugitive Life in an American City*. Chicago: University of Chicago Press.

Goldstein, Robert. [1978] 2001. *Political Repression in Modern America from 1870 to 1976*. Chicago: University of Illinois Press.

Gould-Wartofsky, Michael. 2015. *The Occupiers: The Making of the 99 Percent Movement*. New York: Oxford University Press.

Graeber, David. 2007. *Possibilities: Essays on Hierarchy, Rebellion, and Desire*. Oakland, CA: AK Press.

Graham, Stephen. 2010. *Cities under Siege: The New Military Urbanism*. New York: Verso.

Gramsci, Antonio. 1971. *Selections from the Prison Notebooks*. New York: International Publishers.

Haggerty, Kevin, and Richard Ericson. 2001. "The Military Technostructures of Policing." In *Militarizing the American Criminal Justice System: The Changing Roles of the Armed Forces and the Police*, edited by Peter Kraska, 43–64. Boston: Northeastern University Press.

Hall, Stuart. 1981. "The Whites of Their Eyes: Racist Ideologies in the Media." In *Silver Linings: Some Strategies for the Eighties*, edited by George Bridges and Rosalind Brunt, 28–52. London: Lawrence & Wishart.

Hall, Stuart, Chas Citcher, Tony Jefferson, John Clarke, and Brian Roberts. [1978] 2013. *Policing the Crisis: Mugging, the State, and Law & Order*. New York: Palgrave Macmillan.

Harcourt, Bernard. 2001. *Illusion of Order: The False Promise of Broken Windows Policing*. Cambridge, MA: Harvard University Press.

Harvey, David. 2005. *A Brief History of Neoliberalism*. New York: Oxford University Press.

Herbert, Steve. 1997. *Policing Space: Territoriality and the Los Angeles Police Department*. Minneapolis: University of Minnesota Press.

Jackson, Jonathan, Ben Bradford, Mike Hough, Andy Myhill, Paul Quinton, and Tom Tyler. 2012. "Why Do People Comply with the Law?: Legitimacy and the Influence of Legal Institutions." *British Journal of Criminology* 52: 1051–1071.

Jay, Scott. 2014. "Who Gives the Orders?: Oakland Police, City Hall, and Occupy." *libcom.org*, last modified December 21, 2014, https://libcom.org/library/who-gives-orders-oakland-police-city-hall-occupy.

King, Martin Luther. [1963] 2003. "Letter from Birmingham Jail." In *Reporting Civil Rights: Part One*. New York: Library of America.

King, Mike. 2010. "Redrawing the Line on 'Outside Agitators': The Coming Mehserle Sentencing." *San Francisco Bay View*, last modified November 1, 2010, http://sfbayview.com/2010/11/the-coming -mehserle-sentencing-redrawing-the-line—on-outside-agitators/.

———. 2012. "Occupy Oakland and State Repression: The Struggle for Public Space." *Progressive Planning* 191 (Spring): 20–23.

———. 2013a. "'Broken Windows,' Urban Policing, and the Social Contexts of Race and Neighborhood (Dis-)Empowerment." *Critical Criminology* 21, no. 4: 533–538.

———. 2013b. "Disruption Is Not Permitted: The Policing and Social Control of Occupy Oakland." *Critical Criminology* 21, no. 4: 463–475.

King, Mike, and Emily Brissette. 2017. "Kindling Waiting for a Spark: Eros and Emergent Consciousness in Occupy Oakland." In *Spontaneous Combustion: The Eros Effect and Global Revolution*, edited by Jason Del Gandio and AK Thompson. Albany: SUNY Press.

King, Mike, and George Ciccariello-Maher. 2011. "Oakland on Strike!" *Counterpunch*, last modified October 27, 2011, http://www .counterpunch.org/2011/10/27/oakland-on-strike/.

King, Mike, and David Waddington. 2006. "The Policing of Protest in Canada." In *Policing of Transnational Protest*, edited by Donatella della Porta, Abby Peterson, and Herbert Reiter, 75–96. Abingdon, UK: Ashgate.

Kraska, Peter. 2001. *Militarizing the American Justice System: The Changing Roles of Armed Forces and Police*. Boston: Northeastern University Press, 2001.

Machiavelli, Niccolo. 1961. *The Prince*. New York: Penguin Books.

Maeckelbergh, Marianne. 2011. "Doing Is Believing: Prefiguration as Strategic Practice in the Alterglobalization Movement." *Social Movement Studies* 10, no. 1: 1–20.

———. 2012. "Horizontal Democracy Now: From Alterglobalization to Occupation." *Interface* 4, no. 1: 207–234.

Marx, Gary. 1988. *Undercover: Police Surveillance in America*. Berkeley: University of California Press.

———. 1998. "Some Reflections on the Democratic Policing of Demonstrations." In *Policing Protest: The Control of Mass Demonstrations in Western Democracies*, edited by Donatella della Porta and Herbert Reiner, 253–270. Minneapolis: University of Minnesota Press.

Marx, Karl, and Frederick Engels. [1947] 2001. *The German Ideology*. New York: International Publishers.

McCarthy, John, and Clark McPhail. 1998. "The Institutionalization of Protest in the United States." In *The Social Movement Society:*

Contentious Politics for a New Century, edited by David Meyer and Sidney Tarrow, 83–110. Lanham, MD: Rowman & Littlefield.

McNally, David. 2011. *Global Slump: The Economics and Politics of Crisis and Resistance.* Oakland, CA: PM Press.

McPhail, Clark, and John McCarthy. 2005. "Protest Mobilization, Protest Repression, and Their Interaction." In *Repression and Mobilization*, edited by Christian Davenport, Hank Johnston, and Carol Mueller, 3–32. Minneapolis: University of Minnesota Press.

McPhail, Clark, David Schweingruber, and John McCarthy. 1998. "Policing Protest in the United States: 1960–1995." In *Policing Protest: The Control of Mass Demonstrations in Western Democracies*, edited by Donatella della Porta and Herbert Reiner, 49–69. Minneapolis: University of Minnesota Press.

Mitchell, Don. 2003. *The Right to the City: Social Justice and the Fight for Public Space.* New York: Guilford Press.

Murch, Donna. 2010. *Living for the City: Migration, Education, and the Rise of the Black Panther Party in Oakland, California.* Chapel Hill: University of North Carolina Press.

National Advisory Committee on Civil Disorders. 1968. *Report of the National Advisory Committee on Civil Disorders.* New York: Bantam Books.

National District Attorneys' Association. 2009. *Civil Gang Injunctions: A Guide for Prosecutors.* Washington, DC: US Department of Justice.

Neocleous, Mark, and George Rigakos, eds. 2011. *Anti-Security.* Ottawa: Red Quill Books.

Noakes, John, and Patrick Gillham. 2006. "Aspects of 'New Penology' in the Police Response to Major Political Protests in the United States, 1999–2000." In *Policing of Transnational Protest*, edited by Donatella della Porta, Abby Peterson, and Herbert Reiter, 97–115. Abingdon, UK: Ashgate.

Noakes, John, Brian Klocke, and Patrick Gillham. 2005. "Whose Streets?: Police and Protester Struggles Over Space in Washington, DC, 29–30 September 2001." *Policing & Society* 15, no. 3: 235–254.

Oliver, Pamela. 2008. "Repression and Crime Control: Why Social Movements Scholars Should Pay Attention to Policing of Crime as a Form of Repression." *Mobilization* 13, no. 1: 1–24.

O'Reilly, Kenneth. 1989. *Racial Matters: The FBI's Secret File on Black America, 1960—1972.* New York: Free Press.

Parenti, Christian. 1999. *Lockdown America: Police and Prison in the Age of Crisis.* New York: Verso.

———. 2003. *The Soft Cage: Surveillance in America, From Slave Passes to the War on Terror.* New York: Basic Books.

Peterson, Susan Rae. 1977. "Coercion and Rape: The State as Male Protection Racket." In *Feminism and Philosophy*, edited by Mary

Vetterling–Braggin, Frederick Elliston, and Jane English, 360–376. Totowa, NJ: Littlefield, Adams & Co.

Piven, Frances Fox. 2006. *Challenging Authority: How Ordinary People Change America.* New York: Rowman & Littlefield.

Piven, Frances Fox, and Richard Cloward. 1977. *Poor Peoples' Movements: Why They Succeed, How They Fail.* New York: Pantheon Books.

Platt, Anthony, ed. 1971. *The Politics of Riot Commissions.* New York: Collier Books.

Platt, Anthony, Lynn Cooper, Elliott Currie, Jon Frappier, Betty Ryan, Richard Schauffler, Joy Scruggs, Larry Trujillo, Bill Bigelow, Michael Klare, Nancy Stein, and Millie Thayer. 1975. *The Iron Fist and the Velvet Glove: An Analysis of the U.S. Police.* San Francisco: Synthesis Publications.

Poletta, Francesca. 2002. *Freedom Is an Endless Meeting: Democracy in American Social Movements.* Chicago: University of Chicago Press.

Police Executive Research Forum. 2011. *Managing Major Events: Best Practices from the Field.* Critical Issues in Policing Series. Washington, DC: Police Executive Research Forum.

Potter, Will. 2011. *Green Is the New Red: An Insider's Account of a Social Movement under Siege.* San Francisco: City Lights Books.

Putnam, Robert. 2000. *Bowling Alone: The Collapse and Revival of American Community.* New York: Simon & Schuster.

Raider Nation Collective. 2010. *Raider Nation,* Volume 1: *From the January Rebellions to Lovelle Mixon and Beyond.* Oakland, CA: 1984 Printing.

Redden, Jim. 2002. "Police State Targets the Left." In *The Battle of Seattle: The New Challenges to Capitalist Globalization,* edited by Eddie Yuen, George Katsiaficas, and Daniel Burton Rose, 139–152. New York: Soft Skull Press.

Rigakos, George. 2011. "'To Extend the Scope of Productive Labor': Pacification as Police Project." In *Anti-Security,* edited by Mark Neocleous and George Rigakos, 57–84. Ottawa: Red Quill Books.

Rimke, Heidi. 2011. "Security: Resistance." In *Anti-Security,* edited by Mark Neocleous and George Rigakos, 191–216. Ottawa: Red Quill Books.

Rios, Victor. 2011. *Punished: Policing the Lives of Black and Latino Boys.* New York: New York University Press.

Ryan, Charlotte. 1991. *Prime Time Activism: Media Strategies for Grassroots Organizing.* Boston: South End Press.

Schultz, Bud, and Ruth Schultz. 2001. *The Price of Dissent: Testimonies to Political Repression in America.* Berkeley: University of California Press.

Seferiades, Seraphim, and Hank Johnston. 2012. Violent Protest, Contentious Politics, and the Neoliberal State. Burlington, VT: Ashgate.

Simon, Jonathan. 2007. *Governing Through Crime: How the War on Crime Transformed American Democracy and Created a Culture of Fear.* New York: Oxford University Press.

Sitrin, Marina. 2006. *Horizontalism: Voices of Popular Power in Argentina.* Oakland, CA: AK Press.

Skolnick, Jerome. 1969. *The Politics of Protest.* New York: Ballantine Books.

Slack, Jennifer Daryl. 1996. "The Theory and Method of Articulation in Cultural Studies." In *Stuart Hall: Critical Dialogues in Cultural Studies,* edited by David Morley and Kuan-Hsing Chen, 112–130. New York: Routledge.

Smith, Neil. 1996. *The New Urban Frontier: Gentrification and the Revanchist City.* New York: Routledge.

Sobieraj, Sarah. 2011. *Soundbitten: The Perils of Media-Centered Political Activism.* New York: New York University Press.

Soule, Sarah, and Christian Davenport. 2009. "Velvet Glove, Iron Fist, or Even Hand?: Protest Policing in the United States, 1960–1990." *Mobilization* 14, no. 1: 1–22.

Starr, Amory. 2006. "'. . . (Excepting Barricades Erected to Prevent Us from Peacefully Assembling)': So-called 'Violence' in the Global North Alterglobalization Movement." *Social Movement Studies* 5, no. 1: 61–81.

Starr, Amory, Luis Fernandez, Randall Amster, Lesley Wood, and Manuel Caro. 2008. "The Impacts of State Surveillance on Political Assembly and Association: A Socio-Legal Analysis." *Qualitative Sociology* 31: 251–270.

Starr, Amory, Luis Fernandez, and Christian Scholl. 2011. *Shutting Down the Streets: Political Violence and Social Control in the Global Era.* New York: New York University Press.

Sun Tzu. 1971. *The Art of War.* Translated and introduced by Samuel Griffith. New York: Oxford University Press.

Szasz, Andrew. 2007. *Shopping Our Way to Safety: How We Changed from Protecting the Environment to Protecting Ourselves.* Minneapolis: University of Minnesota Press.

Thomas, Peter. 2009. *The Gramscian Moment: Philosophy, Hegemony, and Marxism.* Chicago: Haymarket Books.

Thompson, E. P. 2001. *The Essential E. P. Thompson.* Edited by Dorothy Thompson. New York: New Press.

Tilly, Charles. 1985. "War Making and State Making as Organized Crime." In *Bringing the State Back In,* edited by Peter Evans, Dietrich Rueschemeyer, and Theda Skocpol, 169–191. New York: Cambridge University Press.

Tirman, John, ed. 2004. *The Maze of Fear: Security and Migration after 9/11.* New York: New Press.

Vitale, Alex. 2005. "From Negotiated Management to Command and Control: How the New York Police Department Polices Protest." *Policing and Society* 15, no. 3: 283–304.

———. 2007. "The Command and Control and Miami Models at the 2004 Republican National Convention: New Forms of Policing Protests." *Mobilization* 12, no. 4: 403–415.

Wacquant, Loïc. 2001. "Deadly Symbiosis: When Ghetto and Prison Meet and Mesh." *Punishment & Society* 3, no. 1: 95–134.

———. 2009. *Punishing the Poor: The Neoliberal Government of Social Insecurity.* Durham, NC: Duke University Press.

Waddington, P.A.J. 1998. "Controlling Protest in Contemporary Historical Perspective." In *Policing Protest: The Control of Mass Demonstrations in Western Democracies,* edited by Donatella della Porta and Herbert Reiner, 117–142. Minneapolis: University of Minnesota Press.

Weber, Max. 1946. *From Max Weber: Essays in Sociology.* Edited by H. H. Gerth and C. Wright Mills. New York: Oxford University Press.

Werdegar, Matthew. 1999. "Enjoining the Constitution: The Use of Public Nuisance Abatement Injunctions against Urban Street Gangs." *Stanford Law Review* 51, no. 2: 409–445.

Williams, Kristian. 2006. *American Methods: Torture and the Logic of Domination.* Boston: South End Press.

———. 2007. *Our Enemies in Blue: Police and Power in America.* Boston: South End Press.

———. 2011. "The Other Side of the COIN: Counterinsurgency and Community Policing." *Interface* 3, no. 1: 81–117.

Williams, Kristian, Will Munger, and Lara Messersmith-Glavin. 2013. *Life during Wartime: Resisting Counterinsurgency.* Oakland, CA: AK Press.

Wood, Lesley. 2007. "Breaking the Wave: Repression, Identity, and Seattle Tactics." *Mobilization* 12, no. 4: 377–388.

———. 2014. *Crisis and Control: The Militarization of Protest Policing.* New York: Pluto Press.

Young, Iris Marion. 2003. "The Logic of Masculinist Protection: Reflections on the Current Security State." *Signs: Journal of Women in Culture and Society* 29, no. 1: 1–26.

Index

About the Author

Mike King is an assistant professor in the Criminal Justice Department at Bridgewater State University, Bridgewater, Massachusetts. He received his PhD in sociology from the University of California–Santa Cruz in 2013. His research generally focuses on social movements, policing, and race. His writing has recently been featured in the journals *Race & Class* and *Critical Criminology*, and he is also a regular contributor to the online magazine *Counterpunch*. He is currently working on a book that examines race, political affect, and the rise of far-Right political movements.